KRIEGSMARINE

HISTORY • UNIFORMS • HEADGEAR
INSIGNIA • EQUIPMENT
1935-1945

Großadmiral Karl Dönitz
(1891-1980)
(Private collection)

KRIEGSMARINE

HISTORY • UNIFORMS • HEADGEAR
INSIGNIA • EQUIPMENT
1935-1945

Enzo Berrafato and Laurent Berrafato

Color photographs by Marc de Fromont

Schiffer Military History
Atglen, PA

This work is dedicated to all those members of the Marine *(Navy) who lost their lives during the Second World War.*

Translation from the German by Mary Burdman.

The original French edition appeared in 2010 under the title,
La Kriegsmarine 1935-1945,
by REGI ARM, Paris, France.

This book was also published in German under the title,
Die Uniformen Der Deutschen Kriegsmarine: 1935-1945,
by Zeughaus Verlag, Berlin, Germany.

Book design by Joël Leroux and Claire Dupont.

Library of Congress Control Number: 2012943466

Printed in Hong Kong.
ISBN: 978-0-7643-4274-5

We are interested in hearing from authors with book ideas on related topics.

Published by Schiffer Publishing Ltd.
4880 Lower Valley Road
Atglen, PA 19310
Phone: (610) 593-1777
FAX: (610) 593-2002
E-mail: Info@schifferbooks.com.
Visit our web site at: **www.schifferbooks.com**
Please write for a free catalog.
This book may be purchased from the publisher.
Try your bookstore first.

In Europe, Schiffer books are distributed by:
Bushwood Books
6 Marksbury Avenue
Kew Gardens
Surrey TW9 4JF, England
Phone: 44 (0) 20 8392-8585
FAX: 44 (0) 20 8392-9876
E-mail: Info@bushwoodbooks.co.uk.
Visit our website at: www.bushwoodbooks.co.uk

CONTENTS

Introduction

No single book could be sufficient to present a comprehensive history of the German *Kriegsmarine* between 1935 and 1945. Therefore, this work takes a more modest approach, namely, to bring this relatively neglected branch of the *Wehrmacht* (the Third *Reich* Armed Forces, 1934-45) closer to the reader, since the *Kriegsmarine*, despite its limited resources, actually represented the only serious threat to the Allies.

During the six years of war, the *Kriegsmarine* was a force on all the world's oceans, and during this time, inflicted far greater losses on its enemies than it suffered itself, while meeting all the new challenges posed by modern warfare.

Thanks to its outstanding leadership and well-trained and equipped troops, the German *Marine* was respected and admired by its opponents themselves.

We wanted to focus especially on all the nameless seamen who served on the minelayers, *Schnellboote* (fast attack boats), minehunters, cruisers, *U-Boote* (submarines), and so on. Therefore we have selected as yet generally unknown contemporary records, which come from private archives. The pictures of uniforms and pieces of equipment we present here are all originals from the period, and likewise come from private collections. We also want to take a more detailed look at "*Kantinenware*" (canteen goods), which were very popular with the *Kriegsmarine* personnel, and with which they carried on the traditions of their predecessors. But now, enough of introductory words ...

Acknowledgments

The authors would like to take this opportunity to thank the collectors, without whom all the articles presented in this work would have disappeared by now. They are:

- Benoit Abbas	***- Laurent Charbonneau***	***- Pierre-Marie Rousseau***
- Franck Bachmann	***- D. Descordes***	***- Jacques Scipion***
- Christian Boldt (Germany)	***- Frédéric Finel***	***- Christian Tollet***

We also would like to thank Christophe Deschodt (curator of the "*Musée de la seconde guerre mondiale d'Ambleteuse*"), the Parisian specialty stores Overlord and Le Poilu for their expert advice, Xavier Aiolfi, and the auction house Hermann Historica, Munich, for making available a number of photographs.

Propaganda postcard for the *Kaiserliche Marine* (Imperial Navy). (Private collection)

Propaganda postcards for the *Reichsmarine* (German Navy 1922-35) (1933). (Private collection)

***Großadmiral* Erich Raeder (1876-1960). (Private collection)**

***Großadmiral* Dönitz replaced Raeder in January 1943 as *Oberbefehlshaber* (commander-in-chief) of the *Kriegsmarine*. (Private collection)**

Germany is a relatively young nation. The different German states only closed ranks in 1870, to support the King of Prussia after the French emperor Napoleon III declared war on him. With the song "Lieb' Vaterland, magst ruhig sein, fest steht und treu die Wacht am Rhein" ("Dear Fatherland, have no fear, the watch on the Rhine is strong and true") on their lips, the soldiers of the allied German states marched on Paris, with the consciousness of belonging to a united nation. When King Wilhelm I of Prussia was proclaimed the German Kaiser in the Hall of Mirrors in Versailles on January 18, 1871, the German Reich was born, the first unified German nation-state.

Before 1871, there were six nations on the German North Sea coast: Oldenburg, Hanover, Schleswig-Holstein, Mecklenburg, Pomerania, and Prussia. They had a few warships to protect their own coastlines, but these played no great role militarily, as demonstrated in the 1848 Schleswig-Holstein war against Denmark, in which the warships took part as the Reichsflotte (Imperial Fleet). In 1867, after the war against Austria, the North German Bundesmarine (Federal Navy) was created from the navies of the North German Confederation, under the command of Prussia. After the German Reich was founded, the federal states' naval forces were united in 1872 under the name Kaiserliche Marine (Imperial Navy), and retained that name until the Kaiser abdicated in 1918. A year later, these forces were renamed the Vorläufige Reichsmarine (Provisional Navy), and in 1921 became the Reichsmarine, (the German Navy during the Weimar Republic and Nazi period until 1935). Then, on June 1, 1935, the Kriegsmarine was born, and five months later, the black-white-red of the new swastika flag was hoisted aboard its ships. This flag, of course, disappeared after the surrender.

After the German Democratic Republic (East Germany) was founded in 1949, the (official) founding of its own naval forces took until March 1, 1956. The land force – the Nationale Volksarmee (National People's Army) – was first formed on July 1, 1956, and on Nov. 3,1960, the name Volksmarine (People's Navy) was conferred on the naval forces. In the German Federal Republic (West Germany), the Bundeswehr (Federal Armed Forces) was founded as early as November 12, 1955, and already in January 1956, the Bundesmarine (Federal Navy) was created. In 1995, after the reunification of Germany, the Bundesmarine was renamed the Deutsche Marine (German Navy), after taking a part of the staff and ships of the Volksmarine into an all-German naval force. We wish to limit ourselves here, to the history of the Kriegsmarine from 1935 to 1945, although Germany was already re-acquiring a fleet in 1919, after the Treaty of Versailles. The restrictive conditions of this Treaty aroused a great deal of resentment among the Germans, and as time passed, the Reichsmarine began to increasingly circumvent or ignore its terms. The Treaty prohibited replacement of warships which had been put into service less than twenty years before, while, for new ships, predetermined limits of displacement were set: for battleships at 10,000 tons (1,016 kilograms), 6,000 tons for cruisers, 800 tons for destroyers, and 200 tons for torpedo boats.

The new design of *Reichskriegsflagge* (*Reich* war flag) was introduced by a decree of October 31, 1935 (MV ("*Mit Verfügung*" "By decree") 35, No.394). (Collection of P.-M. Rousseau)

Because the tonnage specified in the Washington Naval Treaty, signed in December 1921, was calculated in U.S. tons, which are slightly smaller than the British, the *Reichsmarine* could build their ships 15% larger, without violating the Treaty of Versailles.

The *Reichsmarine,* therefore, was soon moving to build *Panzerschiffe* (pocket battleships), the first being the DEUTSCHLAND, which was launched on May 19, 1931. The ship was faster than the fastest battleship of its time and was, with its six 28-cm guns, able to do battle with enemy cruisers from a distance where the enemy guns could not yet reach. The DEUTSCHLAND's diesel engines gave her a top speed of twenty-eight knots and a cruising range of 10,000 nautical miles.

The signing of the Anglo-German Naval Agreement on June 18, 1935 by Sir Samuel Hoare and Joachim von Ribbentrop, was a happy day for Adolf Hitler, even while this agreement stipulated that German naval strength could not exceed 35% of that of the Royal Navy, when Germany had wanted the limit to be 45% for *U-Boote*. This treaty allowed the *Reich*, among other things, to build warships which had been prohibited by the Versailles provisions, such as aircraft carriers. The first of these, the GRAF ZEPPELIN, was launched on December 8, 1938, but was never put into service. The construction of a sister ship had indeed also been started, but the half-finished ship was scrapped two years later.

On January 27, 1939, the *Reich* apprised H.M. government of Britain of its intention to make the number of German *U-Boote* equal to those of the Royal Navy. On April 27, Adolf Hitler declared in a memorandum that he wanted to revoke the Anglo-German Naval Agreement and ordered the *Kriegsmarine*'s warships back to their military ports. When *Großadmiral* Erich Raeder learned of the British declaration of war on the morning of September 3, 1939 from the *Reich* Chancellery, this was a severe blow to him. He wrote in the war journal of the *Seekriegsleitung* (Naval War Command), that the German *Überwasserstreitkräfte* (Surface Forces), because of their inferiority to those of the British, could only show that they would understand how to die well.

1.) Different stamped markings on *Reich* war flags of the *Kriegsmarine*. The measurements can be readily recognized, as can the *Marine* acceptance stamp (national emblem + 'M'). (Collection of P.-M. Rousseau). 2.) Warship pennants. (Collection of P.-M. Rousseau). 3.) Pennant of the minesweeper R19. (Private collection)

This *Reich* service flag was "found" by a French soldier on May 9, 1945 in the fortress of La Rochelle-La Pallice.

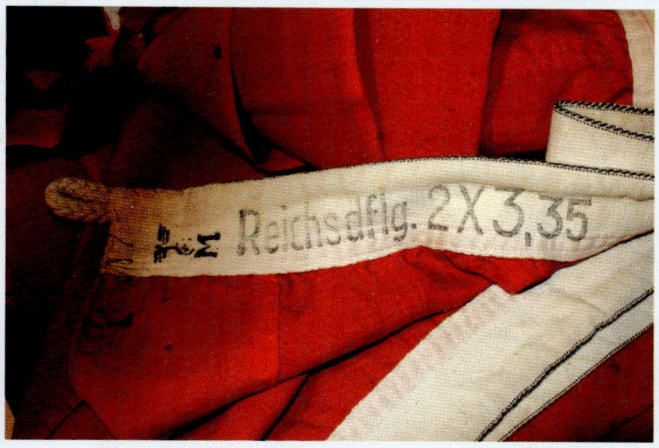

Stamped markings on a *Reich* service flag (2 meters x 3.35 m). (Private collection)

Großadmiral Raeder during a visit aboard ship. He became *Chef der Marineleitung* (head of the *Marine* Command) in October 1928, and retained his position, which was renamed in 1935 *Oberbefehlshaber* (commander-in-chief) of the *Kriegsmarine*, until 1943. (Private collection)

During a visit to a cruiser in 1935, Adolf Hitler had his photograph taken together with the ship's officers. The latter do not yet wear any gold embroidery on their peaked caps, since this was only introduced as of July 1, 1936. (Private collection)

1

2

3

4

5

1.) Command flag for an *Admiral*'s flagship (mounted front left). (Collection of P.-M. Rousseau)

2.) Flag of a *Generaladmiral* (U.S. Four Star Admiral). (Private collection)

3.) Flag of the *Kriegsmarine Oberbefehlshaber*. (Private collection)

4.) Flag of the *Admiralinspekteur* (Admiral Inspector). (Private collection)

5.) *Großadmiral* (Fleet Admiral, U.S. Five Star)'s flag. This flag, like the three previous, was displayed at the bow of the vessels used by *Kriegsmarine* admirals. (Private collection)

U 25, a type IA ocean-going vessel, near the coast in 1936. (Private collection)

The *Reich*'s New Battle Flags

By the decree of October 5, 1935 (MV 35, No.395), the new-design *Reich* battle flag was flown for the first time on November 7 aboard the light cruiser *NÜRNBERG* in the port of Kiel. The new flag was a red rectangle with a black-white bordered white circle at the central axis, which was shifted slightly to the flagpole side. A black swastika, standing on one point, was set in the middle of the circle. A black *Balkenkreuz* (stylized Iron Cross) with a white-black-white border was set by the central circle.

Großadmirale had the right to hoist a square white flags an insignia of rank, which displayed a black *Eisernes Kreuz* (Iron Cross) with black and white border, and on it, two crossed *Großadmiral* batons and a golden *Wehrmacht* eagle. The *Kriegsmarine Oberbefehlshaber* (if he were not a *Großadmiral*) had two crossed golden swords in place of the batons and eagle. The *Admiral*'s flag showed only a black *Eisernes Kreuz. Viczeadmirale* (Vice Admirals) had, by the *Eisernes Kreuz*, another black sphere in the inner upper corner, and *Konteradmirale* (Rear Admirals) also had a second sphere in the inner lower corner.

The *Marineflieger* (*Marine* Pilots)

Germany was not allowed any *Marinefliegerei* (Naval Air Force) under the Treaty of Versailles. However, this branch of the military was re-formed already in 1935, first as the *Luftkreis IV* (Air Group IV), which was soon transformed by the *Luftwaffe* into the *Luftwaffenkommando See* (Naval Air Force Command). Because of *Luftwaffe* chief Hermann Göring's rejection of any *Marinefliegerei* which might operate independently of "his *Luftwaffe*," and not be subordinate to him, and his personal aversion to *Admiral* Raeder, only a few small naval air units were created, which were anyway too insignificant to affect the course of the war. It is also the case that the *Kriegsmarine*'s lack of enthusiasm for aircraft carriers played a role in the failure to build up any *Marinefliegerei*. Despite this, the aircraft manufacturers Heinkel, Fieseler, and Arado, all developed different models of maritime reconnaissance aircraft (primarily seaplanes). In addition, they also worked on the possibilities for adapting existing models for use on aircraft carriers, including as dive-bombers (the Ar 81, Ju 87, and He 118). For fighter aircraft, they considered the Messerschmitt Bf 109, the Heinkel He 112, and the Focke-Wulf 159. Beyond this, a reconnaissance aircraft that could be catapult-launched had been available since 193: the He 60A, a biplane with floats, which was first replaced by the He 60C, and finally by the He 114A.

These light seaplanes were deployed on heavy cruisers, on some light cruisers, and on designated auxiliary cruisers, such as two each of the He 114 V2 on the "*Atlantis*", the "*Widder*" (Ram), and the "*Pinguin*" (Penguin). The low-wing Arado Ar 196 airplane was usually found aboard battleships and pocket battleships and cruisers; this plane had a BMW radial engine 132Dc with 880 hp (which was replaced by the model Ar 196A-1, with a BMW 132K engine with 960 hp). The original weaponry – two 50-kg bombs and one 7.92-mm machine gun – was reinforced with an additional 7.92-mm machine gun and two 2-cm machine guns. The Ar 196A-2 was used predominantly for coastal reconnaissance.

The *Uberwasserstreitkräfte* (Surface Forces)

There were two glaring miscalculations in the fleet buildup which began in 1936: One, the idea that Great Britain would not be a future opponent; the other, was the use of steam turbines to power the battleships and heavy cruisers, instead of the diesel propulsion used for the pocket battleships, which made a significantly greater cruising range possible. Hitler revealed his hopes of being able to reach an amicable solution with England at, among other places, a meeting on November 5, 1937, to which he had summoned the top military leadership and the *Reich* Minister of Foreign Affairs, and where he expounded his expansionary policy plans to those present. These plans impelled the repeatedly amended plans for naval armament, known as "Plan Z."

Großadmiral **Karl Dönitz' automobile standard. (Photo: Hermann Historica auction house, Munich)**

Interim baton of *Großadmiral* Karl Dönitz. (Photo: Hermann Historica auction house, Munich)

Service pennant for an *Admiral*. This pennant was usually flown from the left fender of the service car. Here, the celluloid case to cover the pennant is missing. (Private collection)

Border detail of the *Admiral*'s service pennant. (Private collection)

Even so, Karl Dönitz and Hellmuth Heye spoke against it, arguing that the German fleet would not succeed in beating the British, and they would only be able to disrupt vulnerable British maritime trade. They were supported in these views by the fleet commander Admiral Hermann Boehm, and the Chef der Aufklärungsstreit Kräfte (Chief of Reconnaissance Forces) K.A. Hermann Densch. Hitler, however, supported the faction that wanted to focus on building pocket battleships and battleships, to the detriment of the *U-Boot* forces, and so on January 27, 1939, the "Z-Plan" was set into motion, which, according to the will of its author, was to have been realized by 1949. However, the British declaration of war on September 3, 1939 put an immediate end to "Plan Z."

Version of the service pennant for officers, here with leather border. (Private collection)

Service pennant for an officer's motor vehicle (or for officials of officer rank). (Private collection)

Quadruple-barreled *Flak* aboard a *Kriegsmarine* escort boat.

The *U-Boote*

By 1934 already, a whole range of almost completely finished *U-Boote* were waiting in warehouses, only needing to be rapidly assembled. This situation had been made possible by the "*Ingenieurskantoor voor Scheepsbouw,*" (Shipbuilding Engineering Office) a German R&D bureau for *U-Boot* development, which, operating under the cover of a Dutch company in the Netherlands, was able to incorporate the latest developments in the field in its work. This company had developed *U-Boote* for several countries (including Turkey, Finland, and Spain), which had undergone extensive testing by German crews. In this way, it was possible to train many *U-Boot* experts, who would later form the nucleus of the *Kriegsmarine U-Boot* crews. Thus, on June 15, 1935, two days before the Anglo-German Naval Agreement was signed, the first new German *U-Boot* – U 1 – was launched. Two weeks later, it was put into service under the command of *Kapitänleutnant* (Navy Lieutenant) Klaus Ewerth, and initially used as a training boat. On September 25, 1935, the first *U-Boote-Flotille*, (submarine flotilla) "Weddigen" was deployed in Kiel; it was named after a celebrated German *U-Boot* commander of World War I. Their first flotilla leader was *Fregattenkapitän* (Frigate Captain) Karl Dönitz, who was appointed *Konteradmiral* (Rear Admiral) in October 1939, and held the position of *U-Boot Befehlshaber* (commander) *(B.d.U.)*.

The *Marine* Artillery

This force was responsible for protecting the harbors of strategically important coastal areas. It was armed with German Krupp guns and all possible captured weapons: Bofors, Cockevill, Putilov, Saint-Chamond, Schneider, Skoda and others, from the 6.5-cm C/1902 to the 40.6-cm SK C/34, depending on the task at hand. The batteries were housed in casemates (fortified gun emplacements), in armored or concrete gun turrets, in open positions, and even on armored trains. The *Kriegsmarine* deployed three different types of artillery:

- *Marine-Artillerie-Abteilungen* (Naval Artillery Battalions) *(M.A.A.)*. These were responsible for coastal defense and attacked enemy convoys or single ships crossing their section of the coast.

- *Leichte Marine-Artillerie-Abteilungen* (Light Naval Artillery Battalions) *(le.M.A.A.)*. These were also used for coastal defense, against attacks by ground troops.

- *Marine-Flak-Abteilungen* (Naval anti-aircraft battalions) (*M.FLA.*). Responsible for protecting the airspace over harbors and *Kriegsmarine* facilities.

On February 4, 1938, the "Führer" Hitler made himself *Oberbefehlshaber* (commander-in-chief) of the *Wehrmacht* (Armed Forces). Even though they had sworn their allegiance to Hitler, the *Kriegsmarine*, true to their traditions, always filtered the commands they received. Karl Dönitz was one of the few senior officers who dared to express his own views, even if these did not exactly coincide with those of Adolf Hitler. At the head of this branch of the *Wehrmacht* stood the *Oberbefehlshaber der Marine* (*Ob.d.M.*), initially *Generaladmiral* Erich Raeder, who was quickly promoted to *Großadmiral*, and, from February 1943, Karl Dönitz. Subordinate to the *Ob.d.M.* was the *Oberkommando der Marine* (*OKM*); until 1939, this consisted of three central departments:

- *Allgemeines Marineamt Operationsabteilung* (General Navy Department (Operations))
- *Marinewehramt Marinewaffenamt* (Naval Armed Forces Ordnance Bureau)
- *Marineverwaltungsamt Marinekonstruktionsamt* (Navy Administration Office for Naval Construction)

At the beginning of the war, the geographical authority of the *Marine Oberkommando* was distributed as follows:

- *Marinegruppenkommando Ost* (Naval Group Command East) was the operative command post for the Baltic region, with staff headquartered in Swinemünde (now Świnoujscie, Poland).
- *Marinegruppenkommando West* was responsible for the German Bucht (Bight), the North Sea, and the Atlantic Ocean, with headquarters at Sengwarden, north of Wilhelmshaven.

Großadmiral **Raeder and** ***Kommodore*** **(Commodore) Dönitz in 1939. (Private collection)**

Admirale **Raeder und Dönitz on an inspection tour in Angers, 1941. (Private collection)**

Kriegsmarine propaganda poster.
(Private collection)

Gunner manning a quadruple-barrelled *Flak* on board a warship. (Private collection)

Functioning as the supreme command of the *Marine* on land:

- *Marinestation der Ostsee* (Baltic Sea Naval Station)
- *Marinestation der Nordsee* (North Sea Naval Station)

A German cruiser fires on enemy ships in the Atlantic.

In the course of the war, the *Kriegsmarine* also set up command authorities in the occupied countries and regions. In Denmark, this was the *Marinebefehlshaber* (*Marine* commander) *Dänemark* (from 1943: *Kommandierenden Admiral* (Commanding Admiral for Denmark). He commanded three sectors: North Jutland, South Jutland, and the Danish islands.
The *Marinebefehlshaber Südwest* (Southwest) was responsible for the Netherlands and Belgium (from June 1940: *Marinebefehlshaber Niederlande-Belgien*).
In Norway, numerous duty stations and units answered to the *Kommandierenden Admiral Norwegen* (from 1943: *Marineoberkommando Norwegen* (*Marine* High Command Norway).
In June 1940, the *Kommandierenden Admiral Frankreich* was made responsible for the occupied zone of France, with his command headquarters in Paris; under his command were the *Marinebefehlshaber* for northern France, the Channel coast, Brittany, and western France. These, in turn, held command of the duty stations and facilities at Ostend by Dunkirk, Boulogne, Cherbourg, Brest, Lorient, Saint-Nazaire, La Pallice-La Rochelle, and Bordeaux. Some 30,000 French and foreign workers worked in and around these bases.

In the Mediterranean Region

In France: Port-Vendres, Sete, Port-de-Bouc, Marseille, Toulon, Saint-Tropez, Cannes, and Nice, from November 1942. In Italy: Genoa, La Spezia, Livorno, the island of Elba, Naples, and Palermo. On the Adriatic Sea: Ancona, Ravenna, Venice, and Trieste. In Tunisia: Bizerte, Ferryville (now Menzel Bourguiba), Tunis, Sousse, and Sfax from 1942-1943. Libya: Tripoli, Benghazi, and Tobruk, from the formation of the *Afrikakorps* (Africa Corps).
In Greece: Preveza, Patras, Kaiamata, Piraeus, Thessaloniki, Salamis, Chalcis, as well as on many Greek islands, including Samos, Corfu, and Crete; after the Italian capitulation, Syros, Rhodes, and Leros were added. In Albania: Vlora and Durres.
In Dalmatia: Kotor, Dubrovnik, Split, Sibenik, Zadar, Senj and Pula, since the end of 1943.

On the *Ostfront* (Eastern Front)

On the Black Sea (Romanian side): Varna, Constanta; on the Soviet side: Odessa, Sevastopol, Balaklava, Yalta, and Feodosia, as well as many smaller bases.
Many skilled and unskilled workers from the local population worked at these bases, even those that were in use only for a relatively short time.
The *Kriegsmarine Oberbefehlshaber* was also in charge of the *Flottenchef* (Fleet Commander) – Admiral Hermann Boehm at the outbreak of the war – who had his staff in Kiel. When war broke out, the fleet forces were structured as follows:

- *Befehlshaber der Panzerschiffe* (pocket battleships) (*Konteradmiral* Wilhelm Marshall), with staff in Wilhelmshaven.

- *Führer der U-Boote* (*Kommodore* Karl Dönitz), with staff in Kiel.

- *Befehlshaber der Aufklärungsstreitkräfte* (Reconnaissance Forces) (*Vizeadmiral* (Vice Admiral) Hermann Densch), with staff in Kiel. Answering to him were also, in addition to the cruisers, the following command headquarters:

- *Führer der Torpedoboote* (*Konteradmiral* Günther Lütjens), in Swinemünde.

- *Führer der Minensuchboote* (minehunters) (*Fregattenkapitän* Friedrich Rüge), in Cuxhaven.

Admiral Dönitz at a meeting with Italian comrades in arms in 1942. (Private collection)

At the outbreak of war, the fleet consisted of twelve battleships, heavy and light cruisers, sixty-one *U-Boote* (including twenty-seven ocean-going boats), twenty-one destroyers, twelve torpedo boats, seventeen *Schnellboote* (fast attack boats) and twelve minehunters. The initial structure of the *Kriegsmarine* underwent several significant changes during the course of the war.

THE *KRIEGSFLOTTE*

The war fleet was subdivided into three major sectors:

• The *Flottenstreitkräfte* (Fleet Forces), i.e.

- Battleships and cruisers
- Destroyers
- Torpedo boats
- *Schnellboote*
- Auxiliary cruisers
- Fleet supply ships
- Training ships

• The *Sicherungsstreitkräfte* (Security Forces) (divided into flotillas)

- Minehunters
- Minesweepers
- Minefield breakers
- Patrol boats
- Security boats
- *Unterseebootsjäger* (submarine hunters)
- Escort vessels
- Harbor protection vessels
- Coastal protection vessels

• The *Unterseeboote* (divided into flotillas)

The Fleet at the Beginning of the War in 1939

***Flottenstreitkräfte* (battleships, heavy cruisers, light cruisers), their commanders and anchorages**

- The old battleship SCHLESWIG-HOLSTEIN (*Kapitän zur See* (Captain) Gustav Kleikamp), as a training ship on the Baltic Sea.
- ADMIRAL GRAF SPEE (*Kapitän zur See* Hans Langsdorff), had left Wilhelmshaven on August 21 sailing towards the South Atlantic.
- ADMIRAL SCHEER (*Kapitän zur See* Hans-Heinrich Wurmbach), anchored off Schilling-Reede by Wilhelmshaven.
- DEUTSCHLAND (*Kapitän zur See* Paul Wenneker), in the North Atlantic.
- EMDEN (*Kapitän zur See* Werner Lange), anchored off Wilhelmshaven.
- GNEISENAU (*Kapitän zur See* Erich Förste), anchored off Kiel.
- KÖLN (*Kapitän zur See* Theodore Burchardi), on the Baltic Sea.
- KÖNIGSBERG (*Kapitän zur See* Kurt Caesar Hoffmann), as a training ship on the Baltic Sea.
- LEIPZIG (*Kapitän zur See* Heinz Nordmann), on the North Sea.

One of the great names of German *U-Boot* force: *Kapitänleutnant* (Navy Lieutenant) Otto Kretschmer, *Kommandant* (commander) of U 99. With forty-seven ships sunk and six damaged on only sixteen patrols, he was the most successful *U-Boot* commander of the Second World War. (Private collection)

- NÜRNBERG (*Kapitän zur See* Otto Klüber), on the Baltic Sea.
- SCHARNHORST (*Kapitän zur See* Otto Ciliax), anchored off Wilhelmshaven.
- SCHLESIEN (*Kapitän zur See* Kurt Utke), on the Baltic Sea.

***Sicherungsstreitkräfte* (Security forces) (destroyers, torpedo boats, *Schnellboote*, minehunters)**

- Destroyers: twenty-one units (identification numbers from Z 1 to Z 21)
- Torpedo boats: twelve units (animal names from "Albatross" to "Wolf")
- *Schnellboote*: seventeen units (identification numbers from S 6 to S 22)
- Minehunters: twelve units (identification numbers from M 1 to M 12)

Unterseeboote

U-Boote: sixty-one units (identification numbers from U 1 to U 61), including thirty coastal *U-Boote*, eleven of which were used for training. The remaining boats, four of them still in trials, were ocean-going.

The Fleet at the End of 1941

Two old *Kaiserliche Marine* battleships, which had been in service since 1908, were from then on used as school and training vessels:

- SCHLESIEN,
- SCHLESWIG-HOLSTEIN.

The *Uberwasserstreitkräfte* (Surface Forces)

Four battleships
- GNEISENAU, built in Kiel, commissioned on May 21, 1938.
- SCHARNHORST, built in Wilhelmshaven, commissioned on January 7, 1939.
- BISMARCK, built in Hamburg, commissioned on August 24, 1940.
- TIRPITZ, built in Wilhelmshaven, commissioned on February 25, 1941.

Three *Panzerschiffe* (pocket battleships) (later counted among the heavy cruisers)
- DEUTSCHLAND (LÜTZOW after February 1940), built in Kiel, commissioned on April 1, 1933.
- ADMIRAL SCHEER, built in Wilhelmshaven, commissioned on November 12, 1934.
- ADMIRAL GRAF SPEE, built in Wilhelmshaven, commissioned on January 6, 1936.

Three heavy cruisers
- ADMIRAL HIPPER, built in Hamburg, commissioned on April 29, 1939.
- BLÜCHER, built in Kiel, commissioned on September 20, 1939.
- PRINZ EUGEN, built in Kiel, commissioned on August 1, 1940.

Six light cruisers
- EMDEN, built in Wilhelmshaven, commissioned on October 15, 1925.
- KÖNIGSBERG, built in Wilhelmshaven, commissioned on April 17, 1929.
- KARLSRUHE, built in Kiel, commissioned on November 6, 1929.
- KÖLN, built in Wilhelmshaven, commissioned on January 15, 1930.
- LEIPZIG, built in Wilhelmshaven, commissioned on October 8, 1931.
- NÜRNBERG, built in Kiel, commissioned on November 2, 1935.

Thirty destroyers

Identification numbers from Z 1 to Z 30, divided into eight flotillas

Thirty-one torpedo boats

"*Raubvogel*" – ("bird of prey") and "*Raubtier*" – ("beast of prey") classes: twelve units of torpedo boat-class type 1935: Identification numbers T 1 to T 12.

Torpedo boat-class type 1937: Identification numbers from T 13 to T 19.

Additional types were introduced during the war, and from 1942, fleet torpedo boats were put into service. The captured foreign torpedo boats which the *Kriegsmarine* put into service, carried the identification "TA" before the identification number.

Schnellboot in action. (Private collection)

Schnellboote

At the beginning of the war, the *Schnellboote* (on troop duty), were still under the command of the *Führer der Torpedoboote*, and the command headquarters of the *Führer der Schnellboote* was created only in April 1942. By the end of 1941, seven *Schnellboote* flottillas had been drawn up, which were primarily deployed in the North and Baltic Seas and English Channel. A French-speaking German officer described them, referring to Victor Hugo's novel "*Les Travailleurs de la mer*," as "the workers of the sea," since their crews operated courageously and continually.

Auxiliary cruisers

Initially, these "*Kaperfahrer*" (a *Kaperschiff* was a privateer) were designated as *Handelsschutzkreuzer* (merchant navy protection cruiser), and later as *Handelsstörkreuzer* (trade disruption cruiser, better known as a merchant raider) (HSK). These refitted and armed ships of civilian origin were used for trade war against enemy merchant ships. Their identification numbers ran from HSK 1 to HSK 10.

Minehunters

Besides old minehunters from the First World War, which were designated as auxiliary minehunters, there were *M-Boote* of the types 1935 and 1940, which were numbered from M 1 to M 36 (the type 1943 was added later). Small minehunters were designated as minesweepers and carried the ID "R" before the identification number. *Sperrbrecher*, or minefield breakers, were also deployed for defense against mines.

Patrol boats and security patrol boats

These small boats were divided into many flotillas.

U-Bootjäger (submarine hunters)

The early *U-Boot* hunter flotillas were deployed in the North Sea, the Baltic Sea, off Norway, in the Western region, and in the Aegean Sea. The boats usually carried the designation "UJ" before the identification number.

Escort boats

These operated in the Black Sea, the Mediterranean, the Adriatic, and, until the last day of the war, in the Baltic.

Sailing training vessels

These were three-masted barks with a sail area of 1,797 to 1,973 square meters, and a four-stroke diesel system of 520 to 750 hp as an auxiliary engine:

- The GORCH-FOCK with 1,545 tons water displacement
- the ALBERT LEO SCHLAGETER with a displacement of 1,750 tons
- the HORST WESSEL, also with 1,750 tons water displacement.

Artillery training ships

They were named BREMSE, BRUMMER, and MARS. There was also a number of smaller artillery training boats. Old boats were used for torpedo boat training.

Tenders and escort vessels

There were always at least seventeen of these in service. The *Uberwasserstreitkräfte* also included hospital ships, gunboats, fleet escorts, lighters, and small barges or scows.

The destroyer Z 21 WILHELM HEIDKAMP. (Private collection)

The development of the *U-Boot* forces, from the first *U-Flotille* "Weddigen," to what became almost a "fourth branch of the *Wehrmacht*," went ahead very rapidly during the war. A total of twenty-eight *U-Boot* flotillas were drawn up, of which thirteen served as training flotillas, so that no more than fourteen combat front flotillas were deployed in the various theaters of war, since the *18. U-Flotille* existed for only three months.

In 1936, Karl Dönitz was appointed *Führer der Unterseeboote* (F.d.U.) (*U-Boot* leader) and drove forward, among other things, the development of the new *Rudeltaktik* ("pack tactics"). On Sept. 19, 1939, Dönitz was appointed *Befehlshaber der U-Boote* (B.d.U.) and took over both organizational and operational leadership of the *U-Boot* forces. The *Oberkommando der Marine* was responsible all pertaining to the construction, repair, and supply for its *U-Boote*, as well as their bases.

The *Kriegsmarine* used Roman numerals to denote the different *U-Boot* types (or classes). These type designations were, however, not continuous, because not all the designs planned on the drawing board actually went into production. Improved versions of each type were usually identified by a letter, such as type VII C, of which over 650 units were built. The type IX, intended for the Battle of the Atlantic, was indeed similar to the type VII C, but significantly larger. Three versions of this were constructed:

Right: **A *Korvettenkapitän* (Lieutenant Commander) of the *Kriegsmarine* addressing veterans at a meeting of the *Reichskriegerbund* (German war veterans' association) in 1935. (Private collection)**

***Kapitänleutnant* Günther Prien among the victorious crew of U 47, after their successful attack on Scapa Flow in October 1939. Interesting to note is that the men are not yet wearing the uniform cap bands with the inscription "*Kriegsmarine*," but rather still wear the peacetime inscription. (Private collection)**

Type IX A, B, and C. In the successor version in 1944, type IX D1, the torpedo tubes were removed and the boat was deployed as a fuel cargo vessel. The next version was the type IX D2, which could cover a distance of almost 32,000 nautical miles above water. The Type X B was developed as a minelayer and supply boat for ships on the front; the XIV was also intended as a supply vessel, namely as a tanker. The types XXI and XXIII were the most advanced *U-Boote* of their time, but only came into service towards the end of the war.

Boats of the *1. Unterseeboot-Flottille* in Kiel, 1935. (Private collection)

Types of German *U-Boote* and Their Technical Information

Type UA
Units built: 1
Displacement, submerged: 1,248 tons
Length: 86.70 meters
Beam: 6.80 meters
Maximum surface speed: 18 knots
Maximum submerged speed: 8.5 knots
Surface range: 13,100 nautical miles
Maximum diving depth: 100 meters
Torpedo tubes: 6
Torpedoes on board: 12
Guns: 2x2-cm *Flak*
Crew: 45 men
This boat, actually intended for Turkey, was put into service in September 1939 and sank a total of 40,706 GRT (gross registered tons). It was itself scuttled in May 1945 in Kiel

Type I A
Units built: 2
Displacement, submerged: 983 tons
Length: 72.39 meters
Beam: 6.21 meters
Maximum surface speed: 18.6 knots
Maximum submerged speed: 8.3 knots
Surface range: 7,900 nautical miles
Maximum diving depth: 200 meters
Torpedo tubes: 6
Torpedoes on board: 14
Guns: 1x10.5-cm L/54, 1x2-cm single *Flak*
Crew: 43 men
Both ships of this type were put into service in 1936, initially as training ships, but in 1940 were commandeered for the war effort. U 26 sank in July of that year; U 25 only a month later.

Adolf Hitler awarding Günther Prien the *Ritterkreuz* (Knight's Cross) after his daring exploit at Scapa Flow. (Private collection)

Type II A
Units built: 6
Displacement, submerged: 303 tons
Length: 40.90 meters
Beam: 4.08 meters
Maximum surface speed: 13 knots
Maximum submerged speed: 7 knots
Surface range: 3,100 nautical miles
Maximum diving depth: 150 meters
Torpedo tubes: 3
Torpedoes on board: 5-6
Guns: 1x2-cm single *Flak* (from 1944: 2x2-cm double *Flak*)
Crew: 25 men

Type II were the first *U-Boote* that the new *Kriegsmarine* built. This type had already been developed in the 1920s by the *Ingenieurskantors voor Scheepbow* in The Hague, which was secretly run by the German *Reichsmarine.* The six boats were built in Kiel in the summer of 1935 and put into service with the numbers U 1-U 6. Production of this boat, designed as a coastal vessel, was stopped as from 1941.

Type II B
Units built: 20
Displacement, submerged: 328 tons
Length: 42.70 meters
Beam: 4.08 meters
Maximum surface speed: 13 knots
Maximum submerged speed: 7 knots
Surface range: 3,100 nautical miles
Maximum diving depth: 150 meters
Torpedo tubes and guns: as for Type II A
Crew: 25 men

The first eighteen boats of this type were numbered U 7-U 24. The other two, which had originally been built for China, and therefore called "China boats," carried the numbers U 120 and 121. One of U 19's first commanders was *Kapitänleutnant (Kptlt).* Joachim Schepke, while *Kptlt.* Otto Kretschmer was the third of U 23 – both officers later became German *U-Boot* aces. On February 18, 1940, U 23 sank the British destroyer HMS DARING.

After their former *Kommandanten* took command of type VII boats, these two boats joined their sister vessels U 9, U 18, U 20. and U 24 in the *30. U-Flotille* in the Black Sea, where they fought successfully against the Soviet Navy. Under the command of *Kptlt.* Hans Jenisch, on Jan. 21, 1940, U 22 sank the destroyer HMS EXMOUTH. The last successful boat of this type, was U 19 under *O.z.S. Oberleutnant zur See* (Lieutenant junior grade) Willy Ohlenburg; on Sept. 2, 1944, U 19 sank the Soviet minehunter VZRYV BTSC-410. After the flotilla was disbanded one week later, five of the Black Sea boats were scuttled, and the sixth was sunk by the Soviets. Between December 1939 and June 1940, U 9 was under the command of *O.z.S.* Wolfgang Lüth, who later commanded other *U-Boote* (138, 43, and 181) and sank a total of 48 ships, comprising 229,469 GRT. Some of the remaining boats served in the *U-Boot* training flotilla. The *Kommandant* of U 23, *Kptlt.* Otto Kretschmer, who later took over command of U 99, became, after sinking 263,228 GRT of shipping, the "tonnage king" of the war.

Above: **Propaganda postcard with the text of the famous soldiers' song "*denn wir fahren gegen Engeland*" ("... 'cause we are sailing against England.") (Private collection)** ***Bottom:*** **Propaganda postcard with the flag of the *Kriegsmarine* land troops. (Private collection)**

Type II C
Units built: 8
Displacement, submerged: 341 tons
Length: 43.90 meters
Beam: 4.08 meters
Maximum surface speed: 12 knots
Maximum submerged speed: 7 knots
Surface range: 3,800 nautical miles
Maximum diving depth: 150 meters
Torpedo tubes and guns: as for Type II A
Crew: 25 men

Type II D
Units built: 16
Displacement, submerged: 364 tons
Length: 43.97 meters
Beam: 4.920 meters
Maximum surface speed: 12.7 knots
Maximum submerged speed: 7.4 knots
Surface range: 5,650 nautical miles
(The type II D had almost twice the cruising range as the type II A)
Maximum diving depth: 150 meters
Torpedo tubes and guns: as for Type II A
Crew: 25 men

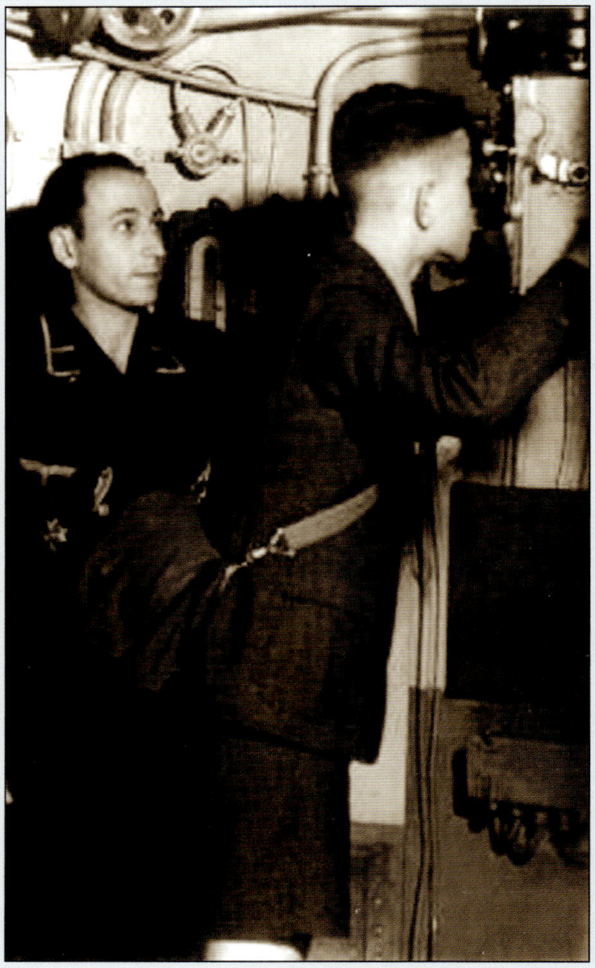

Right: **"Torpedo launched!" ... as this boy would like to think while visiting aboard a *U-Boot*, as he looks through the attack periscope. (Private collection)**

"Alarm!" – during an emergency dive, all the *U-Boot* hatches had to be closed in lightning speed. (Private collection)

Crewmembers of U 552, Erich Topp's boat, gathered on the tower before sailing into their operational port. The two torch-carrying red devils were the boat's emblem. (Private collection)

Type VII A
Units built: 10
Displacement, submerged: 745 tons
Length: 64.51 meters
Beam: 5.85 meters
Maximum surface speed: 17 knots
Maximum submerged speed:8 knots
Surface range: 6,200 nautical miles
Maximum diving depth: 200 meters
Torpedo tubes: 5
Torpedoes on board: 11
Guns: 1x8.8-cm L/45* and 1x2-cm single *Flak*
Crew: 44-50 men

Type VII A boats carried the numbers U 27-U 36. The first boat of this type was put into service on August 12, 1936. U 30 (under the command of *Kptlt.* Fritz-Julius Lemp) sank the first British ship of all, the steamer ATHENIA, on September 3, 1939. Lemp sank a total of twenty ships, comprising 95,507 GRT. On her first patrol against the enemy, U 29 under *Kptlt.* Otto Schuhart, sent the British aircraft carrier HMS COURAGEOUS to the bottom of the sea. The good seaworthiness of the Type VII A and the comparatively low construction costs, prompted the *Kriegsmarine*, until the end of the war, to build five more versions of the VII type.

The officers of U 758, commanded by *Kptlt.* Helmut Manseck, prior to the visit of an *Admiral* on board. (Private collection)

A German *U-Boot* in the Norwegian ice, winter 1940-41. (Private collection)

Type VII B
Units built:24
Displacement, submerged: 857 tons
Length: 66.50 meters
Beam: 6.20 meters
Maximum surface speed: 17.9 knots
Maximum submerged speed:8 knots
Surface range: 8,700 nautical miles
Maximum diving depth: 200 meters
Torpedo tubes: 5
Torpedoes on board: 14
Guns: 1x8.8-cm L/45* and 1x2-cm single *Flak*
Crew: 48-50 men

Type VII B boats carried the numbers U45-U 55, U 73-U 76, U 83-U 87, and U 99-U 102. U 48, whose first commander was *Kptlt.* Herbert Schultze, was the most successful *U-Boot* of the war, and sank fifty-two ships with a total of 307,935 GRT. After she was taken out of frontline service, U 48 served as a school and training boat in service in the Baltic. With his boat U 99, *Kptlt.* Otto Kretschmer achieved twenty-six of his total of forty-three victories, but then was taken as a British prisoner of war after his boat was seriously damaged by HMS WALKER. *Kptlt.* Joachim Schepke scored twenty-six of his thirty-seven victories as *Kommandant* of U 100, going down with his boat after she was rammed by HMS VANOC. The most famous victory of all, was doubtless that of *Kptlt.* Günther Prien as *Kommandant* of U 47 in October 1939, when he penetrated the British naval base at Scapa Flow and there sank the battleship HMS ROYAL OAK. Over the next seventeen months, Prien sank with his VII B *U-Boot* another twenty-seven vessels, with a total of 157,573 GRT. U 47 was lost in the North Atlantic for reasons still unclear today. The loss of these three German *U-Boot* aces in March 1941 marked a turning point in the *U-Boot* war.

Distributing the mail aboard a *U-Boot*. (Private collection)

Types VII C and C/41
Units built: 661 (the most-built *U-Boot* in the world)
Displacement, submerged: 871 tons
Length: 67.10 meters
Beam: 6.20 meters
Maximum surface speed: 17.7 knots
Maximum submerged speed: 7.6 knots
Surface range: 8,500 nautical miles
Maximum diving depth: 250 meters
Torpedo tubes: 5
Torpedoes on board: 14
Guns: 1x8.8-cm L/45* and 1x2-cm single *Flak*
Crew: 48-50 men
The VII C/41 was developed with a number of improvements in the area of the tower, the torpedo tubes, and the guns, (with ninety-one units built); in addition, the second hull and the pressure hull were strengthened, making it possible to increase diving depth to 250 meters. The next version, the VII C/42, was to have succeeded this type; however, it was never completed. The boats of types VII C and C/41 carried the numbers U 69-U 72, U 77-U 82, U 88-U 98, U 132-U 136, U 201-U 212, U 221-U 232, U 235-U 329, U 331-U 458, U 465-U 486, U 551-U 683, U 701-U 722, U 731-U 779, U 821 and U 822, U 825-U 828, U 901-U 908, U 921-U 930, U 951-U 1032, U 1051-U 1058, U 1063, 1064 and 1065, U 1101-U 1110, 1131 and U 1132. U 1161-U 1172, U 1191-U 1210, U 1271-U 1279, and, finally, from U 1301-U 1308.

Among the type VII C *U-Boote* that served in the *29. U-Flotille*, which operated in the Mediterranean, the following boats were especially outstanding: U 81 under *Kptlt.* Guggenberger, that, on November 13, 1941, sank the aircraft carrier HMS ARK ROYAL in the vicinity of Malta in broad daylight; then, U 331 under *Kptlt.* von Tiesenhausen, which also sank in daylight the battleship HMS BARHAM with a crew of 862, while she was underway north of Bardia with two other British battleships. U 522 under *Kptlt.* Erich Topp, scored twenty-nine sinkings, comprising 155,738 GRT; U 96, under *Kptlt.* Heinrich Lehmann-Willenbrock, had twenty-five victories, totaling 183,223 GRT; and U 203. under *Kptlt.* Mützelburg, twenty-one sinkings with 83,302 GRT.

Yet with all the many successes of type VII C *U-Boote* , all those should not be forgotten, which did not return from their patrols or could not boast of any sinkings. The final victory of a German *U-Boot* in the Mediterranean was won by *O.z.S.* Dierk Lührs with his U 453, which torpedoed the British steamer FORT MISSANABIE. The last sinking in the Baltic Sea was by U 370, which sank the Finnish minelayer LOUHI. On April 29, 1945, in the last convoy battle of the war, *O.z.S.* Dietrich, with his boat U 286, torpedoed the British frigate HMS GOODALL in the Barents Sea. On May 2, U 979 under *Kptlt.* Johannes Meermeier sank the British armed trawler EBOR WYKE in the Atlantic. Finally, on May 7, U 1023 under *Kptlt.* Heinrich- Andreas Schroeteler, sank the Norwegian minehunter NYMS 382. The last German *U-Boot* that was defeated in battle during the Second World War, was the VII- C/4l boat U 320 under *O.z.S.* Emmrich, which was damaged on May 8, 1945 by depth charges. The units U 471 and U 766 were put back in service in 1946 by the French Navy under the names MILLE and LAUBIE.

The triumphant return of U 47 under Günther Prien after his daring raid on Scapa Flow, where he sank the British battleship HMS ROYAL OAK and other ships. (Private collection)

The victory pennants fastened on the tower of U 47 give a good impression of the success of German *U-Boote* men during the first years of the war. (Private collection)

Type VII D
Units built: 6
Displacement, submerged: 1,080 tons
Length: 76.90 meters
Beam: 6.38 meters
Maximum surface speed: 16.7 knots
Maximum submerged speed: 7.3 knots
Surface range: 11,200 nautical miles
Maximum diving depth: 200 meters
Torpedo tubes: 5
Torpedoes on board: 12 or 4 torpedoes and 15 mines
Guns: 1x8.8-cm L/45* and 1x2-cm single *Flak*
Crew: 44 men
The D type, designed as a minelayer, was a full ten meters longer and approximately 20-cm broader than the Type VII C. The six ships carried the numbers U 213-U 218.

Type VII F
Units built: 4
Displacement, submerged: 1,181 tons
Length: 77.63 meters
Beam: 7.30 meters
Maximum surface speed: 17.6 knots
Maximum submerged speed: 7.9 knots
Surface range: 14,700 nautical miles
Maximum diving depth: 200 meters
Torpedo tubes: 5
Torpedoes on board: 14 (plus another 21 for supplying other boats)
Guns: 1x8.8-cm L/45*, 1x3.7-cm *Flak*, 2x2-cm *Flak*
Crew: 46 men
This type was deployed as torpedo transporters, to supply front-line ships at sea and was therefore more than ten meters longer and 1.10 meters broader than the Type VII C. The numbers of these boats ranged from U 1059-U 1062.
*The 8.8-cm deck gun used on the *U-Boote* had nothing to do with the famous "8.8-*Flak*", and did not even use the same ammunition.

Type IX A
Units built: 8
Displacement, submerged: 1,153 tons
Length: 76.50 meters
Beam: 6.51 meters
Maximum surface speed: 18.2 knots
Maximum submerged speed: 7.7 knots
Surface range: 10,500 nautical miles
Maximum diving depth: 200 m
Torpedo tubes: 6
Torpedoes on board: 22
Guns: 1x10.5-cm, 1x3.7-cm *Flak*, 1x2-cm double *Flak* (from 1943: 2x 2-cm instead of the 10.5 cm)
Crew: 48 men
The first German *U-Boot* which was sunk during the war was a type IX A, the U 39 under *Kptlt.* Glattes, which was lost on September 14, 1939. This design, oriented to the Ms type (*Mobilmachungstyp* (mobilization boat type)) U 81-U 86 of the First World War, was a two-hull boat and therefore more seaworthy than the Type VII. Type IX A boats carried the numbers U 37-U 44.

Type IX B
Units built: 14
Displacement, submerged: 1,178 tons
Length: 76.50 meters
Beam: 6.51 meters
Maximum surface speed: 18.2 knots
Maximum submerged speed: 7.3 knots
Surface range: 12,000 nautical miles
Maximum diving depth: 200 meters
Torpedo tubes: 6
Torpedoes on board: 22
Guns: as for Type IX A
Crew: 48 men
Boats of this type carried the numbers U 64 and U 65, U 103-U 111, and U 122-U 1242 and were under the command of the *2. U-Flotille* in Wilhelmshaven, which was later transferred to Lorient. During the Battle of the Atlantic, the type IX B proved its outstanding quality: four of these boats were among the six most successful *U-Boote* in terms of tonnage sunk. These were the boats U 103 under *Korvettenkapitän* (Lieutenant Commander) (*K.K.*) Viktor Schütze, U 123, U 124, and U 107, which under their respective *Kommdanten*, sank a total of 174 vessels with altogether 2,860,958 GRT. U 123 was put back into service in 1946 under the name BLAISON in the French Navy.

Type IX C
Units built: 145
Displacement, submerged: 1,232 tons
Length: 76.76 meters
Beam: 6.76 meters
Maximum surface speed: 18.3 knots
Maximum submerged speed: 7.3 knots
Surface range: 13,450 nautical miles
Maximum diving depth: 200 meters
Torpedo tubes: 6
Torpedoes on board: 22
Guns: as for Type IX A
Crew: 48 men
The boat numbers of this type were U 66-U 68, U 125-U 131, U 153-U 166, U 171-U 176, U 501-U 524, U 801-U 806, U 841-U 846, U 853-U 858, U 865-U 870, U 877-U 881, U 889-U 891, and U 1221-1235. The *U-Boot* U 155 under *Kptlt.* Adolf Piening sank the British escort aircraft carrier HMS AVENGER in November 1942. After U 167, boats were built with various improvements (such as increased range due to larger fuel tanks); these were put into service under the designation type IX C/40 from 1942 on. On May 14, 1944, U 549 under *Kptlt.* Detlev Krankenhagen sank the escort aircraft carrier USS BLOCK ISLAND. In the Indian Ocean, U 510 under *Kptlt.* Alfred Eick sank the Canadian steamer POINT PLEASANT PARK on February 23, 1945, while U 853 under *O.z.S.* Helmut Frömsdorf sank the American freighter SS BLACK POINT on May 5 in the Atlantic.

Victory pennant with the number '5452,' which boasts of the tonnage of the ships sent to the bottom of the the sea. (Collection of P.-M. Rousseau)

Every *U-Boot* returning victorious from a patrol hoisted its victory pennant as it sailed into its base. The number is '2500' gives the approximate tonnage of the sunken vessels, and in this case also tells who was the victim: a tanker. (Collection of P.-M. Rousseau)

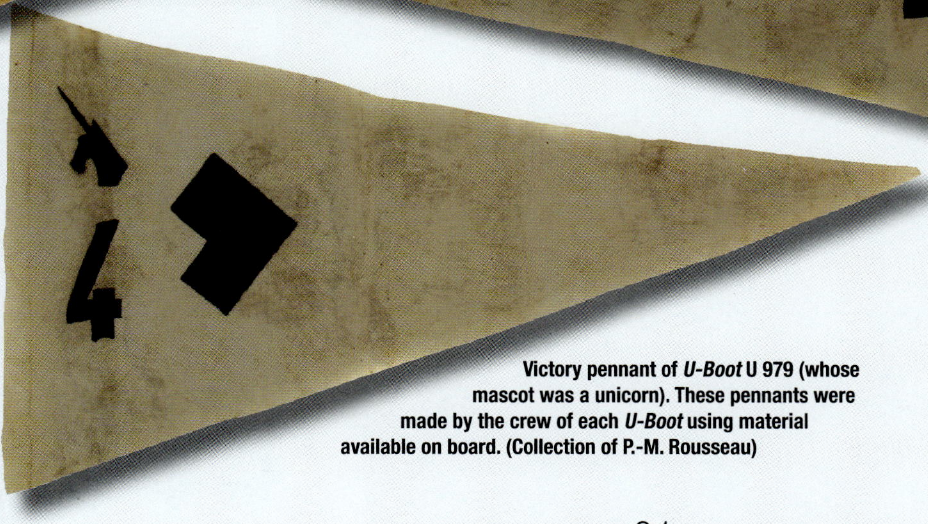

Victory pennant of *U-Boot* U 979 (whose mascot was a unicorn). These pennants were made by the crew of each *U-Boot* using material available on board. (Collection of P.-M. Rousseau)

Type IX DI
Units built: 2
Displacement, submerged: 1,799 tons
Length: 87.58 meters
Beam: 7.50 meters
Maximum surface speed: 16.5 knots
Maximum submerged speed: 6.9 knots
Surface range: 12,750 nautical miles
Maximum diving depth: 200 meters
Torpedo tubes: 6
Torpedoes on board: 24
Guns: 1x10.5-cm, 1x3.7-cm *Flak*, 1x2-cm double *Flak*
Crew: 55 men
Both U 180 and U 195, put into service in 1942, had fast diesel engines, which were at the same time very vulnerable. Therefore, these were dismantled and replaced by slower engines. In 1944, the torpedo tubes were expanded and the two boats afterwards used as fuel suppliers. The 10.5-cm gun aboard was also removed, and the boats then retained only the *Flak* weapons.

Type IX D2
Units built: 28
Displacement, submerged: 1,804 tons
Length: 87.50 meters
Beam: 7.50 meters
Maximum surface speed: 19.2 knots
Maximum submerged speed: 6.9 knots
Surface range: 31,500 nautical miles
Maximum diving depth: 200 meters
Torpedo tubes: 6
Torpedoes on board: 22
Guns: as for Type IX A
Crew: 57 men
Type IX D2 boats were designed as long-haul boats and intended for deployment in the Indian Ocean and the South Atlantic, where they were to attack Allied convoys. Nearly all boats of this Type were, after commissioning, put under the command of the *12. U-Flotille* in Bordeaux. Under the command of *F.K.* Wolfgang Lüth, U 181 sank a total of twenty-seven enemy ships with 138,779 GRT. The longest patrol of any *U-Boot* ever, was that of U 196 under *K.K.* Eitel-Friedrich Kentrat; she was at sea for 225 days before she again sailed into Bordeaux. The last success of the *Kriegsmarine* in the Pacific was achieved by *K.K.* Heinrich Timm aboard U 862, when he sank the U.S. freighter ROBERT J. WALKER. Some of the boats deployed in the Indian Ocean were equipped for reconnaissance with the portable gyro aircraft or copter FA 330 ("*Bachstelze*" ("Wagtail")).

Type X B
Units built: 8
Displacement, submerged: 2,177 tons
Length: 89.80 meters
Beam: 9.20 meters
Maximum surface speed: 17 knots
Maximum submerged speed: 7 knots
Surface range: 18,450 nautical miles
Maximum diving depth: 200 meters
Torpedo tubes: 2 (stern)
Torpedoes on board: 15 and 66 SMA (shaft-launched) mines
Guns: 1x10.5-cm, 1x3.7-cm *Flak*, 1x2-cm double *Flak*. From 1943, the 10.5-cm gun was replaced with a second 2-cm double *Flak*
Crew: 52 men
This type, deployed as a minelayer and supplier for front-line ships, was the largest German *U-Boot* of the Second World War.
Two X B – U 219 and U 234 – were converted into transports, the others carried the numbers U 116-U 119 and U 220-U 233. U 116, U 117, U 118, and U 119 went missing after only a few patrols against the enemy. The last boat of this type was U 233, sunk in July 1944. However, the two transports survived the war: U 219 was taken over by the Japanese and U 234 surrendered on May 16, 1945 to the Americans, who took the boat to Portsmouth (New Hampshire).

U 218 returning from a patrol in 1942, under the command of *Kptlt.* Richard Becker. (Private collection)

Type XIV
Units built: 10
Displacement, submerged: 1,932 tons
Length: 67.10 meters
Beam: 9.35 meters
Maximum surface speed: 14.9 knots
Maximum submerged speed: 6.2 knots
Surface range: 12,350 nautical miles
Maximum diving depth: 240 meters
Torpedo tubes: - none –
Torpedoes on board: 4 (as freight)
Guns: 2x3.7-cm *Flak*, 1x2-cm *Flak* (from 1943, 1x3.7-cm and 2x2-cm)
Crew: 53 men
This *U-Boot* tanker (nicknamed the "*Milchkuh*" ("milk cow")), and intended to replace the types IX D and X B, had only a brief career. In July 1943, four boats were all sunk within just one week, and three more in the same year (the final boat, U 490, was lost on June 11, 1944 in the Atlantic). Construction of other boats was abandoned after that. The boats bore the numbers U 459-U 464 and U 487-U 490.

Type XXI
Units built: 118, but only 113 put into service
Displacement, submerged: 1,819 tons
Length: 76.70 meters
Beam: 8.00 meters
Maximum surface speed: 15.6 knots
Maximum submerged speed: 17.2 knots
Surface range: 15,500 nautical miles
Maximum diving depth: 240 meters
Torpedo tubes: 6
Torpedoes on board: 23
Guns: 4 x 3-cm *Flak*
Crew: 57 men
This was a more developed version of the trial model type XVIII, which had a "Walter Drive," a hydrogen peroxide-powered, external air-independent propulsion system which allowed the boat to remain submerged for substantially longer than before. After a lecture at the *Reichskanzlei* (Chancellery) in Berlin, Hitler gave Dönitz the green light to build two trial type XVIII boats. These extraordinary *U-Boote* were equipped with an electric motor power unit (two Walter motors, each with 7,500 hp), giving them an underwater speed of twenty-four knots(!) and a theoretical cruising range of 16,000 nautical miles. The production costs and high fuel consumption (twenty-five times as much as a conventional diesel) led, however, to the cancellation of the trial project in favor of a model with mixed motor power unit of diesel and electric motors; this aborted the birth of a groundbreaking *U-Boot*, that not only had an extremely fast diving time (eighteen seconds to ten meters), but also could achieve significantly greater speeds under water than on the surface.
A new sonar system and the ability to attack targets without having to surface, gave this boat a considerable advantage. With the also new rapid torpedo-loading device, a new round of ("Aale" ("eels" slang for torpedoes) could be fired off every five to fifteen minutes. The type XXI *U-Boote* carried the numbers U 2501-U 2552, U 3001-U 3025, U 3037-U 3041, U 3044, and finally U 3501-U 3530. The first unit was put into service on June 17, 1944, far too late to have any influence on the outcome of the war. After the war, U 2518 was transferred to the French Navy, where she remained in service under the name ROLAND MORILLOT until 1967.

On board *U-Boot* U 47, which has hoisted its victory pennant for sailing into port, there are also two *Luftwaffe* servicemen, who likely had been fished out of the water. (Private collection)

Type XXIII
Units built: 64, but only 62 put into service
Displacement, submerged: 258 tons
Length: 34.68 meters
Beam: 4 meters
Maximum surface speed: 9.7 knots
Maximum submerged speed: 12.5 knots
Surface range: 4,450 nautical miles
Maximum diving depth: 160 meters
Torpedo tubes: 2
Torpedoes on board: 2
Guns: none
Crew: 14 men
This single-hulled coastal vessel was planned for deployment in the Mediterranean and North Sea; the first unit of type XXIII was launched on April 17, 1944. The boats of this type were numbered throughout as U 2321-U 2371, as 4701-U 4707, and as U-4709-U 4712. Even though it was quite small and could not carry any reserve torpedoes, this type did have a modern streamlined design, with a narrow tower, which enabled the boats to submerge to ten meters in only nine seconds, and also to reach high speeds under water. The German *U-Boot* which scored the fleet's two last sinkings on May 7, 1945, hit both the Norwegian freighter SNELAND I and the Canadian freighter AVONDALE PARK with one torpedo each; this was U 2336 under *Kptlt.* Emil Klusmeier.

Type XXVII

The command for serial production of these midget *U-Boote* was issued only at the end of March 1944. The "*Hecht*" ("pike") (type XXVII A) was built in the Germania shipyard in Kiel. The length was 10.39 meters, the width 1.70 meters; the boat could carry two torpedoes and a two-man crew.

Almost 300 "*Seehunde*" ("seals") (type XXVII B) were finished, some in Kiel and some in Elbingen. The boats had a length of 11.87 meters, a beam of 1.68 meters; they could transport two torpedoes and had a two-man crew. 363 "*Molche*" ("salamanders") were built by Deschimag AG in Bremen. These 10.78 meters long and with a 1.81 meter beam. The boats carried two torpedoes and a one-man crew. Of the "*Biber*," ("beaver"), 324 units were built by the Lübeck Flender-Werke by Deschimag. The boats, nine meters long and with just a 1.57 meters beam, carried two torpedoes and a one-man crew. All of these midget *U-Boote* were deployed in the *K-Flotillen* of the *Kleinkampfverbände* (the small battle or attack units).

Günther Prien, the "Bull of Scapa Flow," was made into the first great war hero by German propaganda. (Private collection)

The other small attack craft, so-called one-man torpedoes, were, however, less *U-Boote* as rather manned torpedoes. The "*Neger* ("Negro") [modern German: Afro-German] was named after its inventor, naval architect Richard Mohr and consisted of two G-7 torpedoes hung one under the other. The upper one was converted to a carrier torpedo for the actual battle torpedo, with the warhead removed and a cockpit with a plexiglass cover installed for the driver, who also wore a Dräger breathing apparatus. An electric motor was installed at the rear of the carrier torpedo, with which the weapon could reach a speed of 3.2 knots. The "*Neger*" was not submersible and could only be used near the coast.

However, the Germans must have soon recognized that the shallow draft of the Allied landing craft meant that the torpedoes had to shoot through under the keel. The first "*Neger*" were still in the *Reich*, and were transported by train to Italy, where they were to be used against the Allied troops landed at Anzio-Nettuno. The fleet of thirty-seven "*Neger*" (*K-Flotille* 361), under the command of *Leutnant zur See* (Ensign) Johann-Otto "Hanno" Krieg, finally arrived in their operational area on April 20, 1944.

Some fourteen of the devices were left behind on sandbanks and were destroyed. The remaining twenty-three were divided into three groups. The first, under the command of *Oberfähnrich zur See* (Senior Midshipman) Koch, was to attack the Allied fleet in the bay before Nettuno. The second, led by *Oberfähnrich zur See* Seibicke, was to attack ships lying in the roads off Anzio, and the third, under the command of *Fähnrich* (Midshipman) Voigt, was to penetrate the port of Anzio, but they found it empty, so that they launched their torpedoes against the quay walls, which were damaged. The *Matrose* (Seaman Recruit) Horst Berger, from the first group, successfully torpedoed a small freighter and *Fähnrich* Potthast an American patrol boat. Only thirteen "*Neger*" returned from their missions.

The discouraging results in Italy accelerated construction of the "*Marder*" ("marten"), but this was never deployed in the Mediterranean. Thanks to a ventilation system, these could dive for a short time up to ten meters deep. These one-man torpedoes were used, among other places, during the Allied landings in Normandy, where *Obergefreiter* (Seaman) Gerhold sank the Polish light cruiser DRAGON.

***Kapitän zur See* Kurt Dobratz, *Kommandant* of *U-Boot* U 1232. (Private collection)**

***Kptlt.* Georg Schewe, *Kommandant* of *U-Boot* U 105. (Private collection)**

Even though German *U-Boote* were deployed on almost all the seas and oceans of the world during the Second World War, their main hunting grounds lay in the Atlantic. It should be remembered, that Great Britain was dependent upon importing raw materials and food supplies to survive and fight – and these had to be brought over the sealanes across the Atlantic. In 1939, during the first months of the war, German *U-Boote* sank some fifty ships, including the aircraft carrier HMS COURAGEOUS. The daring exploit of *Kptlt.* Günther Prien who penetrated Scapa Flow and there, right in the middle of the British Fleet's base, with his U 47, sank the battleship HMS ROYAL OAK on October 14, 1939, was really remarkable. Already on September 5, he had sunk the British steamer BOSNIA in the Bay of Biscay. The balance for the first year of the war came to: 147 enemy ships sunk, totaling more than 500,000 GRT, against nine sunken *U-Boote*, two of them by mines.

In 1940, the *U-Boote* were not very numerous, moved slowly, and had to struggle with too many faulty torpedoes, but they achieved notable success in the Atlantic, not least thanks to the bases along the French coast. At the same time, they avoided sorties into the North Sea, where the sky teemed with RAF aircraft, while the Home Fleet controlled the sea. The occupation of France and its Atlantic coast gave the *U-Boote* direct access to their most important "hunting grounds." On July 7, 1940, the first German *U-Boot*, U 30 under *Kptlt.* Fritz-Julius Lemp, arrived in the Scorff *U-Boot* bunker at Lorient; by the end of August 1940, U 37 under *Kptlt.* Victor Oehrn returned to Lorient, after he had sunk eight ships in the Atlantic.

At the end of September, the British RAF began its air attacks on Lorient, which housed three German *U-Flotille*, thus becoming the most important *U-Boot* base on the French Atlantic coast. From the end of 1940 and during all of 1941, the *Kriegsmarine* was building many *U-Boot* bunkers in the most important French Atlantic harbors. These bases were an important trump card for the *Oberkommando der Marine*, since the geographical position of the German *Reich* had been very unfavorable at the beginning of the war; the *U-Boot*e had to sail around Great Britain via northern Scotland. Since the Strait of Dover was mined and patrolled by countless armed cutters and *U-Boot* hunters, the shortest route to the Atlantic Ocean was also the most dangerous. The work on these massive defensive structures, themselves intended

Fregattenkapitän **Albrecht Brandi commanded, in succession, the boats U 617, U 380, and U 967. (Private collection)**

to be able to withstand even the most powerful bombs, as well as their technical equipment, made these facilities equal of those in the *Reich* itself. At these bases, it was possible to carry out all conceivable repairs and maintenance work, up to the most complex.

Five bases were built in the French Atlantic ports: Brest, Lorient (the most important one, which was consistently expanded until June 1944), Saint-Nazaire, La Pallice, and Bordeaux. A *Kriegsmarine Flotille* and one of the Italian *Regia Marina* were based in Bordeaux. Two other *U-Flottille* were based in Saint-Nazaire, yet another in La Pallice, and then the three mentioned above in Lorient. There were, therefore, eight *U-Boot Flotille* stationed on the French Atlantic coast.

The *U-Boote*'s "halcyon days" began in July 1940, and these lasted until September 1941. In October, Karl Dönitz' so-called *Rudeltaktik* ("pack tactics") brought the *U-Boot* forces good success: a *Rudel* of twelve *U-Boot*e, during four nights, attacked the convoys SC-7 and HX-79 and sank thirty-two ships with a total of 154,661 GRT. Up through the end of 1940, Dönitz' *U-Boote* had sunk 492 enemy ships with a total of more than two-million GRT. Some twenty-six of his boats never returned to their French bases.

In 1941, some 120 *Kriegsmarine U-Boote* operated successfully in the Atlantic, but the *Befehlshaber der U-Boot*e (B.d.U.) also had to deal with a serious setback: Within just ten days, he lost all at the same time his three best *U-Boot Kommandant*en: on March 7 or 8, *K.K.* Günther Prien went down with U 47 and her forty-five crew members south of Iceland, for reasons unknown. *Kptlt.* Joachim Schepke was sunk on March 17 with his U 100 and thirty-seven crewmembers (only five of his men could be rescued), by the destroyers HMS VANOC and HMS WALKER in a nighttime battle. *K.K.* Otto Kretschmer was taken prisoner by the British on the same day with his entire crew (although three men were killed), after he had to give up his severely damaged boat U 99. The British had meanwhile improved their methods of *U-Boot* hunting. They benefitted in this from the capture of a *U-Boot* of type IX B, *Kptlt.* Fritz-Julius Lemp's U 110. She had been badly damaged by depth charges from the destroyer HMS BROADWAY and the corvette HMS AUBRETIA, and forced to surface, whereupon the crew were ordered to abandon ship. The British succeeded in taking all the secret documents and the "*Enigma*" cipher machine they found on board, and keep that fact secret – the Germans had no idea that, from that time on, the British were able to read all their encrypted messages. (The HMS BULLDOG then tried to tow the German *U-Boot* to Iceland, but U 110 sank on the way there.) Already in June, they were able to sink many *Kriegsmarine* tankers and supply ships, as well as weather ships in the Atlantic.

On August 27, U 570 under *Kptlt.* Rahmlow was slightly damaged by the RAF, whereupon the crew surrendered; the boat was subsequently boarded by the Royal Navy, towed to England and eventually put into the service of the British Navy under the name HMS GRAPH. In December, U 567 under *Kptlt.* Engelbert Endrass, along with the entire crew, was lost north of the Azores, sunk by depth charges from the corvette HMS SAMPHIRE and sloop HMS DEPTFORD. Although the number of *U-Boot*e had increased (247 ready for service, of which 50% were in the line of duty at the same time), in the Atlantic, actually, only sixteen boats were operating at the same time, with the exception of June-July 1941, when their numbers rose to thirty-five. In the course of 1941, some thirty-eight *U-Boote* were lost, but the other side lost in return 445 ships, of more than two million GRT.

In April 1943, as Kommandant of U 181, Korvettenkapitän Wolfgang Lüth was awarded the Ritterkreuz (Knight's Cross) with Schwertern zum Eichenlaub (swords with oak leaf cluster) clasp. (Private collection)

A German *U-Boot* puts to sea for a patrol from her *U-Boot* bunker. (Private collection)

1942: The situation changed completely when the United States entered the war at the end of 1941. Freight and other ships were produced in quick succession for supplying Great Britain and securing the convoys. The introduction of new technologies and of frigates which were significantly faster and equipped for *U-Boot* hunting, made it possible to intercept *U-Boote*, allowing the convoys to proceed on their way with their heavily armed escorts when the danger was over. New British anti-submarine weapons — "Hedgehog" and "Squid" — gave the Allied captains more cause for hope. All this was nearly outweighed by the fact that the *U-Boote* were now able to expand their hunting grounds almost up to the American East Coast. In February 1942, U 578 under *Kptlt.* Ernst-August Rehwinkel, sank the destroyer USS JACOB JONES, sending the balance for that month up to seventy-six sunken Allied ships, with a total of 411,500 GRT. In March, the balance exceeded this up-to-then record, with 131 ships sunk totaling 616,904 GRT. In April, *Kptlt.* Max-Martin Teichert torpedoed the cruiser HMS EDINBURGH in the Barents Sea and damaged her seriously. Two days later, the German destroyer Z-24 struck the ship, which was being towed to Murmansk, with the ultimate deathblow. During May and June 1942, German *U-Boote* sank more than 550,000 GRT per month! In June, however, another *U-Boot* ace was lost, after U 158, under her *Kommandant K.K.* Erwin Rostin, was attacked by a U.S. flying boat with depth charges and sunk. In July, a *Wolfsrudel* ("wolf pack") of type VII C *U-Boote* attacked the convoy PQ 17 on its way to Murmansk, and sank sixteen ships, while seven others fell victim to the *Luftwaffe*.

In the night of September 12, *Kapitänleutnant* Werner Hartenstein, *Kommandant* of U 156, torpedoed the British passenger ship LACONIA, 500 nautical miles off the island of Ascension. In addition to her crew, the ship also had sixty civilians, 430 Allied soldiers, military materiel,

Kptlt. Prien standing, here in service dress, on the tower of U 47, not long after being awarded the *Ritterkreuz*. Note the emblem on the tower, the 'bull of Scapa Flow,' which later was displayed on all boats of the 7. *U-Flotille*. (Private collection)

Admiral Dönitz in discussion with *Kptlt.* Prien, before Prien put to sea for a patrol. (Private collection)

and 1,700 Italian prisoners of war on board. When Hartenstein realized that there were Italian allies among the survivors floating in the water, he turned to the *B.d.U.* with a request for further instructions. Dönitz agreed to the rescue of the shipwrecked and had two more German *U-Boote* set course for the site of the sinking. *Kptlt.* Hartenstein sent out an English message to all ships in the area, stating that he would not attack any ship that was taking part in the rescue of the shipwrecked survivors of the LACONIA. Some time later, U 506 and U 507, and the Italian submarine CAPPELLINI reached the place and also took on survivors of the torpedoing. The four *U-Boote* raised Red Cross flags and sailed, with hundreds of survivors on deck and on rafts which they took in tow, towards the African coast, where they wanted to hand the survivors over to Vichy French ships.

On September 16, an American "Liberator" bomber discovered the convoy and was signaled by Hartenstein, that he might need help. The bomber pilot reported the situation to his base, including the fact that boats were sailing under Red Cross flags. Despite this, the U.S. Air Force base still ordered the sinking of the *U-Boote*. This attack caused countless casualties among the shipwrecked, even though the *U-Boote* had time to make emergency dives and thus escape more or less unscathed Most of the Britons survived the attack, and were fished out of the sea by other German ships, and a number of the shipwrecked were handed over to French ships, but the majority of the Italians were killed by the torpedoing and subsequent bombardment. A further consequence of this incident was that Dönitz gave the order that in future, German *U-Boote* were to refrain from any rescue attempts for passengers on sunken enemy ships.

In September, *U-Boote* destroyed three Allied destroyers at the same time: the Canadian HMCS OTTAWA, which was torpedoed on September 14 by U 91 under *Kptlt.* Heinz Walkerling off Newfoundland; then, on September 20, HMS SOMALI by U 703 under *Kptlt.* Heinz Bielfeld off Greenland; finally, HMS VETERAN on September 26, by U 404 under *Kptlt.* Otto von Bülow in the Atlantic. On November 15, U 155 under *Kptlt.* Adolf Piening, shot her four front torpedoes at an Allied convoy off Portugal, and scored two direct hits: One sank the escort aircraft carrier HMS AVENGER, and the other the British troop transport ETTRICK. A third hit badly damaged the cargo ship USS ALMAACK. In December, a "*Wolfsrudel*" of 19 *U-Boote* attacked the convoy ONS-154 in the Atlantic. Ten of them sank fifteen Allied ships. U 435 under *Kptlt.* Siegfried Strelow and U 356 under *Kptlt.* Günther Ruppelt each sank three ships, while U 225 under *Kptlt.* Wolfgang Leimkühler sent two more down. The seven remaining boats each achieved one sinking. By the end of 1942, the tonnage of the ships sunk by the German *U-Boote* was more than what could be produced in the British roadsteads. The "*grauen Wölfe*" ("gray wolves") were about to win victory for the *Kriegsmarine* in the Atlantic, despite the improved methods of reconnaissance and combat the Allies introduced. The year ended with 1,094 sunken Allied ships, comprising more than 5.5 million GRT, while, during the same period, eighty-eight *U-Boote* were lost, thirty-three due to Allied aircraft.

1943: Some 429 *U-Boote* were operational by the end of April 1943, and 110 of these were deployed in the Atlantic. Per month, twenty new units were being finished, and since February, the new, pressure-independent torpedoes were also being delivered. However, the hopes aroused by these developments were not fulfilled, because the Allies also were not asleep, but continued their work as in perfecting radar technology; beyond this, the enormous productive capacity of the United States was running at full blast – and this was made clear by the significant increase in losses of *U-Boote* and experienced *Kommandanten*.

The big reception for Prien in Berlin. On March 7 or 8, 1941, the celebrated *U-Boot Kommandant* and his crew suffered the seaman's death (probably due to depth charges) south of Iceland. (Private collection)

In January, *Kptlt.* Karl Thurmann, who had sunk fifteen ships, and *F.K.* Harro Schacht with eighteen sinkings, died; in March, *Kptlt.* Werner Hartenstein (nineteen ships), was taken. In March 1943, the "*grauen Wölfe*" in a pack of forty-one *U-Boote*, attacked over four days the convoys SC 122 and HX229, and sank twenty-two Allied ships, but themselves lost only a single vessel.

That was, however, the last major battle in the Atlantic. The increasingly improved protection of the convoys, as well as unbroken air monitoring, made possible by the stationing of U.S. long-range bombers in Greenland and Iceland, took their toll on the *U-Boote* from that time on. In April, *Kptlt.* Johann Mohr, who had twenty-nine sinkings to his credit, was lost. During the attack on the convoy ONS-5 in May 1943, while thirteen Allied ships were sunk, yet at the same time, eight *U-Boote* were lost. In May 1942, not only were four more type XIV A "*Milchkühe*" sunk, but also U 954 under *Kptlt.* Odo Loewe. This was an especially heavy blow for *Großadmiral* Dönitz, because his son Peter was serving as Watch Officer on this boat. At the same time, the death toll of the aces kept rising: in August, *Kptlt.* Hans Trojan was killed; in September *Kptlt.* Albrecht Achills; and in November they were followed by *Kapitänleutnante* Georg Staats, Wilhelm Rollmann, and Heinz-Otto Schultze. During the following autumn, two more type XIV A tankers were destroyed. Because of the threat from the air, *U-Boote* in the Bay of Biscay could only sail submerged, as the only way to avoid falling victim to the RAF. The race between the shipping tonnage being sunk and that produced in the U.S. shipyards, was now was running in favor of the Allies.

1944: In late January, the number of *Kriegsmarine U-Boote* ready for service peaked at 447; these also carried the new, homing torpedoes on board, and most of them were equipped or refitted with snorkels, so that they no longer had to surface to recharge their batteries. In April, with U 2501, the first unit of the new type XXI came into service – the most advanced submarine of its time. At the end of May, U 549 under *Kptlt.* Detlev Krankenhagen torpedoed the escort aircraft carrier USS BLOCK ISLAND. Yet at the same time, the number of lost *Kriegsmarine U-Boote* was higher than that of the enemy ships they had sunk, and in June, their last type XIV A "*Milchkuh*" went down. The Germans had plans, in the event of an Allied landing in France, for forty *U-Boote* to cruise the sea off the Atlantic coast, but in reality, no more than six units were in the area on June 6. In view of the total sea and air superiority of the Allies, those boats could achieve nothing at all.

This poster promoted an exhibition on the war at sea, being held in Berlin's "*Museum der Kriegsmarine*," which ran from June 13 to September 30, 1942. In a special show, visitors were able to themselves walk through the 1:1 model of a *U-Boot*. (Private collection)

Encounter between a German *U-Boot* and a sailing school ship in the Baltic. (Private collection)

RAF air attacks on the French Atlantic bases on June 29 destroyed the up to eight snorkel-equipped *U-Boote* which were still lying there. The French *U-Boot* bases, endangered by the Allied landings, were abandoned, yet, of the nine *U-Boote* that tried to fight their way through to Norway, only four actually made it.

In the other theatres of war, the time of *U-Boot* success was also at an end: The last successful sinking in the Mediterranean was on May 19, when U 453 under *O.z.S.* Dierk Lührs torpedoed the steamer FORT MISSANABIE. On September 2, *O.z.S.* Willy Ohlenburg sank the Soviet minehunter VZRYV BTSC-410, thus achieving the final *Kriegsmarine* victory in the Black Sea. On December 24, *K.K.* Heinrich Timm and his boat U 862 sank the U.S. freighter ROBERT J. WALKER in the Pacific. The balance for the last quarter of 1944 was painful: for twenty-four sunken enemy ships, sixty-four *U-Boote* never returned to their bases. During all 1944, while some 131 Allied ships with a total of 700,000 GRT were sunk, yet at the same time, the *Kriegsmarine* itself lost 264 *U-Boote*. Dönitz had to note bitterly, that the successes of the *U-Boot* forces were no longer enough to equal their losses.

1945: In January, the German yards launched thirty-seven new *U-Boote*, more than in no other month of the entire war! The British naval historian Stephen Roskill, a former lieutenant in the Royal Navy, wrote on this: *"As astonishing as it may appear, the first months of 1945 were a worrying time for the British naval authorities, as we knew that the Germans were able to put their new U-Boote into service more rapidly than we could sink them. Beyond this, we assumed that we would have to deal with some boats of the greatly improved types XXI and XXIII, and we knew that since the development of the 'snorkel,' our radar-equipped aircraft had lost much of their efficiency."*

This was a very unequal fight, however, and the few modest successes were of no consequence, in the face of the tremendous losses. Dönitz's order to cease hostilities on May 4 did not reach all the serving *U-Boote* in time, so some of them were only able to respond several days later. On May 5, U 853 under *O.z.S.* Helmut Frömsdorf sank the coal freighter SS BLACK POINT off New York; the next day, the boat itself was destroyed by the destroyer USS ATHERTON and the frigate USS MOBERLEY. On May 7, U 1023 under *Kptlt.* Heinrich Schroeter torpedoed the Norwegian minehunter NYMS 382 in the Bay of Biscay, while the type XXIII U 2336 under the command of *Kptlt.* Emil Klusmeier sank the freighters AVONDALE PARK and SNELAND I off the Scottish Firth of Forth. Two *U-Boote* – U 530 and U 977 – preferred to surrender in Argentina. Those *U-Boote* sailing in Japanese-controlled waters in May 1945, (U 181, U 195, U 219, and U 862), were taken over by the Navy of the "*Tennō*" and then fought on under new names and the flag of the rising sun.

Conclusion: Of the 1,170 *U-Boote* built, only 863 are put into service, yet these sank a total of 2,840 Allied ships and boats, including 148 warships, among which were three aircraft carriers, two battleships, five escort aircraft carriers, six cruisers, forty-one destroyers, fifteen frigates, thirty-four corvettes and dispatch boats. These vessels, taken together, comprised over than fourteen-million GRT.* On the German side, 630 *U-Boote* were lost at sea; another 123 units were sunk in ports or coastal waters, and finally, at the end of the war, 216 *U-Boote*, under Operation *Regenbogen* (Rainbow), followed the order to scuttle themselves. The *U-Boot* crews fought to the bitter end, and they had to pay a terrible toll in lives for this: Of the 41,000 men who manned the *U-Boote*, more than 29,000 lost their lives, usually in dreadful circumstances. At least for a short period, it had appeared as though these comparatively few men could, with their boats, determine the outcome of the war in favor of the German *Reich* – but in this, in the face of their enemies' superior forces, they failed.

***Dimensions of the volume of all space within a ship**

The battleship SCHARNHORST. (Private collection).

SURFACE FORCES

The surface forces were under the command of the *Oberkommando der Marine* and included the armed forces of the fleet and the security forces (minehunters, minesweepers, and so on).

THE GREAT WARSHIPS OF THE *KRIEGSMARINE*

We will present here the technical characteristics and histories of the battleships and pocket battleships, as well as the various cruiser classes up to auxiliary cruisers. The torpedo boats and other small boats of the Kriegsmarine *were already briefly touched on in Chapter II, and we cannot treat them in detail here, because their large numbers would require a work of their own. An overview table of the major warships of the* Kriegsmarine *from 1939-1945 appears at the end of this book.*

Apart from two old ships of the line, which dated back to 1908 – the SCHLESIEN and the SCHLESWIG-HOLSTEIN, which served from 1935 as training ships (although the latter was deployed during the Polish campaign and in *Unternehmen "Weserübung"* ("Operation Exercise on the Weser") – the *Kriegsmarine* had four modern battleships. In the chronological order of their commissioning, these were the GNEISENAU, the SCHARNHORST (both classified abroad as battle cruisers), the BISMARCK, and the TIRPITZ.

In addition to these battleships, there were another three pocket battleships, which had a displacement of about 12,000 tons: The DEUTSCHLAND, which was renamed LÜTZOW on Hitler's orders on November 15, 1939, because he was afraid that it would be bad for morale if the enemy succeeded in sinking a "Deutschland" during a naval battle! In early 1940, the ship was re-standardized as a heavy cruiser. The second German pocket battleship, the ADMIRAL SCHEER, had been activated as a heavy cruiser since 1940. The most famous ship of the Deutschland class, however, was the third pocket battleship, the ADMIRAL GRAF SPEE, whose short time in service was to end off Montevideo.

Initially Germany had only three heavy cruisers, with an actual displacement of around 14,000 tons, but their number rose to five in 1940, due to the re-standardization of the two remaining pocket battleships. The original heavy cruisers were the ADMIRAL HIPPER, the BLÜCHER and the PRINZ EUGEN; the latter gained notoriety because the Americans used her in 1946 as a target ship for their atomic bomb tests on Bikini Atoll. Of the light cruisers with a displacement to 6,000 tons, six units were put into service: EMDEN, KÖLN, KÖNIGSBERG, KARLSRUHE, LEIPZIG, and NÜRNBERG.

The Battleships of the Scharnhorst Class

The SCHARNHORST: The keel for this ship, named for the Prussian general and military reformer Gerhard Johann David von Scharnhorst (1755- 1813), had been first laid in 1934, but construction was stopped and the final keel laying only took place on June 15, 1935. The SCHARNHORST was launched on October 3, 1936.

Another view of the SCHARNHORST. (Private collection).

The ship was christened by the widow of *K.z.S.* Felix Schultz, *Kommandant* of SMS SCHARNHORST, who went down with his *Kaiserliche Marine* ship in the Battle of the Falkland Islands on December 8, 1914. The new ship was commissioned on January 7, 1939. The ship had a standard displacement of 31,840 tons and a loaded displacement of 38,900 tons; the length was 234.90 meters (after conversion); the beam thirty meters; and the draft between 8.2 and 9.9 meters. The machinery consisted of three sets of geared steam turbines from Brown-Boveri, with a capacity of 160,000 horsepower, which allowed her a speed of 31.65 knots and a cruising range of 7,100 nautical miles at nineteen knots. The ship was manned with a crew of between 1,669 and 1,840 men and the weaponry on board consisted of: 9x28-cm guns, 12x15 cm, 14x10.5-cm *Flak*, 16x3.7-cm *Flak*, 8- to 10x2-cm *Flak*, and two triple sets of torpedo tubes of 53.3 cm. At first, she has three, later only two, seaplanes of the Type Arado Ar 196A-4. In addition, there was a FuMO 22 (*Funkmess-Ortungsgerät*) on board – an early radar device which was replaced in 1941 by a FuMO 26.

We will go into more depth below, in the discussion of the GNEISENAU, on the deployment of the SCHARNHORST in *Unternehmen "Weserübung"* (the occupation of Denmark and Norway) and *"Juno"* in northern Norway. On April 9, 1940, there was an exchange of fire between two ships in the Vestfjord, where the British battle cruiser HMS RENOWN received two hits, at the same time that she herself was able to land three hits on the GNEISENAU. During *Unternehmen "Berlin"* (the battle against British convoys in the Atlantic), the SCHARNHORST sank eight of the fourteen British merchant ships destroyed, and then sailed, together with the GNEISENAU, to Brest, suffering a total of five bomb strikes during several air raids by the RAF. The SCHARNHORST was ordered, together with the GNEISENAU and the PRINZ EUGEN, to return to Germany. The group sailed under the protection of six destroyers and *Schnellboote* through the Channel, and reached Wilhelmshaven in mid-February 1942. During this breakout in the English Channel, also called *Unternehmen "Cerberus"* ("Operation Cerberus"), the SCHARNHORST received several mine hits, and repairing them put her out of action for eight months.

She was then to be transferred to Norway in January 1943, but two attempts to break out failed, and only on the third attempt (code named "Paderborn") was she able to break through, along with other units. On March 9, the ship anchored again off Narvik. In April, a momentous accident occurred at the new berth at Langfjord, where the TIRPITZ now also lay, probably caused by an act of sabotage: An explosion on board killed seventeen crewmen, and twenty others were injured.

After the ship was repaired, a battle group of the SCHARNHORST, TIRPITZ, and nine destroyers carried out a mission against Spitsbergen from September 6-9, where they bombarded Allied bases. On the first Christmas Day 1943 (December 25), she sailed from the fjord, accompanied by five destroyers, to intercept the convoy JH-55B, which was on its way to Murmansk (*Unternehmen "Ostfront"* ("Eastern Front"). The *Kriegsmarine* ignored the fact that another convoy was sailing from the opposite direction, this one with a powerful British escort. This escort was made up of three heavy cruisers under the command of Vice Admiral Burnett, and another combat group under Admiral Fraser, commander-in-chief of the British Home Fleet [the Royal Navy Fleet in the area of the British Isles], with the battleship DUKE OF YORK, a cruiser, and a destroyer. This formation, which was coming from Iceland, had taken course for the North Cape. The British, thanks to their reconnaissance, had very accurate information about the SCHARNHORST's mission, while at the same time, the SCHARNHORST's own radar was out of commission due to chance hit by the cruiser HMS NORFOLK. The ships under Vice Admiral Burnett drove the SCHARNHORST towards the DUKE OF YORK, whose ten 35.6-cm guns hit the German battleship three times. She continued the battle against these superior forces, until all her ammunition was expended. The DUKE OF YORK was able to achieve several more hits, and the destroyers MATCHLESS, MUSKETEER, OPPORTUNE, and VIRAGO fired a total of fifty-five torpedoes at the enemy, of which just eleven hit their target. The SCHARNHORST, who had waged a bitter fight against a superior opponent for 3.5 hours and received countless hits, capsized slowly and finally sank in the *Nordmeer* (here, Barents Sea) on December 26, 1943, with 1,932 men of her crew. There were only thirty-six survivors. This was the naval battle at the North Cape.

The SCHARNHORST at sea. (Private collection)

The **Gneisenau:** The keel was laid on February 14, 1934, but building was stopped when the original construction plans were scrapped; the ship's keel was again laid on May 6, 1935, and the ship was launched on December 8, 1936. The ship was christened by the widow of the *Kommandant* of the *Kaiserlichen Marine*'s large cruiser of the same name, which was also sunk on December 8, 1914 off the Falkland Islands. Both ships carried the name of the Prussian *Generalfeldmarschall* August Neidhart von Gneisenau (1760-1831). The battleship went into service on May 21, 1938 under the command of *Kapitän zur See* (Captain) (*K.z.S.*) Erich Förste and undertook the role of fleet flagship.

The ship had a standard displacement of 31,840 tons and a loaded displacement of 38,900 tons, the length was 234.90 meters (after conversion), the beam was thirty meters and the draft between 8.2 to 9.9 meters. The machinery consisted of three sets of Germania geared turbines and twelve Wagner high-pressure boilers with a capacity of 153,897 horsepower, which allowed her a speed of 30.7 knots and a cruising range of 6,200 nautical miles at nineteen knots. The ship was manned with a crew of between 1,669 and 1,840 men, and she carried the following weapons on board: 9x28-cm guns in three triple turrets, 12x15-cm, 14x10.5-cm *Flak*, 16x3.7-cm *Flak*, 8- to 10x2-cm *Flak*, and two triple sets of 53.3-cm torpedo tubes. At first, she had two catapult-capable seaplanes of the type Arado Ar 196A-4, instead of the original Focke-Wulf Fw 62 and Arado Ar 96. In addition, from November 1939, the ship had a FuMO 22 on board.

Officer aboard a cruiser. (Private collection).

The GENEISENAU's first cruise, with the mission to disrupt the maritime traffic between Scandinavia and Great Britain, began on September 7, 1939, with no results. On November 23, 1939, together with her sister ship, the SCHARNHORST, she attacked the Northern Patrol of the Royal Navy south of Iceland, and sank the auxiliary cruiser HMS RAWALPINDI. During a breakout through the strait between the Shetland Islands and Bergen, Norway, the GNEISENAU ran into a heavy storm, in which she suffered considerable damage, causing her to return to the Kiel shipyard.

A *Kriegsmarine* battalion in a preparatory exercise for a parade, presumably in the barracks courtyard. (Private collection)

Two *Kriegsmarine* servicemen talking to an English "Bobby" on the British Channel Islands, which were occupied by the *Wehrmacht* in 1940. (Private collection)

She only returned to her home port of Wilhelmshaven on February 4, 1940. On February 20, 1940 she sailed out for *Unternehemen "Nordmark,"* to fight British convoys off Bergen, but did not encounter any enemy ships. From April 7 to November 12, 1940, the ship took part, as flagship of fleet commander *Vizeadmiral* Lütjens, in *Unternehmen "Weserübung,"* always at the side of the SCHARNHORST. Together with the heavy cruiser ADMIRAL HIPPER and ten destroyers, both ships landed the *Gebirgsjäger* (mountaineering troops) at Narvik. East of the Lofoten, she met the heavy cruiser HMS RENOWN and the cruiser HMS BIRMINGHAM, taking three strikes in this clash, but the RENKOWN was also hit twice. On May 7, the GNEISENAU, underway in the Baltic Sea, struck a mine, but suffered no serious damage.

During *Unternehmen "Juno,"* which took place during June 4-10, 1940 in the Norwegian Sea, the battleship again served as the flagship. This naval group included, besides the SCHARNHORST, the heavy cruiser ADMIRAL HIPPER, and the destroyers KARL GALSTER, HANS LODY, HERMANN SCHOEMANN, and ERICH STEINBRINCK. On June 8, the German combat formation encountered a task group of the British aircraft carrier HMS GLORIOUS (which had about twenty type Gladiator and Hurricane airplanes on deck), and not only sank the GLORIOUS, but also her two accompanying destroyers, the HMS ACASTA and HMS ARDENT, a tanker, a troop carrier, and a guard ship. On June 20, 1940, the GNEISENAU, together with the ADMIRAL HIPPER, sailed on a foray towards Iceland and the Faroe and Orkney islands, but the German ships encountered the British submarine "Clyde," which was able to land a strike on the GNEISENAU, so that the operation had to be halted and the ship returned for emergency repairs to Trondheim.

Crewmembers of the TIRPITZ photographed in 1942 aboard their ship. The camouflage tarpaulins in the background conceal one the four 38-cm towers. (Private collection).

From here, the GNEISENAU sailed on July 25 to return to Kiel, accompanied by the light cruiser NÜNBERG. The battleship only left the dry dock at Kiel again at the end of December, when she again attempted to break out into the Atlantic, but that mission had to be aborted because of bad weather, so she again turned back.
Together with the SCHARNHORST, the ship took part in *Unternehmen "Berlin,"* from January 22 through March 22, 1941: during this engagement against Allied convoys, the GNEISENAU sank altogether fourteen vessels with a total displacement of 66,300 tons. The GNEISENAU was sighted by the British battleship HMS RODNEY, which was escorting convoy HX-108, and called upon over the radio to identify herself. *K.z.S.* Otto Fein was able to convince the British that he was the HMS EMERALD, thus avoiding a fight, continued on *Unternehmen "Berlin"* unimpeded. In April, a British plane achieved a torpedo hit on the ship, forcing her to return to dry dock in Brest. During *Unternehmen "Cerberus,"* the forcible breakout through the English Channel together with the SCHARNHORST and the PRINZ EUGEN, the ship hit another mine, but was still able to return under its own power to Kiel; however, an RAF bomb attack on February 27, 1942 destroyed the entire foreship. After this, she was deployed to Gotenhafen (today: Gdynia in Poland), where she was to be repaired and equipped with new 38-cm turrets. But already by July, the work had been abandoned and the GNEISENAU decommissioned. In the face of the relentless approach of the Red Army, she was sunk to block the entrance to the Gotenhafen harbor on March 28, 1945.

The Battleships of the Bismarck Class

The **Bismarck:** The keel was laid on July 1, 1936; she was launched on February 14, 1939. The ship's godmother was Dorothea von Löwenfeld, the great-granddaughter of former Chancellor Otto von Bismarck-Schönhausen. On August 24, 1940. the BISMARCK, under the command of the *K.z.S.* Ernst Lindemann, was put into service, and from September 1940, she sailed for practice and test runs in the Baltic Sea. The ship was only fully operational by March 1941. The BISMARK had a standard displacement of 41,676 tons and a loaded displacement of 50,133 tons. Her length was 250.50 meters , the overall beam thirty-six meters , and the maximum draft 10.2 meters. The machinery consisted of three sets of high-pressure reaction turbines from Blohm & Voss, which could produce 138,000 horsepower and made possible an average speed of twenty-nine knots and a top speed of 30.12 knots. Her cruising range was between 4,500 and 8,335 nautical miles, depending on the speed. The armament consisted of 8x38-cm guns in four twin turrets, 12x15-cm guns in six twin turrets and 10x10.5-cm *Flak*. The *Flak* also included a further 16x3.7-cm guns and 12x2-cm guns. The ship had three radar devices (1xFuMO 22, 1xFuMO 23, and 1xFuMO 26) and four catapult-capable aircraft of type Arado Ar 196A-4 on board. On May 5, 1941, Adolf Hitler, accompanied by Fleet Commander *Admiral* Günther Lütjens and *Feldmarschall* Wilhelm Keitel, visited the 2,092-man crew, before the ship sailed.

The battleship sailed from Gotenhafen on May 18, 1941 as the flagship of *Admiral* Lütjens towards the North Atlantic, under the command of *K.z.S.* Lindemann. At the beginning of *Unternehmen "Rhineübung"* ("Operation Rhine Exercise"), she was joined by the PRINZ EUGEN and the destroyers Z 16, Z 23, and Z 10. The German formation was sighted by a Swedish aircraft cruiser in the Kattegat; on May 21, she was then photographed around 13:15 hours by an RAF Spitfire. After the German destroyers veered round, on May 22, the German big ships sighted the cruiser HMS SUFFOLK. The BISMARCK fired five rounds at her without achieving any hits. On May 24 at 05:35 hours, the British naval forces again sighted the two German ships, and the battle cruiser HMS HOOD and battleship HMS PRINCE OF WALES opened fire on them from twenty-three kilometer distance. This was the beginning of the Battle of the Denmark Strait. The Germans responded immediately with a salvo from the PRINZ EUGEN's 20.3-cm guns against the HOOD, and the BISMARCK's 38-cm turrets also fired on her. One shell from the BISMARK's fifth salvo struck an ammunition chamber on the HOOD, and the resulting explosion tore her into three sections and she sank within a very short time, taking with her the lives of 1,412 seamen – only three men of the crew could be rescued.

The battleship TIRPITZ in a Norwegian fjord. (Private collection)

However, the BISMARK had also taken three hits from the PRINCE OF WALES, which put an electrical system out of operation and damaged a fuel bunker, among other things. Some 3,000 tons of seawater started flowing in through the damaged foreship, and *K.z.S.* Ernst Lindemann therefore decided to head for Saint-Nazaire. At 06:20 hours, the PRINCE OF WALES, which had taken eight hits from the German ships, turned round under cover of heavy smoke. The PRINZ EUGEN hoped to draw the British to herself, but this failed. The U.S. Coast Guard boat MODOC discovered the battleship at around 23:00 hours, and at around 24:00 hours, the BISMARK was attacked by nine Fairey Swordfish torpedo bombers, which had taken off from the aircraft carrier HMS VICTORIOUS. They managed to land one strike, although that achieved no effect, but the BISMARK kept taking on more water because of her evasive maneuvers, so that she had to reduce her speed to twenty knots. The next morning, the Royal Navy lost the battleship from its radar screens at around 03:10 hours.
Foolishly, *Admiral* Lütjens sent out a long, encrypted message to the *Seekriegsleitung* (Naval War Command) between 09:12 to 09:48 hours; this message was intercepted and located by the Home Fleet. The British had assumed that the German ship was much further north, but could now adjust their search accordingly, and, on May 26 at 10:30 hours, a Catalina flying boat of the RAF Coastal Command spotted the German battleship, which was taking course for France. Vice Admiral James Somerville immediately sent off fifteen Swordfish torpedo bombers from the aircraft carrier HMS ARK ROYAL, which accidentally fired eleven torpedoes on the HMS SHEFFIELD; the SHEFFIELD had kept contact with the BISMARK, and they had mixed her up with the other ship. The second flight of Swordfish attacked the correct target at 20:47 hours, and, at 21:05 hours, two torpedoes hit the battleship amidships and aft, so that the rudder jammed at 12° portside and the ship was disabled. Two further torpedo hits in the midship caused no major damage. At 21:40 hours, *Admiral* Lütjens gave an initial report to the *OKM* about the situation and also reported to *Großadmiral* Raeder some time later, at 02:17 hours. The wind had risen to a force of 8-9 on the Beaufort wind scale, and at 07:20 hours, the BISMARCK requested that a *U-Boot* be sent to take the logbook to safety. On May 27, 1941, the BISMARK, which was badly hit, was sighted at 08:44 hours by the battleships HMS KING GEORGE V and RODNEY. The latter had nine 40.6-cm guns on the foreship, and now opened fire from all barrels, firing 2,876 shells of all calibers, from 13.3 to 40.6 cm, at the Germans. But the BISMARCK was still afloat, even after the HMS DORSETSHIRE had fired two 53.3-cm torpedoes at her from 3,000 meters distance, and fired a third a quarter of an hour later, at 10:37 hours. The ship went down shortly later, with a crew of 2,077, including the *Flottenchef Admiral* Günther Lütjens, and her *Kommandant, K.z.S.* Ernst Lindemann. Today, it is assumed that *K.z.S.* Lindemann, following German naval tradition, had ordered the BISMARK to be scuttled after she had expended all her ammunition.

The **TIRPITZ**: The keel was laid for this sister ship of the BISMARK on October 24, 1936 in Wilhelmshaven, and the ship was launched on April 1, 1939, christened by the daughter of *Großadmiral* Alfred von Tirpitz, the founder of the German High Seas Fleet. Despite some RAF air attacks, the battleship remained unscathed, giving her an aura of invulnerability.

The TIRPITZ' standard displacement was 46,400 tons; the loaded displacement 52,000 tons. The ship had a length of 253.60 meters, an overall beam of thirty-six meters, and a maximum draft of 9.30 meters. The machinery included twelve Wagner high-pressure boilers and three sets of high-pressure reaction turbines from Brown, Boveri & Cie, with an output of 138,000 horsepower, giving the ship a speed of twenty-nine knots (maximum speed 30.8 knots), and a cruising range of 8,870 nautical miles at nineteen knots. The armament consisted of 8x38-cm guns on four twin turrets and 12x15-cm guns in six twin turrets, as well as sixteen *Flak* of 10.5-cm, 16x3.7-cm, and 46x2-cm (in 1944, increased to seventy-two); she also had two quadruple sets of 53.3-cm torpedo tubes. For reconnaissance, there were between two and four catapult-capable aircraft of type Arado Ar 196A-4 on board. The FuMO 26 and 23 were used as radar devices. The crew was 2,608 men strong.

The ship was commissioned on February 25, 1941. On November 5, 1941, Hitler visited the battleship, which was under the command of *K.z.S.* Friedrich Carl Topp. By Hitler's order, on November 12, 1942, the TIRPITZ was deployed to Norway, more exactly to Trondheim, where the *Kriegsmarine* had built a *U-Boot* bunker comparable to those on the French Atlantic coast. The bunker was intended for boats deployed in the *Nordmeer* (Northern Ocean). The RAF flew its eighteenth air strike against the ship – again without success. In March 1942, the last of the German battleships left her Norwegian fjord to participate in *Unternehmen "Sportpalast"* ("Sports palace") against the Allied convoys PQ-12 and QP-8, but could not sight any of the convoy ships due to poor weather conditions. A British submarine attack on the TIRPITZ was as unsuccessful as the deployment of a dozen Fairey Albacore type torpedo bombers, which took off from the aircraft carrier HMS VICTORIOUS; these shot down two of the battleship's *Flak*.

The pocket battleship ADMIRAL SCHEER was launched on April 1, 1933. (Private collection).

The TIRPITZ, lying at anchor in the Faettenfjord near Trondheim, was attacked by thirty-two Halifax bombers during the night of March 30-31, and British bombers carried out another attack during the night of April 27-28 – again without results. On July 2, 1942, the battleship put to sea on her second deployment, as part of a battle formation: this was *Unternehmen "Rösselsprung"* (chess: "knight's move"), with the mission to intercept the convoys PQ-17 and QP-13. This attack, however, had to be abandoned, after several ships of both German battle formations were stranded. The TIRPITZ returned to her berth in Trondheim. The British decided now to attack the ship with "Chariot" type torpedoes, and brought two of these to Trondheim, under cover aboard the Norwegian fishing trawler ARTHUR, but she broke loose and sank in heavy seas, so that Operation "Tide" had to be called off. In February 1943, *K.z.S.* Hans Meyer replaced Carl Friedrich Topp as *Kommandant* of the battleship, and, under his command, the TIRPITZ sailed from her fjord in September to join forces with the SCHARNHORST and nine destroyers, to carry out *Unternehmen "Sizilien"* ("Sicily"), shelling the Allied garrison and infrastructure in Spitsbergen. The British Admiralty did not want to accept that the TIRPITZ had survived all their attacks more or less unscathed, and determined to do its utmost to change that. As the next move, as part of Operation "Source," three X-class midget submarines of the British 12th Submarine Flotilla attacked the German ship. While "X5" sank, "X6" and "X7" succeeded in getting through the barrier of torpedo nets and penetrating the fjord, where they managed to attach two mines on the battleship's hull. The resulting explosions caused considerable damage to the hull, the turbines, and the artillery fire control system, so that the ship was put out of operation until March 14, 1944. Fifteen Soviet bombers carried out an unsuccessful attack on the TIRPITZ while she was under repair. The Fleet Air Arm [responsible for the RAF carrier aircraft] also continued their attacks, and launched Operation "Tungsten," sending forty-one Fairey Barracuda from the aircraft carriers HMS VICTORIOUS and FURIOUS, which dropped fifteen bombs on the battleship.

The pocket battleship DEUTSCHLAND was renamed LÜTZOW in November 1939. (Private collection).

Hochbrücke bei Levensau mit PANZERSCHIFF "DEUTSCHLAND"

On April 24, Operation "Planet" followed, and Operations "Brown" on May 15 and "Tiger Claw" on May 28, but all three had to be broken off due to bad weather conditions. On June 17, the aircraft carriers HMS FORMIDABLE, FURIOUS, and INDEFATIGABLE sent off a total of forty-four Barracuda, eighteen Corsair,

The pocket battleship ADMIRAL SCHEER off Gibraltar, 1936. (Private collection).

Admiral Scheer in Gibraltar 1936

eighteen Hellcat, and twelve Firefly, but none of these were unable to land any of their bombs on the TIRPITZ, while a Corsair and a Barracuda fell victim to her *Flak*. On July 31, the battleship set out on her last test cruise, and on August 22, the Royal Navy carried out Operation "Goodwood," but with no success. Finally, the Bomber Command [Supreme Command of the RAF Bomber fleet] launched Operation "Paravane," sending twenty-seven Lancaster long-range bombers to drop their Tallboy type bombs (5,456 kilo heavy "bunker busters") on the TIRPITZ; although just one actually scored a hit, it caused such severe damage to the foreship that the battleship was never again operational. The TIRPITZ sailed towards Sorbotn, near Tromso, where she lay within the range of the Lancasters stationed in Great Britain. On November 12, 1944, Operation "Catechism" was launched, in which thirty-one Lancasters dropped a total of twenty-nine Tallboys, three of which struck the ship, making it capsize. Some 1,204 men of the TIRPITZ crew were trapped inside the ship; only eighty-seven could be rescued after the battleship capsized through holes cut through the sidewalls.

The pocket battleship ADMIRAL GRAF SPEE, which was launched on June 30, 1934. (Private collection)

Pocket Battleships and Heavy Cruisers of the Deutschland Class:

The **DEUTSCHLAND** (later: **LÜTZOW**): The keel was laid for this pocket battleship on February 5, 1929. Since the German *Reich* was still bound by the terms of the Versailles Treaty, the entire hull was not riveted but welded, resulting in a weight-saving of around 15%, which was used in favor of the armor and armament. The DEUTSCHLAND was launched on May 19, 1931 and was put into service on April 1, 1933. The standard displacement was 11,750 tons and the loaded displacement 15,900 tons. The ship had a length of 187.90 meters and a beam of 20.70 meters, while its draft was 7.20 meters. The machinery consisted of eight MAN 9 cylinder diesel engines (four for each propeller) and a Vulcan hydraulic transmission. Each engine had a power of 6,049 horsepower at 450 rpm, giving the ship a top speed of twenty-eight knots and a cruising range of 10,000 nautical miles at twenty knots. The armament consisted of two triple turrets with 28-cm Krupp L/52 guns; the range of the thirty-kilo shells was about thirty-five kilometers. The ship also carried 8x15-cm L/55 C/28 guns in single mounts, 4x8.8-cm *Flak* (later exchanged for 10.5 cm), 8x3.7-cm *Flak*, and 10x2-cm *Flak*; the weaponry was completed with two quadruple sets of 53.3-cm torpedo tubes. There were one or two catapult-capable Arado Ar 196A-4 aircraft on board. The crew was between 926 and 1,188 men.

The DEUTSCHLAND carried out her first missions during the Spanish Civil War (1936-39) in the Mediterranean, where she was attacked off Ibiza by Republican aircraft on May 29, 1937. The two bomb hits on the ship cost thirty-one crewmen their lives, and caused some damage. On August 24, the DEUTSCHLAND set out from Wilhelmshaven towards the Atlantic, here, in October, she sank two Allied steamers and took a third as a prize. After her return home, on November 15, 1939, on the orders of Adolf Hitler, the ship was renamed the LÜTZOW in honor of the Prussian *Generalmajor* Adolf *Freiherr* von Lützow (1772-1834). [Apart from the reason of 'war morale' noted at the very beginning of the chapter, this name change was to also hide the fact that one of the heavy cruisers of the HIPPER class with the same name had been sold to the U.S.S.R.]. On February 15, 1940, the ship was restandarized into a heavy cruiser. She took part a short time later, under her *Kommandant K.z.S.* August Thiele, in *Unternehmung Weserübung*, (the occupation of Norway) and was to be part of the Warship Group 5 under *Konteradmiral* (Rear Admiral) Kummetz (who led the attack aboard his flagship, the heavy cruiser BLÜCHER), to break through the Oslo Fjord and take course for the Norwegian capital. As the joint force tried to sail through the Drobak narrows, it was fired upon by well-camouflaged Norwegian coastal and torpedo batteries, which not only damaged the LÜTZOW, but also sank the BLÜCHER. The LÜTZOW was immediately sent back to Germany for repairs, but on the return voyage, on April 11, 1940, in the Kattegat strait, the British submarine "Spearfish" hit her in the stern with a torpedo, destroying her propeller shafts and rudder.

Another view of pocket battleship ADMIRAL GRAF SPEE. (Private collection).

Panzerschiff "ADMIRAL GRAF SPEE"

The resulting repairs and rebuilding took almost a year to complete. In June 1941, the heavy cruiser LÜTZOW was to be sent to Norway, but was attacked and hit by British torpedo aircraft while underway, so that she had to return to Kiel. In 1942, the ship was sent to Narvik, Norway anyway, but then shortly later, due to new damage, had to return to Kiel for renewed repairs. In December 1942, she participated in *Unternehmen "Regenbogen"* ("Rainbow"). The target was a convoy destined for the Soviet Union, but this was a complete failure for the German side. The heavy cruiser was ordered back to Gotenhafen and was from then on used as a training ship. In the beginning of 1945, the LÜTZOW and her ship's guns took part in the fighting retreat from *Ostpreußen* (East Prussia); despite heavy damage, she persevered in the fight until May 4, 1945, when her *Kommandant* ordered her to be scuttled off Swinemünde (now Swinoujscie).

The **ADMIRAL SCHEER**: The keel was laid on June 25, and the ship was launched on April 1, 1933. The ship was named for Admiral Reinhard Scheer, who had commanded the German *Hochseeflotte* (High Seas Fleet) in the Battle of Jutland (May 30, 1916). The standard displacement was 11,900 tons; loaded displacement 16,000 tons; the ship was 187.90 meters long, with an overall beam of 21.30 meters and draft of 7.30 meters. The machinery consisted of eight MAN 9 cylinder diesel engines (four per propeller) with a Vulcan hydraulic transmission, each one with 6,506 horsepower at 450 rpm, giving the ship a top speed of 28.30 knots and a cruising range of 9,100 nautical miles at nineteen knots. The armament consisted of 6x28-cm Krupp L/54 C/28 guns in two triple turrets, 8x15-cm L/55 C/28 SKA, 6x10.5-cm *Flak*, 8x3.7-cm and 26- to 42x2-cm. There were also two quadruple sets of 53.3 cm torpedo tubes. The pocket battleship carried an Arado Ar 196A-4 airplane on board, and a crew of 1,150 men.

The ADMIRAL SCHEER, put into service on November 12, 1934, shelled the port of Almeria on May 31, 1937, as retaliation for the Republican air attack on her sister ship DEUTSCHLAND on May 29, 1937 (see above). Altogether, the ship undertook seven missions during the Spanish Civil War. From February 1 to July 31, 1940, the ship was extensively refitted, in which not only the foreship was extended, but also the bow was given a "clipper stem," the turret over the bridge expanded/emoved (ausgebaut can mean either, expanded or enlarged is the more common meaning); the tower mast replaced with a tubular mast and the Flak reinforced – just to name a few of the renovations. On February 15, 1940 the ship was restandardized as a heavy cruiser, as was the DEUTSCHLAND.

The ADMIRAL SCHEER sailed again from Gotenhafen on October 23, 1940, towards the North Atlantic, where, on November 5, she sank five freighters of a convoy and the British auxiliary cruiser HMS JERVIS BAY. Subsequently she operated in the South Atlantic, where she sank more Allied merchant ships and tankers, before she broke through to the Indian Ocean in January 1941. Here she succeeded in sinking four more ships, and finally returned to the *Reich*. The balance of her successful trade warfare missions: In 161 days at sea, she had traveled 46,000 nautical miles, and in this time sunk seventeen enemy ships with a total tonnage of 113,000 tons. After renewed repair work, at the end of 1941, she joined the so-called *Baltenflotte*, (Baltic Fleet), here, together with the TIRPITZ, she was to prevent the Soviet

Baltic fleet from breaking out towards Great Britain. After this, the ADMIRAL SCHEER was transferred to Norway, where she took part in *Unternehmen "Wunderland"* ("Wonderland") in August 1942. The mission of this operation was for a German joint naval formation attack the Soviet northern Siberian maritime traffic in the Kara Sea, especially convoys, but it did not succeed, due to the adverse weather conditions. Somewhat later, the cruiser shelled the Allied base Port Dickson at the mouth of the Yenisei River, and was able to destroy the land facilities and several ships. In 1943, the cruiser became a training ship and only returned to active duty in late 1944. From the Baltic Sea, she supported the German troops' defensive battle along the Prussian coast, and fought the Soviet forces from the sea. In March 1945, the ship had to return to Kiel, to have her worn-out gun barrels replaced, taking nearly 1,000 refugees and seriously wounded with her. At the beginning of April, the unarmed ship was hit by RAF bombs and capsized.

Schwerer Kreuzer "ADMIRAL HIPPER"

The heavy cruiser "ADMIRAL HIPPER" in dry dock for maintenance. (Private collection).

The heavy cruiser "ADMIRAL HIPPER" after her launching in February 1937. (Private collection)

Schwerer Kreuzer "ADMIRAL HIPPER"

The light cruiser KÖLN – Launched on May 23, 1928. (Private collection)

The **ADMIRAL GRAF SPEE**: She was the most famous of the three pocket battleships, named after *Vizeadmiral* Maximilian von Spee (1861-1914), who had commanded the German East Asia Squadron in 1914. The ADMIRAL GRAF SPEE's keel was laid on October 1, 1932; she was launched on June 30, 1934, and put into service on January 6, 1936. Her standard displacement was 12,000 tons and the loaded displacement 16,000 tons. The ship had a length of 186 meters, a beam of 20.60 meters, and 7.20 meter draft. The machinery comprised eight MAN 9 cylinder diesel engines (four per propeller) and a Vulcan hydraulic transmission, each with 6,750 horsepower (at 450 rpm), so that ship could reach a top speed of 28.50 knots. At this speed, her operating range was 8,900 nautical miles, but it could be increased at just fifteen knots to 18,650 nautical miles. The armament consisted of 6x28-cm Krupp L/54 C/28 guns in two triple turrets, 8x15-cm L/55 C/28 SKA, 6x10.5-cm *Flak*, 8x3.7-cm, 10x2-cm, and eight 53.3 torpedo tubes. She was equipped with a FuMO 22 radar device and had a catapult-capable Arado Ar 196A-1 waterplane on board. Her crew size was 619 men.

In 1936 and 1937, the ADMIRAL GRAF SPEE served as fleet flagship and also undertook security duties during the Spanish Civil War, taking part in a total of five Spanish missions. In 1938 and 1939, she participated in fleet visits to ports including Tangier, Vigo, Lisbon, and Ceuta. Even before the outbreak of the Second World War, the GRAF SPEE left home under her *Kommandant K.z.S.* Hans Langsdorff, and sailing first to the South Atlantic and then the Indian Ocean, sank eight merchant ships comprising 50,089 tons. She was supplied with fuel en route by the fleet supply ship ALTMARK and then pushed on, in search of new targets, to the mouth of the Rio de la Plata. Here the ship encountered a British cruiser formation under the command of Commodore Henry Harwood, which consisted of the heavy cruiser HMS EXETER, the flagship, and the light cruisers HMS ACHILLES and AJAX. These latter could reach speeds of up to thirty-one knots, and thus were faster than the German pocket battleship. On December 13, 1939, fighting began between the British and the GRAF SPEE off the Uruguayan coast. *K.z.S.* Langsdorff opened fire at 06:17 hours and was able to land some heavy hits on the EXETER; meanwhile the two light cruisers attempted to attack the pocket battleship from the east, hitting the GRAF SPEE with two 20.3-cm and one 15.2-cm shells, but these, thanks to her strong armor, did not do much harm. The British flagship was badly damaged and the AJAX had also taken some hits. It is possible that the pocket battleship might have succeeded in neutralizing all three opponents, but with her ammunition running low, *K.z.S.* Hans Langsdorff brought his ship about and took course for the neutral port of Montevideo, where he wanted to make his ship battle-ready again. The GRAF SPEE had received a total of twenty strikes, and suffered thirty-five killed and sixty wounded among the crew. Under pressure from the British, the government of Uruguay only at first allowed the Germans just twenty-four hours sojourn, which was not long enough for the repairs. But it was quickly clear to the Royal Navy that it would be difficult to encounter the pocket battleship again if she left the port within twenty-four hours. Therefore, they delayed the departure by a trick, and in the meantime brought in reinforcements. The British also succeeded in conveying to Langsdorff the impression that the battle cruiser HMS RENOWN and aircraft carrier HMS ARK ROYAL would join the reinforcements. As a result, the commander of the German pocket battleship requested permission from Berlin to sail out of Montevideo and run his ship aground himself, after the crew had been taken to safety. Under the eyes of many onlookers, the ship sailed the ship out of the harbor, and anchored three miles off, where Langsdorff had the prepared explosive charges primed. After the last crewmembers had disembarked, several huge explosions were set off, and on December 17, 1939 at 19:55 hours, the ADMIRAL GRAF SPEE went under. *Kommandant* Hans Langsdorff committed suicide on December 19.

The Heavy Cruisers:

In addition to the two surviving pocket battleships, which had been restandardized on February 15, 1940, the *Kriegsmarine* had three other ships of the heavy cruiser class.

Servicing the guns aboard an escort vessel. (Private collection)

The **ADMIRAL HIPPER**: On July 6, 1935, the ship's keel was laid; she was launched on February 6, 1937. The ship was named for the German *Admiral* Franz Ritter von Hipper (1863-1932), *Befehlshaber* (Commander) of the *Kaiserlichen Marine* reconnaissance forces during the Battle of Jutland in 1916. The ADMIRAL HIPPER was put into service on April 29, 1939, under the command of *K.z.S.* Hellmuth Heye and subsequently went through trials and training in the Baltic Sea. She had a standard displacement of 14,247 tons and loaded displaced of 18,208 tons; was 205.90 meters long, with a beam of 21.30 meters and draft of 7.70 meters. The machinery comprised twelve oil-fired Wagner-La-Mont high-pressure boilers with three sets of Blohm & Voss geared turbines, with a total of 133,631 horsepower, which allowed a top speed of thirty-two knots and a cruising range of 5,500 nautical miles at seventeen knots. The armament consisted of 8x20.3-cm L/60 C/34 guns in four twin turrets, 12x10.5-cm L/65 C/33, 8-10x3.7-cm L/83 C/30 (which were subsequently exchanged for 6x4-cm) and 28-32x2-cm, and in addition 12x53.3-cm torpedo tubes in four triple sets. She also had three Arado Ar 196A-4 seaplanes on board.

After completing the sea trials, the heavy cruiser left the shipyard and sailed to the Baltic Sea, where the crew completed their training program. At this time the ship also visited Sweden and Estonia. On November 6, 1939, the cruiser returned to the shipyard in Hamburg, where a few alterations were made, especially to the stem. After renewed trials in the Baltic Sea, she sailed to Wilhelmshaven, where a radar system was installed. On February 19, 1940, ADMIRAL HIPPER, and the battleships GNEISENAU and SCHARNHORST, three destroyers, and several *U-Boote*, left their home ports to attack an enemy convoy between northern Norway and England, but the operation had to be broken off. Somewhat later, she took part in *Unternehmen "Weserübung,"* forming Warship Group 2 together with four destroyers, under the command of *K.z.S.* Heye. The Group had the mission to occupy Trondheim (for which they had a mountaineering infantry regiment on board), and accomplished this on April 9, 1940, after destroying a Norwegian coastal battery. Other warship groups which participated in this operation had the following objectives: Group 1, Narvik, Group 3, Bergen, Group 4, Kristiansand and Arendal, Group 5 – with the LÜTZOW, the BLÜCHER, and the EMDEN – Oslo, and Group 6, Egersund. Between April 5 and 8, the British Admiralty mined the Norwegian waters (Operation "Wilfred"), and on April 7, British Admiral Forbes, Commander-in-chief of the Home Fleet, with the battleships HMS VALIANT and RODNEY and the light cruisers HMS REPULSE, SHEFFIELD, and PENELOPE, and ten destroyers, sailed from Scapa Flow. They were reinforced a short time later with the cruisers HMS GALATEA and ARETHUSA and four more destroyers. On April 8, this fleet was again, further reinforced with more cruisers and destroyers. The French cruiser EMILE BERTIN and two French destroyers also joined Forbes' formation.

Around 18:30 hours, ADMIRAL HIPPER encountered the destroyer HMS GLOWWORM near Trondheim, and sank the British ship, although she had succeeded in ramming the German cruiser in the bow before finally sinking beneath the waves. The ADMIRAL HIPPER was able to leave Trondheim in good time and returned to Germany, to have the badly damaged bow repaired. On June 4, she was punctually again ready for action in *Unternehmen "Juno,"* which was to relieve the German troops in Narvik and destroy enemy transport. Here, she sank the UJ trawler HMS JUNIPER, the tanker OIL PIONEER, and the troop carrier ORAMA. On August 11, she returned to the shipyard in Wilhelmshaven, for a machinery overhaul. Even after this, however, she had a series of problems with her engine equipment, with the result that this heavy cruiser was only fully ready for action again in mid-November. Under her new commander, *K.z.S.* William Meise, in December 1940 she broke out into the North Atlantic via the Denmark Strait.

A *Korvettenkapitän* and a *Kapitänleutnant* oversee from the bridge their ship's entry into port. (Private collection)

On December 25, 1940, she encountered the convoy WS-5A, 700 nautical miles west of Cape Finisterre, with its escort consisting of the cruisers HMS BERWICK, BONAVENTURE and DUNEDIN, and the aircraft carriers HMS ARGUS and FURIOUS. The ADMIRAL HIPPER achieved four strikes on the BERWICK with her 20.3-cm guns, as well as several well-placed 10.5-cm gun hits on the 13,994 ton troopship EMPIRE TROOPER, and was able to sink another 6,078-ton troop transport. Due to British superiority, however, she ended the battle, and returned to Brest, from where she set off again for the Atlantic on February 1, 1941, this time sinking the 1,236-ton merchant ship ICELAND.

Shortly before midnight on February 11, the ADMIRAL HIPPER's radar equipment located the convoy SLS-64 with nineteen merchant ships, which was sailing unescorted. The German cruiser opened fire the next morning at 06:18 hours and sank seven ships of altogether 32,806 tons, and severely damaged three more. Since ammunition for the 20.3 cm guns was running low and the torpedo tubes could not be reloaded due to the heavy seas, the ship had to return to Brest. On March 15, the ship returned to Germany.

After extensive repairs and test runs, the heavy cruiser again sailed to Trondheim in mid-March 1942, with two torpedo boats and three destroyers. She left the fjord together with the TIRPITZ, to attack convoy PQ-17 as part of *Unternehmen "Rösselsprung."* However, they could not make contact, but a good 2/3 of the convoy was eliminated by *U-Boote* and the *Luftwaffe*. After an offensive mining operation off the Novaya Zemlya archipelago, the ADMIRAL HIPPER, commanded by *K.z.S.* Hans Hartmann, set out against Soviet shipping in the Arctic Ocean, but the mission was without result. Together with the pocket battleship LÜTZOW and six destroyers, on December 30 the ships launched *Unternehmen "Regenbogen"* ("Rainbow"), directed against the British convoy JW-51B, which was spotted at 07:20 hours on December 31. The ADMIRAL Hipper opened fire at 09:39 hours on the destroyer ACHATES – setting off the so-called Battle of the Barents Sea. The ONSLOW was hit four times, the BRAMBLE sunk, and shortly later the German cruiser re-launched its attack on the ACHATES and struck her. Then, however, the British close cover with the light cruisers SHEFFIELD and JAMAICA, joined the battle, and after the ADMIRAL HIPPER had sustained three severe hits, one of them below the waterline, the *Führer* ordered the German battle formation to break off the attack. On January 23, 1943, the heavy cruiser sailed out of the Altafjord to relocate back to Germany and arrived in Kiel on February 8. Some three weeks later, the badly damaged ship was taken out of service, but was reactivated in the following year as a training ship in the Baltic Sea. As a result, on January 30, 1945 she was able to take some 1,500 refugees on board in Gotenhafen, taking them to Kiel. There, the ADMIRAL HIPPER, after several heavy bomb hits by the RAF, was blown up by her own crew on May 3, 1945.

The highest vigilance was always required after putting to sea: Danger threatened from the skies, from the surface of the water, and from below. (Private collection)

The **BLÜCHER**: Her keel was laid on August 15 in Kiel and she was launched on June 8, 1937. She was named for the Prussian *Generalfeldmarschall* Gebhard Leberecht von Blücher (1742-1819), whose intervention in the battle of Waterloo had led to the Allied victory. The cruiser, put into service on September 20, 1939, had a standard displacement of 14,247 tons and loaded displacement of 18,808 tons. The ship's length was 205.90 meters, beam 21.30 meters, and the draft 7.7 meters. The propulsion system consisted of twelve oil-fired La Mont high-pressure boilers with three sets of geared turbines from Blohm & Voss, which gave a performance of 132,000 horsepower on the waves. This allowed a top speed of thirty-two knots and an operating range of 6,100 nautical miles at fifteen knots. The armament consisted of 8x20.3-cm L/60 C/34 guns and 12x10.5-cm L/65 C/33; *Flak*: 12x3.7-cm and 8x2-cm. She also possessed twelve 53.3-cm torpedo tubes in four triple sets, and had a catapult-capable Arado Ar 196A-4 airplane on board.

Training of the full 1,600-man crew still incomplete when the heavy cruiser, under the command of *K.z.S.* Heinrich Woldag, took part in *Unternehmen "Weserübung,"* of which she was to be the most prominent victim. She was the command ship of Warship Group 5 under *Konteradmiral* Kummetz, and, together with the LÜTZOW, on April 9 reached the mouth of the Oslofjord, where the ships were met by inaccurate Norwegian coastal artillery fire. As she sailed forward, the BLÜCHER was hit by two 28-cm shells from the Oscarsborg coastal battery; the first destroyed the foretop and thus the main *Flak* control unit. The cruiser returned fire with its 10.5-cm guns, but the second Norwegian shell had set the airplane hangar on fire. The Norwegian Drebak battery opened fire with their 15-cm guns, and some twenty shells reduced the German cruiser's midships to ruins. To make matters worse, the ship now also took two torpedo hits from a land torpedo battery on the island of Kaholmen, which finally put the helm out of action. The fire in the hangar had now spread to the ammunition brought along by the *Heer* (Army) units on board, including men of the IR 107 and the staff of the 163rd Infantry Division. The ship was now beyond rescue, was listing more and more, and finally sank at 07:22 hours, with at least 550 servicemen losing their lives. The BLÜCHER's brief career was over.

The **PRINZ EUGEN**: The keel of the "fortunate Prince" was laid on April 23, 1936 in Kiel, and she was launched on August 22, 1938, christened by Magda von Horthy, wife of the Hungarian regent Admiral Miklos Horthy. Originally, this most famous of the three heavy cruisers was to have been christened with the name TEGETTHOFF, in honor of the most important Austrian admiral, who on July 20, 1866 – then as a *Konteradmiral* – had defeated the superior Italian fleet in the sea Battle of Lissa (near the Croatian island of Vis). However, in order not to strain relations with his ally Mussolini, Hitler insisted it would be better to name the ship after Eugen Franz, Prince of Savoy-Carignan (1663-

Signalman at waving directions ("*Winkern*"). (Private collection)

1736), who was likely the most famous *Feldherr* (general) of the Austrian Royal House and had distinguished himself by such victories as the relief of Vienna from the Turkish siege in 1683. The ship's standard displacement was 14,240 tons and loaded displacement 18,400 tons; the ship had a length of 212.50 meters, an overall beam of 21.90 meters, and a draft of 7.90 meters. The ship's propulsion system was served by twelve oil-fired Wagner-La Mont boilers and three geared turbines from Brown Boveri & Cie, each of which drove one of the shafts, generating an overall power of 132,000 horsepower. This allowed a top speed of 33.40 knots and an operating range of 6,800 nautical miles at twenty knots. The armament consisted of 8x20.3-cm L/60 C/34 guns in four twin turrets and 12x10.5-cm C/33 in six twin turrets as well as 12x3.7-cm Flak L/83 C/30 in six twin gun mounts (which were later replaced by 18x4-cm) and 28x2-cm (increased to fifty-six pieces!); she also had twelve torpedo tubes of 53.3-cm, in four triple sets. Also on board were one to three catapult-capable seaplanes of the type Arado Ar 196A-4.
On August 1, 1940, under the command of *K.z.S.* Helmuth Brinkmann, the PRINZ EUGEN was put into service, with a crew of 1,350 men. On May 18, 1941, she sailed to take part in *Unternehmen "Rheinübung,"* which she was to carry out together with the BISMARCK under the leadership of *Flottenchef Admiral* Günther Lütjens. However, already on May 20, 1941, British intelligence had obtained information on the sailing of the formation, which two days later was also discovered by British aerial reconnaissance. As a result, a British battle formation of a battleship, one battle cruiser, and six destroyers sailed from Scapa Flow. The Home Fleet, with a battleship, a battle cruiser, an aircraft carrier, four cruisers, and eight destroyers, also put out to sea. The PRINZ EUGEN had meanwhile taken the lead, after the BISMARK's radar system failed. On May 23, the two German ships appeared on the radar of the heavy cruiser HMS SUFFOLK, which was guarding the entry to the Denmark Strait with another heavy cruiser. At 05:52 hours, the approaching battle cruiser HMS HOOD and the battleship HMS PRINCE OF WALES opened fire on the Germans, which was immediately returned by the 20.3-cm guns of the PRINZ EUGEN and the 38-cm guns of the BISMARCK.
After just five minutes, the HOOD began to sink. The two German ships were also able to land a few strikes on the PRINCE OF WALES, but she then, however, laid a smokescreen and veered round. Thus, the PRINZ EUGEN played her part in the sinking of the Home Fleet's most famous battle cruiser, without being hit herself or losing a single man, while the BISMARCK suffered three hits and took on 3,000 tons of sea water.

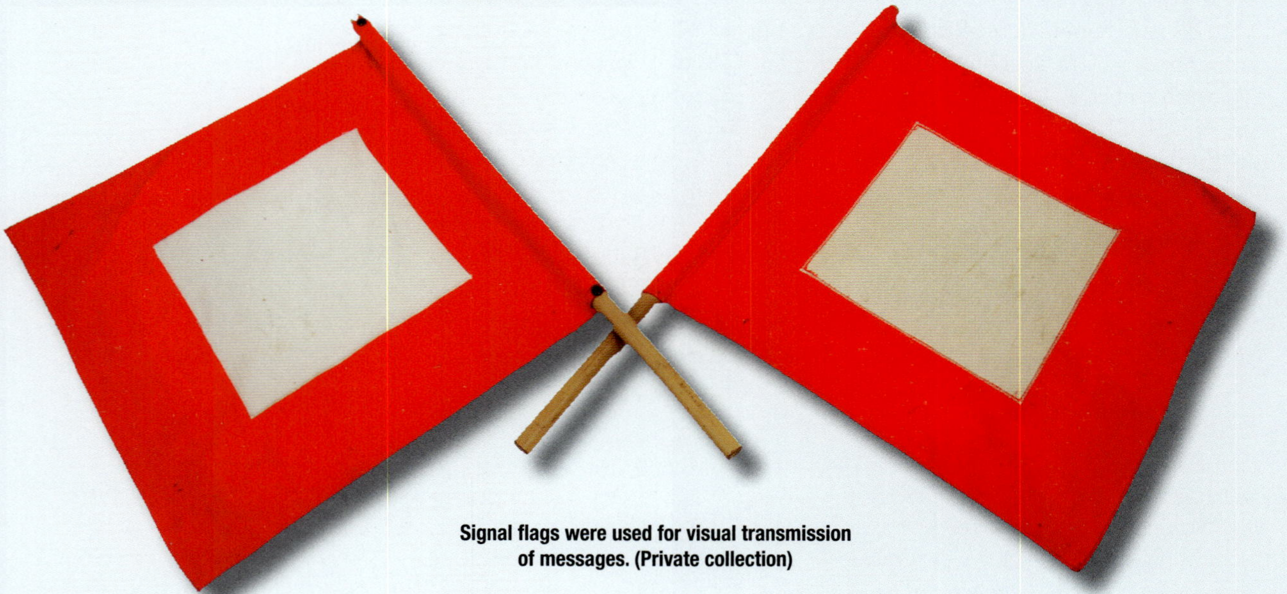

Signal flags were used for visual transmission of messages. (Private collection)

Kriegsmarine **recruits training as signalmen. (Private collection)**

As a result, she could only sail at lowered speed, so that *Admiral* Lütjens ordered the battleship go to Saint-Nazaire for repairs. The PRINZ EUGEN, however, was sent out into the Atlantic, there to carry out an independent war on trade. While the British were now hunting the BISMARCK with every means, and finally sank the battleship, the German cruiser was able to take on oil from the German supply tanker SPICHERN while underway, and after a further fueling at sea, the PRINZ EUGEN returned to Brest on June 1.

At the beginning of January 1942, Hitler ordered the PRINZ EUGEN, the GNEISENAU, and the SCHARNHORST to return to Germany. Not least among the reasons were the RAF's constant air attacks on the base at Brest; half a year before, the heavy cruiser had taken a bomb hit, which had killed sixty crewmen. In the moonless night of February 11, 1942, at 22:45 hours, the heavy units set out from the French harbor for *Unternehmen "Cerberus"* under the command of *Vizeadmiral* Otto Ciliax. They were supported by several torpedo boats and destroyers, while air cover was undertaken by *Luftflotte 3*. The formation made it though the Channel generally undamaged. On February 13, the PRINZ EUGEN reached the Brunsbüttel locks; from here she set off on February 20 together with the heavy cruiser ADMIRAL SCHEER, towards Trondheim, with 200 Army soldiers returning from leave on board. Just before reaching their goal, the PRINZ EUGEN took a torpedo strike in the stern, which required emergency repairs in Trondheim. On May 18, 1942, she arrived back home, where her stern was completely repaired before she sailed out for trials and training in the Baltic Sea. After a brief deployment as a training ship, from August 19-21, 1944, the heavy cruiser took part in the bombardment of the Soviet deployments in the Latvian city of Tukum, before cruising again from September 2, 1944 into Finnish waters. On October 15, she collided with the light cruiser LEIPZIG, and the PRINZ EUGEN had to return for repairs to the shipyard. Under her new commander, *K.z.S.* Hans-Jürgen Reinecke, she participated from mid-January 1945 in the defensive battles against Soviet troops on German territory, including by Königsberg and Danzig, before she left Gotenhafen on March 31, reaching Copenhagen on April 20, 1945. As a result, she was subject to the partial surrender signed by Dönitz's successor, *Generaladmiral* von Friedeburg and British Field Marshal Montgomery, which came into force on May 5; this forbad the German naval forces from putting to sea, scuttling themselves, or damanging their ships. The PRINZ EUGEN fell by lot to the Americans as war booty, and she was initially transferred to the United States. She was finally hauled to Bikini Atoll, where she was used as a test ship for atomic bomb tests. On December 22, 1946 she finally sank at Kwajalein Atoll.

The Light Cruisers:

The **EMDEN**: The light cruiser's keel was laid in December 1921 in Kiel; she was launched on January 7, 1925 and was put into service in October 1925. The EMDEN had a standard displacement of 5,400 tons; the overall length was 155.50 meters; the overall beam 14.30 meters, and the draft 5.80 meters. The propulsion system was served by ten Schultz-Thornycroft steam boilers with a power capacity of 4,500 horsepower, so that she could sail up to twenty-nine knots, while she had a cruising range at fourteen knots of 6,500 nautical miles. The armament consisted of 8x15-cm guns and 3x8.8-cm and 4x2-cm *Flak*, and in addition four 53.3-cm torpedoes. She had a crew of 530 men.

The light cruiser NÜRNBERG taking part in the naval review for the inauguration ceremony for the Laboe Naval Memorial on May 29, 1936. (Private collection)

The **KÖLN**: The keel was laid in August 1926; she was launched on May 23, 1928 and commissioned at the beginning of 1930. The KÖLN had a standard displacement of 6,000 tons; overall length was 173.70 meters; overall beam 15.20 meters and the draft was 5.40 meters. Propulsion was by six double-ended oil boilers, four sets of steam turbines, and two MAN four-stroke diesels. Her turbine output was 65,000 horsepower, which gave her a top speed of thirty-two knots and a cruising range of 9,800 nautical miles at ten knots. The armament consisted of 9x15-cm guns and *Flak* of 6x8.8-cm, 8x3.7-cm, and 8x2-cm. In addition, there were 12x53.3-cm torpedoes on board. The catapult, housed behind the bridge, could catapult the two Arado Ar 196A-4 into the air consecutively. She had a crew of 592 men. Her two sister ships were lost in 1940: The KÖNIGSBERG was sunk by the RAF off Bergen, and the KARLSRUHE sank after torpedo hits from a British submarine off Christiansend.

The **LEIPZIG**: Her keel was laid in April 1928 at Kiel; she was launched on October 18, 1929, but the commissioning was delayed until 1931. She had a standard displacement of 6,000 tons, overall length was 166 meters, overall beam 16.30 meters, and her draft was 4.80 meters. Her propulsion system, with a capacity of 72,000 horsepower, consisted of six oil-fired boilers for two sets of geared turbines of 30,000 horsepower power each, with which there were also four MAN two-stroke diesels of 12,000 horsepower. She could sail up to thirty-two knots and had, at 14.5 knots, a cruising range of 7,000 nautical miles. Her armament consisted of 9x15-cm guns and *Flak* of 8x8.8-cm, 8x3.7-cm, and 4x2-cm, and 12x53.3-cm torpedoes. The catapult for the two onboard Arado Ar 196A-4 aircraft was located in front of the bridge. She had a crew of 632 men.

The **NÜRNBERG**: Her keel was laid in early 1934, the launching followed on December 8, 1934 and she was commissioned in November 1935. She had a standard displacement of 6,000 tons, as her sister ship had also; the overall length was 170 meters, beam 16.40 meters, and her draft 4.30 meters. Her propulsion system, turbine output, and armament were identical to those of the LEIPZIG. For her, however, the catapult for the onboard aircraft was behind the bridge. She had a 655-man crew.

At the beginning of the war, minesweeper R 27 sails out into the North Sea for mine hunting. (Private collection)

The minesweeper R164 at sea. Note the camouflage. (Private collection)

The Auxiliary Cruisers

As heavily armed merchant ships, carrying guns, torpedoes, and naval mines on board and cleverly camouflaged, the German *Hilfskreuzer* (auxiliary cruisers) racked up impressive achievements for themselves on the seven seas. The first victory was in April 1940 by the "Orion"; the last one went to the account of the "Michel" in September 1943.

We have already discussed above the alterations in the designations of the auxiliary cruisers. Below they will be listed alphabetically according to the ship's name, followed by the first commander of each ship, then the "*HSK*" (*Hilfskreuzer* number and the *Kriegsmarine* code, then the Royal Navy code, the original name, and, for those which survived the war, the final name. Given the limited scope of this work, it is unfortunately impossible to go into their privateering operations – these alone would fill a book.

The light cruiser EMDEN was named for the most famous German *Störkreuzer* (merchant raider) of the First World War. (Private collection)

Räumboot-Flottille **(Minesweeper flotilla) at sea. (Private collection)**

Propaganda postcard for the torpedo boat forces. (Private collection)

"Atlantis": *K.z.S.* Bernhard Rogge. *HSK* 2, ship 16, Raider C. (formerly Goldenfels).
"Coronel": F.K. Rudolf Betzendhal. *HSK* 6, ship 14; Raider K. (formerly: Togo; finally: Svalbard).
"Hansa": *K.z.S.* Hans Henigst. *HSK* 6, ship 5. (formerly: Meersburg; finally: Glengarry).
"Komet": K.A. Robert Eyssen. *HSK* 7, ship 45, Raider B. (formerly Ems).
"Kormoran": F.K. Theodor Detmens. *HSK* 8, ship 41, Raider G (formerly Steiermark).
"Michel": *K.z.S.* Hellmuth von Ruckteschell. *HSK* 9, ship 28; Raider H. (formerly: Bielsko).
"Orion": F.K. Kurt Weyher. *HSK* 1, ship 36; Raider A. (formerly Kurmark; finally: Hector).
"Pinguin": *K.z.S.* Ernst-Felix Krüder. *HSK* 5, ship 33; Raider F. (formerly: Kandelfels).
"Stier": *K.z.S.* Horst Gerlach. *HSK* 6, ship 23, Raider J. (formerly: Cairo).
"Thor": *K.z.S.* Otto Kahler. *HSK* 4, ship 10, Raider E. (formerly: Santa Cruz).
"Widder": *K.K.* Hellmuth von Ruckteschell. *HSK* 3, ship 21; Raider D. (formerly: Neumark: finally: Ulysses).
These *Kriegsmarine* "privateers" sank or captured 132 ships, with a total tonnage of 823 080 GRT. Another ten ships that were sunk by mines, which were attributed to the "Penguin" and "Orion," not to forget the Australian cruiser SYDNEY, which became a victim of the "Kormoran."

We have now presented all the large *Kriegsmarine* ships; we might have given the impression of neglecting all the countless medium and small ships and boats, which are also an important part of this branch of the *Wehrmacht*.

The *Zerstörer* (destroyers)
The *Torpedoboote* (torpedo boats)
The *Schnellboote* (fast attack boats)
The *Minensuchboote* (minehunters)
The *Vorpostenboote* (patrol boats)
The *Sicherungsboote* (security boats)
The *Unterseebootjäger* (submarine hunters)
The *Geleitboote* (escort vessels)
The *Begleitschiffe* (escort ships)
The *Schulschiffe* (training ships)
Segelschulschiffe and *Artillerie-Schulschiffe*
(Sailing training ships and artillery training ships)

The majority of these boats were in service significantly more frequently and for longer periods than the large ships that they often enough accompanied. They were often ordered on special missions singly or in formations. It must be borne in mind that on the eve of the Allied landings in Normandy on June 6, 1944, the *Oberbefehlshaber* of the *Marinegruppenkommando* (Naval Group Command) *West*, *Admiral* Krancke and his Chief of Staff, *Konteradmiral* Hoffmann, had no more than a few destroyers, a good dozen torpedo boats, several *Flottile Schnellboote*, and a variety of minehunters, tenders, and supply ships available to them. Indeed, a massive Allied air attack on the quays and *U-Boot* bunkers at Le Havre in the evening of June 14, 1944, destroyed thirty-eight surface ships, including four torpedo boats. The weak air defense had no means to counter the attack. According to *Großadmiral* Karl Dönitz, two weeks later, the *Kriegsmarine* in the West had nothing more than a torpedo boat, twelve security boats, and just eight snorkel-equipped *U-Boote*.

Wasserbombe wird eingestellt   Aufnahme: Burkert

A sailor in "*Arbeitspäckchen*" ("work packaging" (work uniform)) setting a depth charge. (Private collection)

The military situation of the *Kriegsmarine* in the second half of 1944 was like that of all German armed forces: in a word, catastrophic. Control of the sea, which was unattainable at any point, was shrunk to a few strips of coast in northwestern Europe. This extremely unequal battle cost countless young seamen their lives, yet even with this sacrifice, they were only able to delay the collapse of an appalling regime. The *Kriegsmarine* servicemen who still remained in the few German pockets of resistance on the Atlantic Ocean and the Channel Islands of Jersey and Guernsey, were almost all just used as infantry. Only the *U-Boot* bases in Norway remained ready for action almost until the last day of war. Due to the constant Allied air raids, the others were barely able to send anything to sea.

Yet, there was a last stand at the beginning of 1945. The evacuation of millions of soldiers and civilians, who wanted to reach safety from the advancing Red Army, was only made possible by the selfless help of countless ships of the German *Kriegsmarine* and *Handelsmarine*. This logistical and military masterstroke, under the command of *Großadmiral* Dönitz, saved thousands of men and women. Everything that could float, from minelayers to battleships, took part in the largest maritime rescue in history.

Before Adolf Hitler abandoned responsibility by his suicide on April 30, 1945, he named *Großadmiral* Dönitz as his successor, who, as the new head of state, was to attempt to lead the remnants of the Third *Reich* out of the war. In this role Dönitz attempted to negotiate the most favorable terms of surrender – in vain.
On May 7, 1945, the German *Wehrmacht* made its unconditional surrender. Tens of thousands of *Kriegsmarine* servicemen went into POW camps for two to three years, depending on the policies of the victors.

For nearly six years long, the German *Kriegsmarine* had resisted the most powerful fleets in the world – those of the British, the United States, and the Soviets. On all the world's oceans, they dealt their opponents heavy blows, while of necessity taking on twenty to fifty times the number of their own ships. Respected by all their opponents, the *Kriegsmarine* carried out a war without hate, fighting rather to carry out their duty to their fatherland, a fight which, given all the terrible events during the Second World War, may be definitely be considered honorable.

Mustered *Kriegsmarine* formation, 1939 in Berlin, before a military parade in the national capital. (Private collection)

Kriegsmarine recruitment poster.

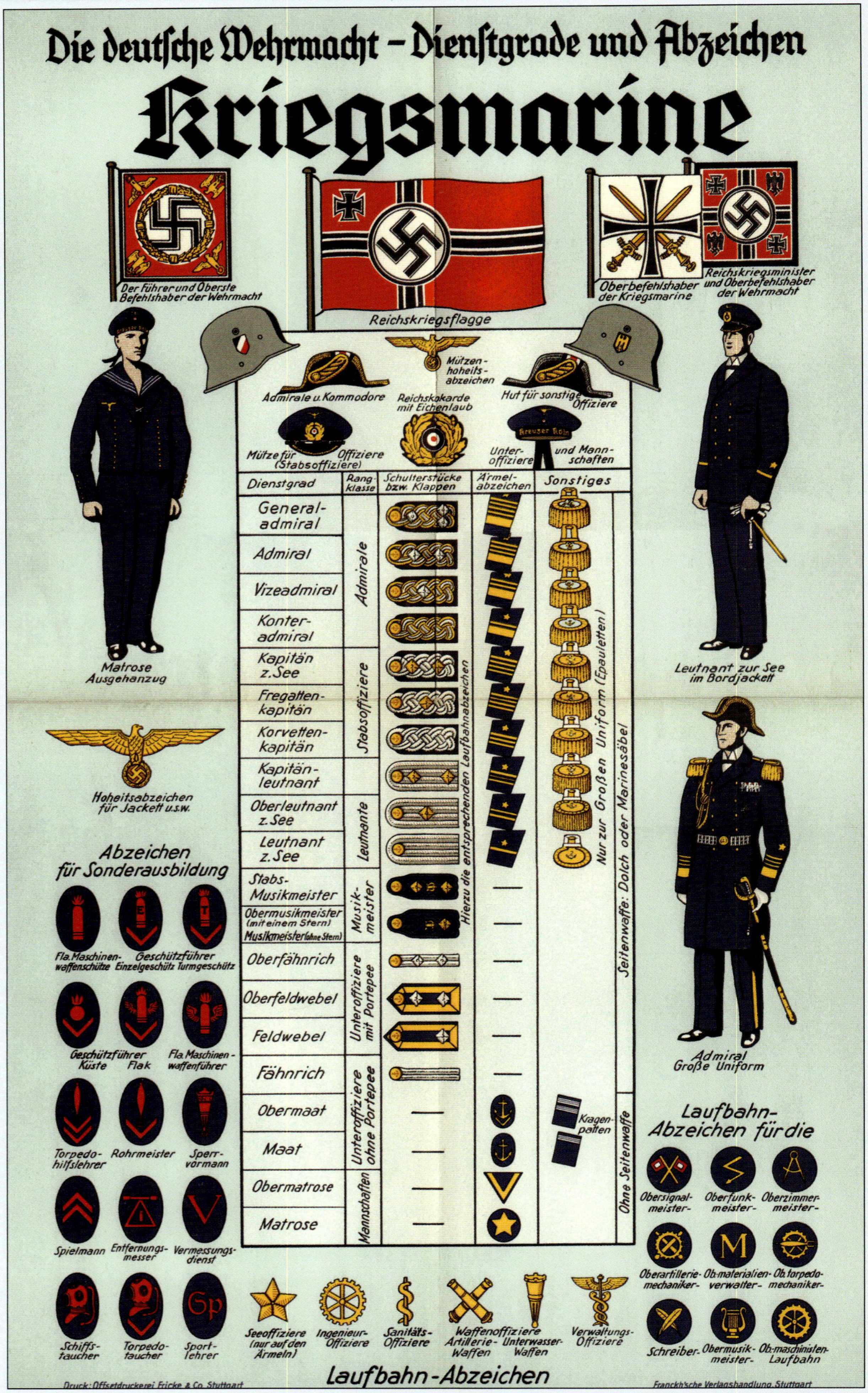

This poster showing *Kriegsmarine* ranks and insignia was displayed in the schools and training facilities of this *Wehrmacht* branch. (Private collection)

COMPARISON OF KRIEGSMARINE SERVICE RANKS (OFFICERS) AND RATES (PETTY OFFICERS AND ENLISTED MEN) (1940) WITH THOSE OF THE HEER (ARMY)

OFFICERS

Kriegsmarine	Heer
Großadmiral (Fleet Admiral Five Star)	*Generalfeldmarschall* (Field Marshal)
Generaladmiral (Four Star Admiral)	*Generaloberst* (Full General)
Admiral (Adm.) (Admiral)	*General der Infanterie usw.* (General of Infantry, etc.)
Vizeadmiral (V.Adm.) (Vice Admiral)	*Generalleutnant* (Major General/Lieutenant General)
Konteradmiral (K.A.) (Rear Admiral)	*Generalmajor* (Brigadier General/Major General)
Kommodore (K.) (Commodore)	No equivalent
Kapitän zur See (K.z.S.) (Captain)	*Oberst* (Colonel)
Fregattenkapitän (F.K.) (Commander)	*Oberstleutnant* (Lieutenant Colonel)
Korvettenkapitän (K.K.) (Lieutenant Commander)	*Major* (Major)
Kapitänleutnant (Kptlt.) (Lieutenant)	*Hauptmann, Rittmeister* (Captain, Calvary Captain)
Oberleutnant zur See (O.z.S.) (Lieutenant junior grade)	*Oberleutnant* (First Lieutenant)
Leutnant zur See (L.z.S.) (Ensign)	*Leutnant* (Second Lieutenant)

PETTY OFFICERS

Stabsoberfeldwebel
(Staff Technical Sergeant)

Stabsfeldwebel
(Master Sergeant/Chief Sergeant)

Oberfeldwebel
(Senior Sergeant)

Oberfeldwebel
(Senior Sergeant)

Oberfähnrich zur See
(Senior midshipman/
Chief Warrant Officer 2)

Oberfähnrich
(Master Sergeant/officer candidate)

Stabsfeldwebel
(Master Sergeant/Chief
Sergeant) –No equivalent

Feldwebel
(Technical Sergeant)

Feldwebel
(Technical Sergeant)

Fähnrich zur See
(Cadet/Midshipman)

Fähnrich
(Officer candidate)

Obermaat
(Petty officer 2nd class)

Unterfeldwebel
(Staff Sergeant)

Maat
(Petty Officer, 3rd class)

Unteroffizier
(Non-Commissioned
Officer/Sergeant)
(*as per 1944 dictionary; other sources say 2nd class*)

ENLISTED MEN

Oberstabsgefreiter
(Petty Officer 3rd class U.S.)
No equivalent

Stabsgefreiter
(Petty Officer 3rd class U.S.)
No equivalent

Hauptgefreiter (Seaman 1st class)
Stabsgefreiter
(Staff Lance Corporal, no U.S. equivalent)

Obergefreiter
(Seaman 1st class)

Obergefreiter (Corporal)

Gefreiter (Seaman 2nd class)

Gefreiter (Acting Corporal)
- No equivalent

Obersoldat
(Senior Private)

Matrose
(Seaman apprentice)

Soldat
(Soldier/Enlisted man)

The abbreviations in parentheses are also used in this book.
***The service rate and rating designations for enlisted men and petty officers went through a number of alterations between 1933 and 1940. To ensure consistency within the Wehrmacht, up to July 1940, the designations (and insignia) were made broadly equivalent to those of the Heer (Army) and Luftwaffe (Air Force). For the sake of convenience, we use these throughout.**
In addition, it should be noted for this work on uniforms that the land-based Kriegsmarine units and their uniforms are only touched on very briefly, since this theme would require a separate volume.

The Insignia of Rank

The enlisted rates (with the exception of seamen) wore their rate insignia on the left upper arm. These insignia consisted of one or more "V"-shaped chevrons. The *Laufbahnabzeichen* (rating badges) were sewn on above the chevron, and the badges for specific training below. The land units used the same rate insignia and wore the distinguishing badges of the *Marine* units embroidered in golden thread on the shoulder straps of their field-gray uniforms. Petty officers *ohne Portepee* ("without sword knot" (lower ranks) also wore their rate badges on the left upper arm, also combined with the respective rating badges. The entire insignia was either embroidered of yellow thread or struck from yellow metal. They were also identified by a gold-colored braid sewn on the jacket sleeve cuff and around the collar of their pea coats.
The *Portepee* petty officers ("with sword knot" (higher ranks)) wore their rating insignia (in the form of 1-3 silver rank stars) on their shoulder straps, which were decorated all around with bands of gold-colored braid. The rating badges, also attached to the shoulder straps, were stamped out of gold-colored metal.
Officers could be recognized by the golden embroidery on their peaked cap bands, introduced in 1936; those for *Leutnante, Ober-* and *Kapitänleutnante* consisted of a narrow strip with serrated edge, for *Stabsoffiziere* (staff officers) of an *Eichenlaub* (oak leaf) border and for *Kommodore* and *Admirale*, of a double *Eichenlaubranke* (oak leaf tendril). The exact rank could be read from the gold-colored sleeve stripes, which were worn on both sleeve forearms of their coats and blue jackets (and mess jackets). The gold-embroidered rating badge was sewn about 4-cm above this. The shoulder boards of bright silver or bright aluminum-colored flat cording, corresponded generally in style those of the *Heer*, but usually had a navy blue cloth backing. *Admirale* wore shoulder boards made of braiding of three round cords, i.e., a silvered braid between two gilded ones. Here, too, the number of rank stars of gilded metal (since 1938) indicated the exact rank.

Maschinengefreiter (engine room seaman 2nd class) of the torpedo boat TIGER. Above his *Gefreiter* stripe, his rating badge (here: Machinery rating) is sewn on. He is wearing walking-out uniform with jacket. (Private collection)

Enlisted men's rate insignia:
a) *Gefreiter*
b) *Obergefreiter*
c) *Obergefreiter*, for the white shirt
d) *Hauptgefreiter* (Seaman 1st class), for the tropical field tunic

e) *Stabsgefreiter* (new style)
f) as above, but for the white shirt (Collection of P.-M. Rousseau)

Stabsgefreiter of a *Marine* artillery unit. He wears the service rank insignia on his navy blue pea coat. (Private collection)

Dienstgradabzeichen der Kriegsmarine

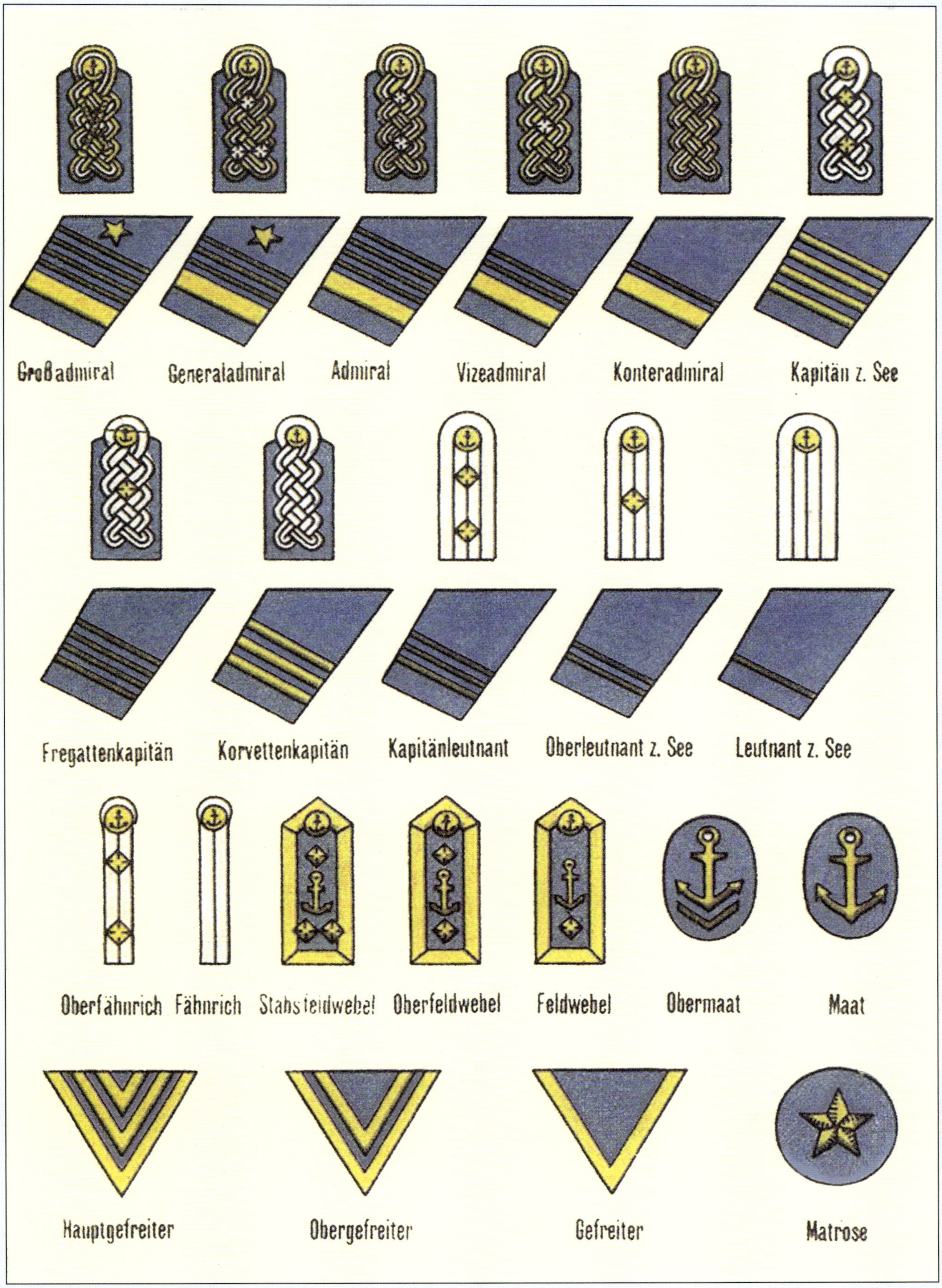

Table of *Kriegsmarine* rank insignia (1940). (Private collection)

Badge for a *Gefreiter, Marine* Artillery. The rating badge is here sewn directly on the upper-extended cloth patch backing for the rank insignia. (Private collection)

Machinery *Obergefreiter* proudly facing the photographer with his newly awarded *Eisernes Kreuz* (Iron Cross) 2. *Klasse*. (Private collection)

This *Hauptgefreiter*'s decorations (torpedo mechanic rating) include the *Eisernes Kreuz* 1. and 2. *Klasse*, the *U-Boot* war badge and those for minehunter, *U-Boot* hunter, and security units. (Private collection)

Rating and rank insignia for a machinery *Oberstabsgefreiter*. (Private collection)

Signalmaat (signalman). (Private collection)

The rank of this *Maat* (petty officer 3rd class) can be seen from the single cord on the collar flap. Petty officers *ohne Portepee* (without sword knot) also wore a gold-colored braid around the pea coat collar. (Private collection)

Maat's collar tab (after October 1939). (Private collection)

Torpedo *Obermechanikersmaat* (Chief Mechanic's Mate) His rank can be seen both from the two cords on the collar tabs as well as his sleeve insignia. (Private collection)

RATING BADGES FOR ENLISTED MEN

BADGES FOR SPECIFIC TRAINING FROM 1940

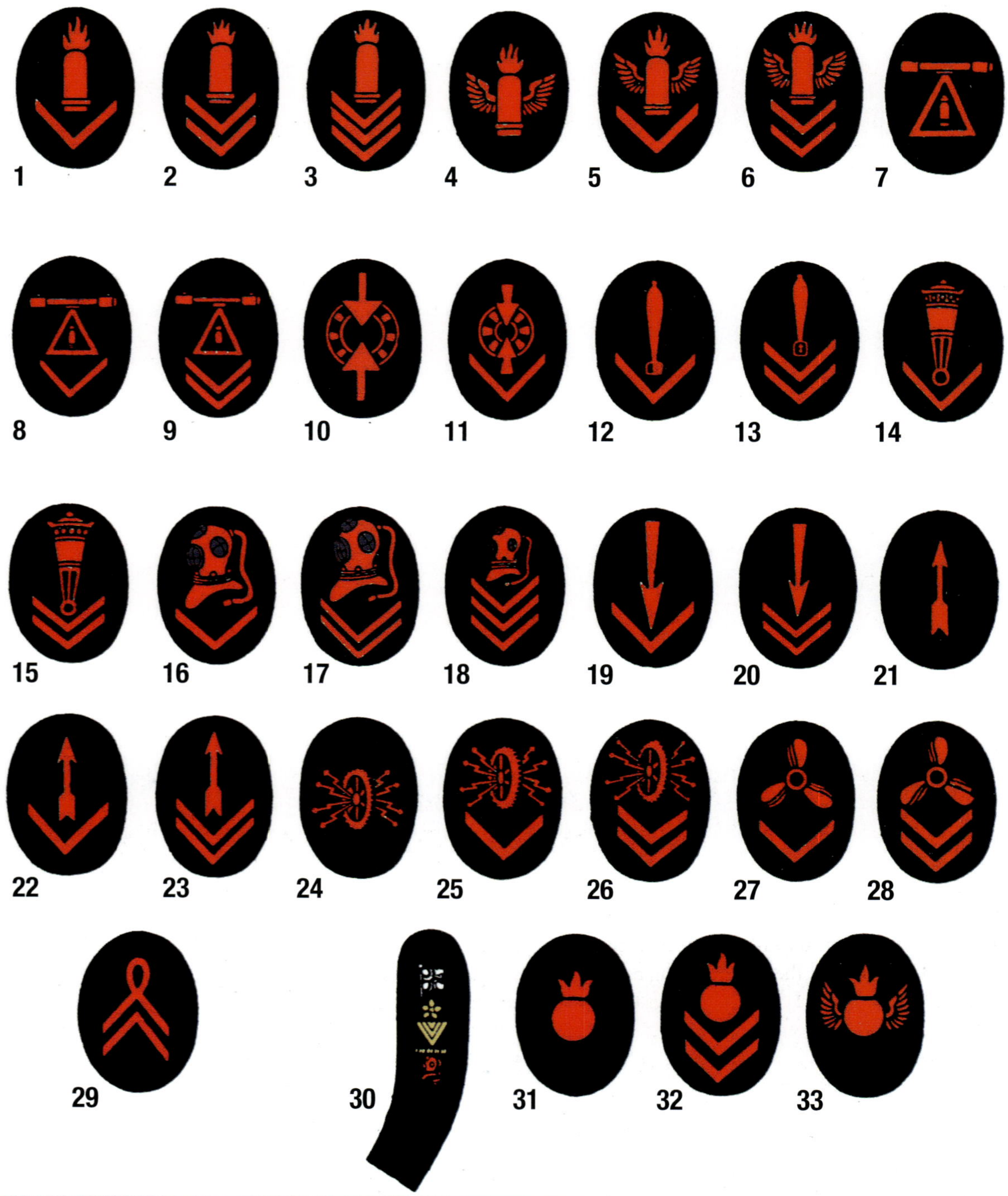

RATING BADGES FOR ENLISTED MEN

A) *Bootsmannslaufbahn* Boatswain rating (Seaman service rate) ("Botswain's")
B) *Maschinenlaufbahn* Machine operator rating ("Machinist's-")
C) *Steuermannslaufbahn* Helmsman rating ("Helmsman's")
D) *Signallaufbahn* Signalman rating ("Signal")
E) *Funklaufbahn* Radio operator rating ("Radio operator")
F) *Fernschreiblaufbahn* Teletype operator rating (Teletype")
G) *Zimmermannlaufbahn* Carpentry rating ("Carpenter's")
H) *Feuerwerkerlaufbahn* Gunnery/Technical specialist ("Gunner's")
I) *Artillermechanikerlaufbahn* Artillery mechanic rating ("Mechanic's")
J) *Torpedomechanikerlaufbahn* Torpedo mechanic rating ("Mechanic's")
K) *Sperrmechanikerlaufbahn* Blockade weapons mechanic rating ("Mechanic's")
L) *Verwaltungs-, Sachverwalter-, Verpflegungslaufbahn* Administration, special (legal etc.) administration, supply corps rating ("Administration man")
M) *Schreiberlaufbahn* Clerical rating ("Clerk")
N) *Sanitätslaufbahn* Paramedic rating ("Paramedic- or Corpsman")
O) *Musiklaufbahn* Musician rating ("Musician")
P) *Marineartillerielaufbahn* Naval artillery rating ("Artilleryman")
Q) *Kraftfahrerlaufbahn* Motor transport rating ("Motor transport operator")
R) *Flugmeldelaufbahn* Aircraft reporting rating "Aircraft reporter")

BADGES FOR SPECIFIC TRAINING from 1940
(Petty officers ohne Portepee and Enlisted Men)

1) Gunner for anti-ship and Flak artillery smaller craft (GF III)
2) Gunner for middle-caliber ship (GF IIa) or destroyer (GF lib) artillery.
3) Gunner for heavy artillery for ships (GF I)
4) Rifleman or observer for light Flak artillery (Flak S bzw. B)
5) Gunner for light Flak artillery (GF Flak II)
6) Gunner for heavy Flak artillery (GF Flak I)
7) Rangefinder with anti-ship and rangefinder training
8) Rangefinder with anti-ship and Flak rangefinder training
9) Rangefinder with petty officer training course
10) Weapons control foreman (troop training)
11) Weapons control foreman (artillery, Flak, coast)
12) Torpedo control foreman III
13) Torpedo control foreman II
14) Blockade and mine weapons foreman
15) Blockade weapons foreman
16) Ship's diver
17) Torpedo diver
18) *U-Boot* and salvage and rescue diver
19) Underwater sound locator enlisted man
20) Flak sound locator petty officer
21) Flak sound locator (troop training)
22) Flak sound locator
23) Flak searchlight operator
24) Technical coastal searchlight training course
25) Electrical engineering III
26) Electrical engineering II
27) Motor course III
28) Motor course II
29) Bandsman/musician
30) Mode of wearing various badges on the left sleeve
31) Coastal defense gunner (troop training)
32) Coastal defense gunner
33) Flak gunner (troop training)

Rating Badges and Insignia for Specific Training

The rating badges were worn by the enlisted ranks and petty officers *ohne Portepee* on the left upper arm while *Portepee* petty officers (petty officers with sword knot) wore these on their shoulder straps; Officers wore them on both lower sleeves (above the sleeve stripes), and, for certain types of uniforms, attached to the shoulder boards and epaulettes. For enlisted men, the rating badges were stitched on a round cloth backing of about 6-cm diameter; for the blue apparel, golden embroidery on navy blue backing was used, and cornflower-blue embroidery on white backing for the white shirt and work shirt. Very often, the rating badges were sewn onto the upper-extended cloth base patch for the rank or rate insignia.

For *Maate* and *Obermaate*, the corresponding badges were displayed on one or two anchors. *Portepee* petty officers wore rate badges of gold-colored metal on their shoulder boards. Officers used gold thread hand-embroidered badges on both forearms, while gilded metal insignia were attached to the shoulder boards, and silver-plated metal insignia to the epaulettes (from 1938).

Badges for specific training were also worn on the left sleeve, but only by enlisted men and petty officers *ohne Portepee*. These were made of red yarn and were stitched onto an oval backing patch (height 9-cm, width 7-cm). These patches were blue for the blue apparel, and white for the white. In 1940, these sleeve badges were newly re-ordered, in part altered somewhat, and some were given a new designation.

House pattern badge with seal attached, from the firm Thiele & Steinert of Berlin, here for the badges for *U-Boot* and salvage or rescue divers. (Private collection)

Mode of wearing rating badges, rank chevron, and badge for specific training on the blue uniform. (Private collection)

This ship's diver – in a white work shirt – wears the badge for his special training (diving helmet of red cotton), under his *Obergefreiter* stripe. Note the diving equipment on the wall. (Private collection)

A ship's diver in diving suit and with Dräger breathing apparatus at work inspecting the ship's hull. (Private collection)

Specific training badges (From left to right): Ship's diver (for the blue uniform), torpedo diver (for the blue uniform) and *U-Boot* and salvage or rescue diver (for the white shirt or work shirt). (Private collection)

Sonderführer (specialist leader) (*Leutnant zur See*) in cloth coat. From mid-1940, *Sonderführer* were distinguished by a golden fouled anchor, which they wore on both sides of the collar of the particular uniform. Their position and its rank were limited to the length of their assignment; they were, as soon as possible, to return to their military training. (Private collection)

Collar badge for a *Sonderführer* (specialist leader) (from 1940). (Private collection)

Badge for staff *Unterpersonal* (personnel) (worn on the left upper arm above all other insignia). (Private collection)

RANK AND CAREER INSIGNIA FOR PETTY OFFICERS OHNE PORTEPEE (from 1938)

1) *Bootsmannsmaat* (Boatswain's mate)
2) *Oberbootsmannsmaat* (Chief Boatswain's mate)
3) *Maschinenmaat* (Machinist's mate)
4) *Obermaschinenmaat* (Chief machinist's mate)
5) *Steuermannsmaat* (Quartermaster)
6) *Obersteuermannsmaat* (Chief quartermaster)
7) *Vermessungsteuermannsmaat* (Quartermaster navigation)
8) *Obervermessungsteuermannsmaat* (Chief quartermaster navigation)
9) *Signalmaat* (Signalman mate)
10) *Obersignalmaat* (Chief signalman)
11) *Funkmaat* (Radioman)
12) *Oberfunkmaat* (Chief radioman)
13) *Fernschreibmaat* (Teletype operator)
14) *Oberfernschreibmaat* (Chief teletype operator)
15) *Zimmermansmaat* (Carpenter's mate)
16) *Oberzimmermannsmaat* (Chief carpenter's mate)
17) *Feuerwerksmaat* (Gunner's mate)
18) *Oberfeuerwerksmaat* (Chief gunner's mate)
19) *Mechanikermaat* (Mechanic's mate)
20) *Obermechanikermaat* (Chief mechanic's mate)
21) *Mechanikermaat* (Mechanic's mate)
22) *Obermechanikermaat* (Chief mechanic's mate)
23) *Mechanikermaat* (Mechanic's mate)
24) *Obermechanikermaat* (Chief mechanic's mate)
25) *Verwaltungsmaat* (Administration petty officer)
26) *Verwaltungsobermaat* (Chief administration petty officer)
27) *Schreibermaat* (Clerical petty officer)
28) *Schreiberobermaat* (Chief clerical petty officer)
29) *Sanitätsmaat* (Navy Corpsman/Paramedic)
30) *Sanitätsobermaat* (Chief corpsman/paramedic)
31) *Musikmaat* (Musician petty officer)
32) *Musikobermaat* (Chief musician petty officer)
33) *Marineartilleriemaat* (Artilleryman)
34) *Marineartillerieobermaat* (Chief artilleryman)
35) *Kraftfahrmaat* (Motor transport mate)
36) *Kraftfahrobermaat* (Chief motor transport mate)
37) *Maat* (Petty Officer, 2nd class)
38) *Obermaat* (Petty officer 1st class)
39) *Flugmeldemaat* (Aircraft spotter)
40) *Flugmeldeobermaat* (Chief aircraft spotter)

A *Matrosen-Obergefreiter* (the embroidered yellow star above the *Obergefreiter* stripe is for the *Bootsmann* rating) with two badges for specific training (embroidered in red wool), which are sewn under the rank insignia: *Geschützführer* (gunner) for anti-ship and Flak artillery for smaller vessels (top) and below *Geschützführer* in the light Flak artillery. (Private collection)

This *Obermaat* had already fought in the First World War, because he is wearing the *Ordensband des Ehrenkreuze* (medal ribbon of the badge of honor) for front-line soldiers on his pea coat. The rating badge sewn on his left sleeve is that for the *Marineartillerie.* (Private collection)

Rating badges for petty officers (rows 1 to 3) and enlisted men (rows 4 and 5). For blue apparel, these were appliqued on a blue backing, and for the white shirt and work shirt, on a white backing. (Private collection)

Shoulder straps for a *Feuerwerker* (gunnery or technical sergeant) (*Feldwebel*) blue dress (left) and a *Sanitätsfeldwebel*, tropical dress (right). (Private collection)

Shoulder straps (left to right): *Verwaltung feldwebel*, (administrative sergeant), *Kraftfahrfeldwebel*, *Oberfunkmeister*, *Maschinist.* (Collection of P.-M. Rousseau)

Back view of several shoulder straps: The shoulder strap at left was once sewn into the shoulder seam, while the two others were buttoned on, since they were worn on apparel which had to be washed more frequently (white jacket or brown tropical uniform). (Private collection)

Portepee petty officer in tropical dress (shorts and shirt), Italy, summer 1944. On his sand-colored shirt, he wears shoulder straps of the same material and also the blockade runner badge and the war badge for minehunter, *U-Boot* hunter, and security units.
(Private collection)

Obermaschinist in blue jacket. The shoulder straps were sewn into the shoulder seams in this article of apparel.
(Private collection)

A selection of rating insignia for officers, which were to be worn on the forearm (from left to right and from top to bottom): *Seeoffiziere* (Naval officers), *Seeoffiziere* (variant), *Ingenieuroffizier* (engineering officer), *Ingenieuroffizier* (variant), officers in the *Truppensonderdienst* (Special Troop Service TSD) - recognizable from the horizontal braid, *Verwaltungsoffiziere* (Administrative officers), *Nachrichtentechnische Offiziere* (telecommunications officers), *Waffenoffiziere der Sperrwaffen* (blockade weaponry officers), *Waffenoffiziere (Artilleriewaffen)* (Artillery), *Marineartillerieoffiziere.* (Private collection)

Detail of the rating badge for a *Torpedotechnisch* officer, which was sewn 4-cm above the top sleeve stripe. (Private collection)

The braid below the rating badge of this officer reveals that he is a *Marineoberstabsintendant* (Naval senior staff director) of the TSD *(Truppensonderdienst)* (corresponding to a *Korvettenkapitän*). (Private collection)

Shoulder boards for officers (from left to right): *Oberfähnrich des Marineingenieurwesens* (Naval engineering), *Leutnant* (still with manufacturer's wrapping band), *Kapitänleutnant des Marineingenieurwesens, Kapitänleutnant des Sperrwaffenwesen, Fregattenkapitän.* (Collection of P.-M. Rousseau)

Konteradmiral's shoulder boards, for buttoning on. (Private collection)

Fähnrich (officer candidate) in cloth coat with narrow shoulder braids corresponding to his rank. (Private collection)

Kapitän des Marineingenieurwesens (Naval engineering), ***Leutnant for Nachrichtentechnik*** (Communications engineering). (Private collection)

Oberleutnant zur See wearing his shoulder boards on the gray leather jacket for Naval personnel. (Private collection)

This *Portepee* petty officer is wearing the W.O. rank insignia (*Wachhabender Offizier* (Watch Officer)) for officers on his coat, according to regulations, in the second buttonhole from the top. (Private collection)

W.O. rank insignia for officers. This rank insignia was usually worn on the left side of the chest and identified the relevant duty/watch officer on board; on land, it was worn by the particular officer on duty. (Private collection)

These three back views of the insignia show different ways to fasten it to the uniform. The *Bundesmarine*, incidentally, still uses the same insignia. (Collection of P.-M. Rousseau)

THE CLOTH CAP

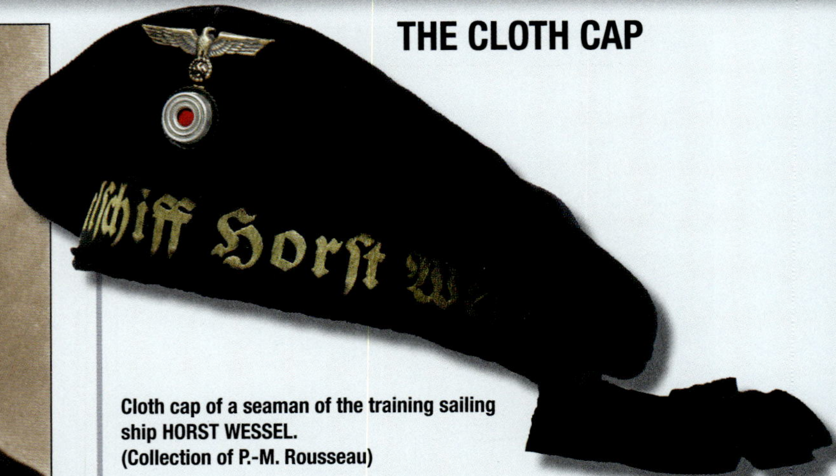

Cloth cap of a seaman of the training sailing ship HORST WESSEL. (Collection of P.-M. Rousseau)

A *Matrose* of the *4. Schiffsstammabteilung 4* (*Marine* units stationed on the coast, responsible for the military and seaman's basic training for the Fleet) wearing the cap band of his unit on his blue seaman's cap. (Private collection)

Two *U-Boot* men in gray *"Lederpäckchen"* ("leather package") and the seaman's cap, here with white cover. Unfortunately, you cannot see from the cap bands, to which *Unterseebootsflottille* they belong. Before the war, the cloth cap was often worn also by *U-Boot* crews, but shortly after the outbreak of war, they disappeared almost completely onboard. (Private collection)

Headgear

In peacetime, the seamen's cap, also known as a cloth cap, was the sailors' general headgear. The cap had a black cap band, which showed, in *Fraktur* (gothic) script (of gold thread – later, rayon thread) the type and name of the ship or boat, and the *Division, Halbflottille* or *Flotille*. These were also named for the land troop units, or their respective departments, schools, etc. For security and secrecy reasons, a new, uniform cap band with the word '*Kriegsmarine* ,' also in *Fraktur* script, was introduced on September 5, 1939. The *Hoheitsabzeichen* (the national emblem) (introduced in March 1934) was pinned onto the front over the black-white-red *Reich* cockade.

Shortly after the war began, the blue *Bordmütze* ("on board cap"; U.S. equivalent "garrison cap" or "overseas cap") was introduced, for practical considerations, for all soldiers up to the rank of *Admiral*; this was the Navy's version of the "*Schiffchen*" ("little ship"/side cap). As its name suggests, they were especially designed to be worn aboard ship. The version for seamen

This picture of a Matrose from a *Marineartillerieabteilung* dates from 1933. He is still wearing the uniform of the *Reichsmarine* and the *Reich* eagle cockade of the Weimar Republic is also on his cloth cap. (Private collection)

This seaman also belongs to a *Marineartillerieabteilung*, but this photo dates from 1935. On his seaman's cap he wears the first design of the Nazi National Emblem. (Private collection)

A blue and a white cover for the enlisted men's cap. The first comes from the *Kriegsmarine* arsenal in Cherbourg. The white cap cover was worn within *Reich* territory during the summer uniform period (April 20 to September 30), in foreign waters and in the tropics, depending upon the climate. (Private collection)

and petty officers had a golden yellow, woven National Emblem on it, while officers mostly used a gold-embroidered badge. In 1940, a border of woven braid (*Gespinstlitze*) (gold or silver) was introduced, which ran around the upper edge of the flap. For the Mediterranean and the Black Sea theatres, the *Kriegsmarine* introduced in 1942 a tropical field cap with visor, which resembled the *Afrika Korps* field cap, but was, however, made from the *Marine*'s tropical brown material. Already around 1940, a white garrison cap was introduced, which was intended for tropical waters. The "sou'wester," made of rubberized fabric, was part of the rain gear and was issued during appropriate weather to the men on board duty. During cold weather, the seafaring crew on board wore wool or bobble caps that were knitted from thick, dark blue wool, and had a wool bobble on top. The men also wore self-furnished items of different colored wool. Winter clothing also included fur caps, for which there was likely no official design – the men simply wore whatever was warm and looked fairly militarily.

Two of the seamen in this 1942 photo are wearing blue enlisted men's cap with ***'Kriegsmarine'***; the third, a blue garrison cap. As the war continued, these displaced cloth caps more and more. (Private collection)

Inside of a personal cap, with the manufacturer's label. (Collection of P.-M. Rousseau)

Inside of an item issued by the Naval supply depot, with the corresponding acceptance mark. (Private collection)

A small selection of over 300 different capbands, which were worn in the *Kriegsmarine* between 1933 and 1939. Until the beginning of the war, the name of the ship, boat, military unit, school, etc. where the wearer was serving, was worked into the band in *Fraktur*. (Private collection)

Photo of a *Maat* of the *U-Boot Flottile Hundius* from peacetime. The width of the cap band was 3.2-cm, its length could be 116-150-cm. (Private collection)

Sailor in the blue uniform. His cloth cap has a band bearing the lettering *"Kriegsmarine."* (Private collection)

Two hat-bands of the pre-war period and a cap band of the *"Kriegsmarine,"* introduced for the duration of the war. (Private collection)

THE "ON BOARD" CAP (GARRISON CAP)

White garrison cap for petty officers and seamen. This headgear should – in theory – be worn with white work clothing. (Collection of P.-M. Rousseau)

The national emblem for the white garrison cap, of cornflower blue cotton or rayon on a white backing. (Collection of P.-M. Rousseau)

Manufacturer's label in another white garrison cap. (Private collection)

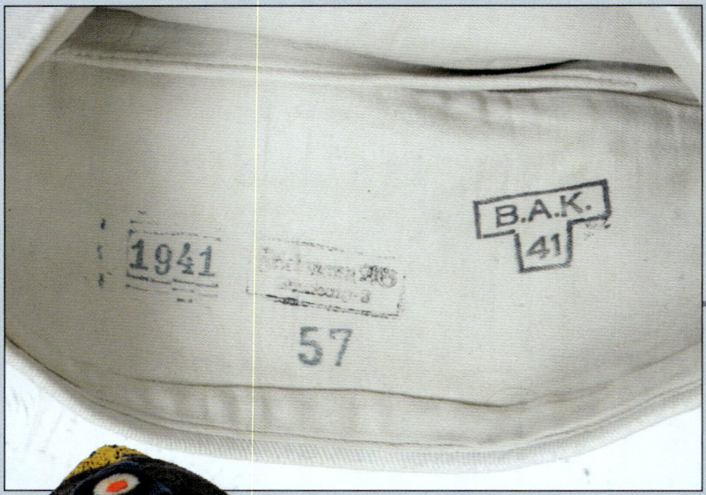

The stamp on the lining of a white garrison cap: On the one hand, the year of manufacture (1941), size (57), the manufacturer's label (here unfortunately illegible) and the acceptance stamp of the relevant *Marinebekleidungsamt* (Navy uniform supply depot) *('B.A.K' - Bekleidungsamt Kiel)*. (Collection of P.-M. Rousseau)

Blue garrison cap for petty officers and enlisted men with blue lining. (Private collection)

White garrison cap for petty officers and enlisted men, but here with the insignia on a blue backing. These insignia were actually intended for the blue version of garrison cap, but are found sometimes on white caps. (Private collection)

An officer wearing a white garrison cap and gold-colored border on the upper flap edge. (Private collection)

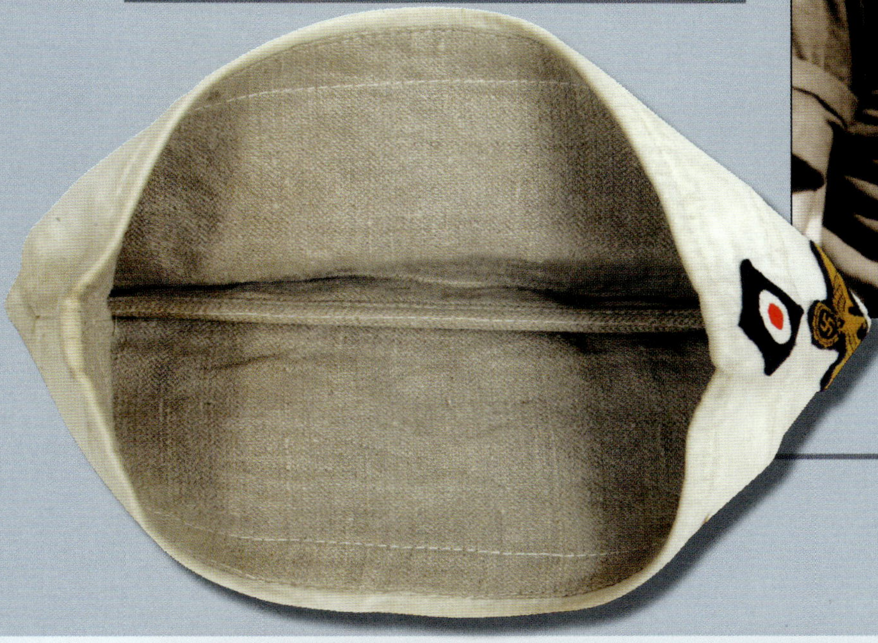

Inside of a white garrison cap. There are no stamps to be seen on the gray lining. (Private collection)

National emblems and cockades from different manufacturers for the blue garrison cap. (Private collection)

Size notation on the lining of a blue garrison cap. The 'W' before it indicates the uniform supply depot in Wilhelmshaven. (Private collection)

This young seaman, just awarded the *EK II*, is wearing the usual garrison cap for petty officers and enlisted men of navy blue cloth. (Private collection)

Blue garrison cap for petty officers and enlisted men with the insignia of *Räumboot 162* (minesweeper) of the *22. U-Jagdflottille*, which was stationed in Italy in May 1943. (Private collection)

Garrison cap of an officer of the *1. U-Flotille*. The gold border on the upper edge of the flap identifies *Kriegsmarine* officers (and from September 1943, also *Oberfähnriche*). The badge on this cap, however, is of the so-called *BeVo* (woven) version for enlisted men and petty officers. (Collection of P.-M. Rousseau)

Korvettenkapitän in blue jacket and garrison cap for officers. Officers did not generally wear the garrison caps; they preferred the more elegant peaked cap. (Private collection)

THE FIELD CAP WITH VISOR

Field cap with visor of blue cloth. This rare model was only issued in early 1945 and may reflect the attempt of the German leadership to introduce a standard uniform for all Wehrmacht branches. It was only issued to a few land-based units.
(Collection of P.-M. Rousseau)

Detail of the insignia and anchor buttons on the blue field cap.
(Collection of P.-M. Rousseau)

One of the few photos showing members of the German Marine with navy blue "Einheitsfeldmütze" (uniform field caps). This picture shows a group of prisoners of war in 1945, who were photographed after burying a comrade. This also explains why the headgear and uniforms show no national or other insignia. (Private collection)

FUR HATS

This *Portepee* petty officer is wearing a really unusual fur hat. (Private collection)

Two other petty officers with fur hats, this time of sheepskin (which look much more "militaristic"). The man at right has even added the national emblem, oak wreath, and cockade of the peaked cap. (Private collection)

TROPICAL HEADGEAR

Tropical field cap with visor (enlisted men's version) of khaki cloth, which has anyway been sun-bleached to almost white. In this example, the national emblem is woven onto a brown backing and the cockade is on the same khaki material as the cap. This piece was captured by a French soldier in exactly this state. Since the national emblem is hardly faded, it might have been "upgraded" by the original owner. (Private collection)

The inner lining of the field cap is made of khaki colored satin. This style is typical of items manufactured in occupied France. (Private collection)

Detail of the jacquard woven national emblem (enlisted men's version) for tropical field caps. (Private collection)

Obergefreiter in tropical shirt and field cap with jacquard woven national emblem ("BeVo" version). (Private collection)

A young seaman in the tropical field cap with visor. Contrary to regulations, he is wearing a national emblem of gold colored metal. (Private collection)

This photograph of a group of *Marine* personnel was taken some time in the summer of 1944 in the Mediterranean. Particularly interesting here are the different shades of colors to be seen in the tropical field caps. (Private collection)

Some of these *Portepee* petty officers photographed in Greece, are wearing tropical peaked caps (Private collection)

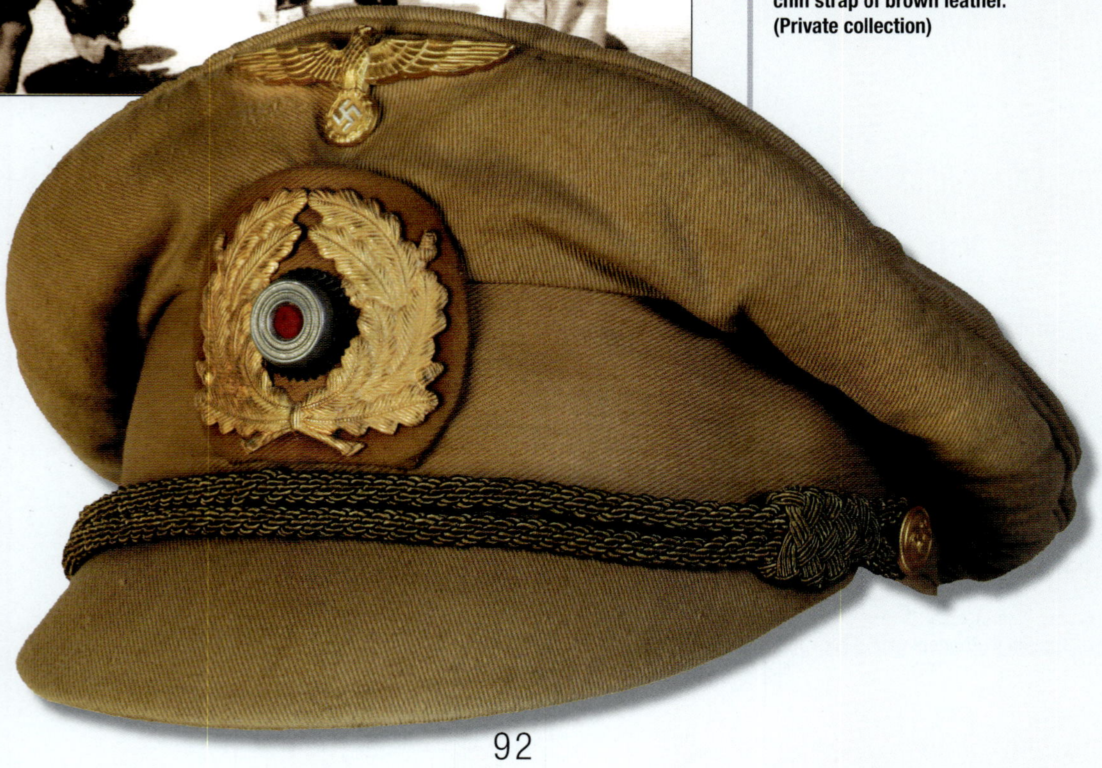

An *Admiral's* tropical peaked cap. This headgear of khaki tropical cloth could only be worn in the Mediterranean, the Black Sea, North Africa, and the tropics. The *Admiral's* version can be recognized by the gold-colored cap braid, while officers and *Portepee* petty officers wore an aluminum-colored cap cord and a chin strap of brown leather. (Private collection)

This 1944 photo shows two *Portepee* petty officers wearing the tropical peaked cap with brown leather chin strap. (Private collection)

Inside of an *Admiral's* tropical peaked cap. (Private collection)

Group photo of members of a sea-going unit, aboard their ship in the Mediterranean. Two of them, (*Portepee* petty officers), wear the tropical peaked cap, with the regulation leather chin strap (Private collection)

HELMETS

The shield/blazon with the gold-colored *Wehrmacht* eagle, was worn on the left side of the tropical helmet. (Collection of P.-M. Rousseau)

Tropical helmet with both *Marine* shields of aluminum. (Collection of P.-M. Rousseau)

Servicing the guns of a 10.5-cm SK *(Schnellladenkanone)* (fast-loading guns) aboard an escort vessel. The soldiers are wearing *Stahlhelme* (steel helmets) painted a light gray color, as was used for the warships themselves. (Private collection)

THE STAHLHELM (STEEL HELMET)

Stahlhelm 35, with the characteristic *Kriegsmarine* gold national emblem. In February 1934, new insignia were introduced for the *Stahlhelm*: The black-white-red *Reich* shield/blazon on the right side and the golden *Wehrmacht* eagle, on black background on the left. By an order of July 17, 1941, the *Reich* shield was eliminated for the *Kriegsmarine*, or was to be removed by painting it over, and from August 28, 1943, the gold national emblem could no longer be applied. Theoretically from this time, no more insignia could be worn on the steel helmets, yet in practice there were still helmets with one or the other insignia until the end of the war. (Private collection)

Detail of the gold-colored *Wehrmacht* eagle, here in almost perfectly preserved condition. (Private collection)

Stahlhelm "M42" of an Italian volunteer, who were deployed between 1943-45 with the *Kriegsmarine* in the Atlantic. The insignia was hand-painted on. (Private collection)

PEAKED CAPS

Peaked cap of a *Portepee* petty officer with embroidered wreath but metal-embossed national emblem. This was also often used by officers in place of the embroidered version. For the lining, the usual light blue rayon was used, and the brown leather sweat band matches the usual style. (Private collection)

This peaked cap of a *Portepee* petty officer is from the "Fortress Lorient." In addition to a rare version of the oak leaf wreath, this cap also has traces of a bullet or in grenade splinter its cap cover. (Private collection)

The peaked cap was worn by officers and *Portepee* petty officers. The design was generally the same, except that officers' caps usually made of better material: The peaked caps of black vulcanized fiber or leather, bands made of black mohair, and tops of blue or white material (the latter for the summer period or the tropics. There were caps with either a permanent or a removable cover. In war, it became usual for the commanders of boats and ships to wear peaked caps with a white cover, in order to be more quickly recognized in their function. The chin strap made of black leather was buttoned on the side with two small gold anchor buttons. The national emblem was of gold or celleon thread and hand-embroidered (for the white cover, a gold-colored metal eagle was compulsory) and mounted centrally on the upper part of the cap. The oak wreath and the black-white-red *Reich* cockade were set on the front band. In 1936, gold cap border embroidery for officers was introduced, so that the visor was now covered on top with blue cloth (the peaked cap of the *Portepee* petty officers kept the normal leather visor). Subaltern officers (*Leutnante, Ober-* and *Kapitänleutnante*) wore a round serrated stripe, staff officers from *Korvettenkapitän* up to *Kapitän zur See* a 1.8-cm wide oak leaf tendril and *Kommodore* and *Admirale* a double oak leaf tendril. Officers' peaked caps increasingly reflected personal preferences and fashion influences, so that these can show major differences in these respects in workmanship and materials used. Thus, we find some in which instead of the usual light-blue silk or rayon lining, other colors such as dark blue, white, yellow or ivory were used. Pieces that were made by French manufacturers can be recognized by the black lining, which also had been used for the caps of the French "*Marine Nationale*." In addition, there was the hat (also called 'gala hat') worn by officers with the full dress uniform. This bicorn hat, then still worn by many navies around the world, was rarely seen after the outbreak of the war, as the full dress uniforms were no longer worn.

Peaked cap for a *Portepee* petty officer, here with permanent blue top. The insignia are embroidered in celleon and the chinstrap of black leather is buttoned on with gold anchor buttons. (Collection of P.-M. Rousseau)

In this 1944 photo, a young ensign is wearing a peaked cap with rim and national emblem embroidered of gold colored celleon. (Private collection)

Inner lining the cap shown above, of blue rayon and with sweatband of brown leather. (Collection of P.-M. Rousseau)

Peaked cap for *Portepee* petty officers. The oak leaf cluster and cockade are metal-embossed, the national emblem, instead, is hand-embroidered. (Collection of P.-M. Rousseau)

Portepee petty officer in walking-out dress. On his peaked cap he wears exactly the above insignia combination. (Private collection)

The lining material for this cap is – rather unusually – of originally yellowish silk. Here, the manufacturer's name is printed on the so-called celluloid sweat plate. (Collection of P.-M. Rousseau)

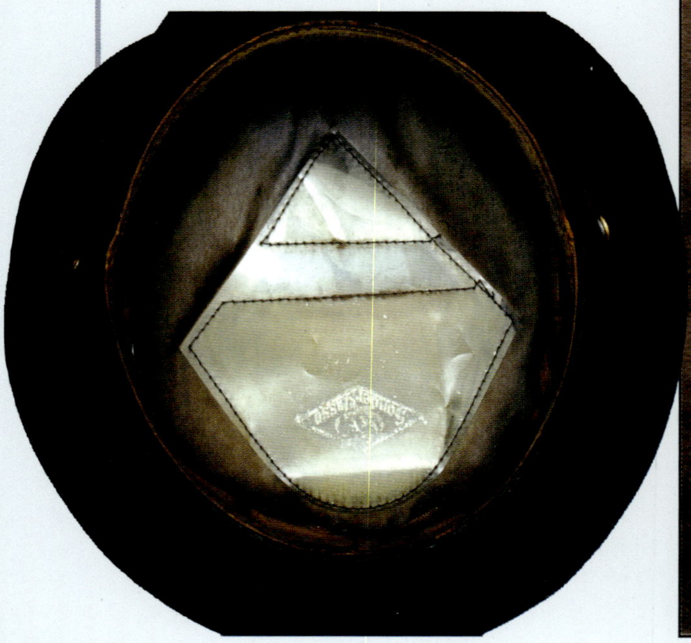

Peaked cap for *Portepee* petty officers from a French manufacturer. The national emblem is here again hand-embroidered, the wreath and cockade metal-embossed. Pinned on the black mohair band of this cap, is the insignia of the *22. U-Jagdflottille,* which in 1942 was deployed in Marseille, where the cap's maker had his workshop. (Private collection)

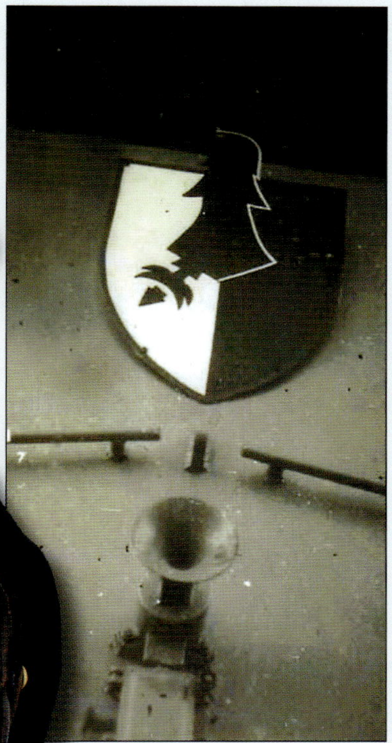

This picture from 1944 shows the insignia of the *22. U-Jagdflottille* on board the *U-Jäger* UJ 2207. (Private collection)

The insignia on the blue peaked cap of this *Portepee* petty officer are all embroidered. Note the checkered shirt he is wearing under his jacket, which was at least tolerated since 1941. (Private collection)

Oberfähnrich in a peaked cap. Up to the visor embroidery, it corresponds to the officers' style. (Private collection)

Hans Rudolf Rösing, *Kommandant* of U 48, returning from a mission. The originally white cover of his peaked cap shows, after many weeks at sea, a dirty-gray film. Actually, for the white caps a metal embossed insignia was compulsory, but here, Rösing is wearing a hand-embroidered design. (Private collection)

Leutnant zur See. Around his cap visor is the regulation, blunt jagged gold embroidery. (Private collection)

Peaked cap with a blue cover, here in the style for *Leutnant zur See* up to *Kapitänleutnant.* National emblem and oak wreath are embroidered of regulation gold thread. (Collection of P.-M. Rousseau)

Usually the hat lining was of blue rayon and had a sweat band of celluloid. (Collection of P.-M. Rousseau)

This U-boat *Kommandant* wears a peaked cap with white cover. After the outbreak of the war, it was allowed for commanders of boats and ships to wear this cap at all times, to distinguish them. Our man is wearing on it the first design of the national emblem, which had shorter wings than those on the in April 1935 introduced second design. (Private collection)

Kapitän zur See with peaked cap in the style for staff officers, with white cover. For the white cap, a national emblem of gold colored metal was required. This could be more easily removed for cleaning the cover, since it was of course, more easily soiled. (Private collection)

Peaked cap with a blue cover, in the style for a *Leutnant zur See* to *Kapitänleutnant*. Due to the many manufacturers of uniform caps, who did not all use the exact same materials, there were some pretty significant differences among the caps worn. (Private collection)

The inner lining used by this cap maker from Cuxhaven is exceptionally elegant. On the sweatband are the initials of the wearer fastened. (Private collection)

An *Oberleutnant zur See* with the *Eisernes Kreuz I. Klasse* and two war badges on his jacket. He also wears a peaked cap with a blue cover and the regulation gold thread embroidered insignia. (Private collection)

Peaked cap with white cover and embroidered visor. The lining is of blue rayon. This headgear once belonged to *Kapitänleutnant* Hermann Lamby. (Collection of P.-M. Rousseau)

Peaked cap with a white cover and visor embroidery, here in the style for staff officers, from *Korvettenkapitän* up to *Kapitän zur See*. The gold-embroidered visor for officers was introduced on May 13, 1936 by order of the *OKC*. (Collection of P.-M. Rousseau)

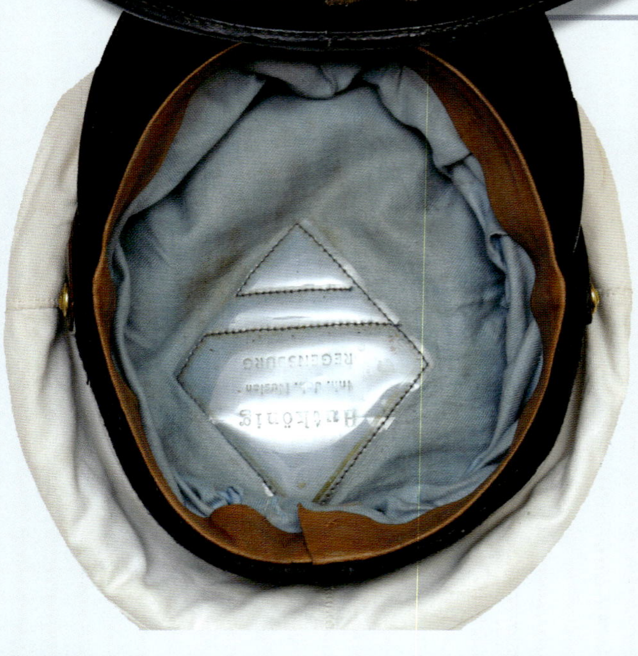

Light blue cap lining with diamond-shaped sweat plate and brown sweatband. (Collection of P.-M. Rousseau)

A woman *Kriegsmarine* auxilliary member greets with flowers *Korvettenkapitän* Dommes, *Kommandant* of U 178, after he carried out a *"Kaperfahrt"* (privateering mission). Here, it is easy to see the visor embroidery for staff officers on his white cap. (Private collection)

Blue peaked cap for a staff officer. The cover cannot be removed. (Private collection)

A *Kapitän zur See* (left) and a *Korvettenkapitän* (right), both with the blue peaked cap for staff officers. (Private collection)

HEADGEAR FOR *ADMIRALE*

Hat (also called gala-hat) of *Generaladmiral* Alfred Saalwächter. The lower end of the agraffe or ornamented clasp, is fastened to the right side of the hat with a gold button showing the national emblem. (Auction house Hermann Historica, Munich)

Peaked cap with removable white cover from the estate of *Admiral* Alfred Saalwächter (1883-1945). Instead of the metal national emblem, Saälwächter wore on his cap a hand-embroidered insignia on a white background – he would have hardly been questioned about this. The embroidery on the visor is the double oak tendril for *Admirale* and *Kommodoren.* Note the yellow-white cap lining. (Hermann Historica auction house, Munich)

Here, *Großadmiral* Dönitz good-humoredly gives a young "fan" – a leader in the Deutschen Jugend (German Youth Alliance) – an autograph. His blue *Admiral's* peaked cap has the regulation double oak leaf tendril on the visor. (Private collection)

UNOFFICIAL CAP INSIGNIA

Locally made *9. U-Flottille* cap badges. This version, cut from aluminum, was issued to the flotilla's seamen. (Collection of P.-M. Rousseau)

An officer's peaked cap, with the *9. U-Flottille* emblem pinned on it. This flotilla was stationed in Brest. (Collection of P.-M. Rousseau)

The propaganda magazine *"Signal"* liked to adorn its front pages with *U-Boot* men. This photo shows a *Portepee* petty officer whose cap is decorated with a locally made badge, as were issued to the unit members. (Private collection)

Enameled badge of the *9. U-Flotille*. The "laughing swordfish" was originally the turret mascot of U 96, commanded by *Kapitänleutnant* Heinrich Lehmann-Willenbrock until March 1942. After he was appointed commander of the *9. U-Flotille* in Brest, Lehmann-Willenbrock adopted this emblem for the whole flotilla. Some eighteen other *U-Boote* also had a swordfish as their mascot. (Collection of P.-M. Rousseau)

Cap insignia of the ***18. Vorpostenflottille*** (Outpost flotilla) set up in July 1940 as the ***18. Vorposten-gruppe*** (Outpost group), and expanded into a flotilla on October 3, 1940. As the inscription ***'Abschnitt Kanal'*** ('Channel Division') shows, this formation was deployed in the English Channel. (Private collection)

A ***U-Boot*** crew have their photo taken after a successful patrol, beneath the oversized mascot of the ***9. U-Flotille.*** (Collection of P.-M. Rousseau)

Insignia of U 118 (commissioned on 12/6/41, sunk on 6/12/43) from the estate of *Kptlt. (Ing.),* Felix Miller, who had also been involved in the *U-Boot's* construction. During his health leave in the Austrian town of Bad Gastein, the community approached him with the proposal that they become sponsors for the future boat. The spa then made this badge for the crew, designed with an *Edelweiß* on the city coat of arms and a banner inscribed "Sponsored by Bad Gastein 1942." (Private collection)

Unofficial Cap Insignia

This topic is so broad and exciting that you could write an entire book about it. In the spring of 1940, badges began to appear on the crew's on board and peaked caps, showing the mascot or emblem of the boat or formation in which the wearer was serving. [Translator's note: The first of these was the *Edelweiß* insignia of the mountain troops; after the battle at Narvik, the "*Jäger*" ("hunters") shared this insignia with their *Marine* comrades who had fought at their sides on land after their ships had been sunk]. Even if this practice was against regulations, there was no stopping it – it was sometimes approved by superiors, to increase morale. There were many designs, from simple badges cut out of tin cans to professionally made and enameled pieces ordered from local makers.

Unattributed badge, possibly from a land unit (it is sometimes ascribed to a coastal artillery unit). This badge was also made with a red-white pennant or a blue pennant with a yellow cross. The photo shows another version, painted on a railroad car or truck. (Private collection)

The *Kommandant* of U 97, *Kptlt.* Udo Heilmann, returning to base. U 97's symbol was a sea horse, which Heilmann here wears on the band of his peaked cap. (Private collection)

The *Kommandant* of U 333, *Kptlt.* Peter-Erich "Ali" Cremer, getting an appropriate reception after returning from a successful patrol with his crew. His boat's emblem was three small fish, after one of Cremer's most frequent expressions: *"Alles kleine Fische..."* ("[We're] All small fish..."). On July 31, 1944, U 333 was sunk in the North Atlantic by British depth charges. (Private collection)

From left to right and top to bottom: Badges of U 128 (commissioned in May 1941, sunk on May 17, 1943). This badge is certainly similar to that of U 68, but the contemporary piece of paper attached to it named U 126 instead; we unfortunately have no further information. Brass badges of U 67 (*2. U-Flotille* in Lorient in January 1941; sunk on July 16, 1943). Aluminum badges from U 505, also of the *2. U-Flotille* in Lorient; capsized on June 4, 1944 by the U.S. Navy. Brass badge of U 521, again, of the Lorient *2. U-Flotille*; sunk on June 2, 1943. (Private collection)

Many *U-Boote* (U 22, U 23, U 24, U 59, U 105, U 128, U 192, U 203, U 228, U 306...) used the Olympic rings as their emblem – going back to Crew 36 (graduating year of *Marine* officer candidates). This enameled version is the most commonly found. (Collection of P.-M. Rousseau)

Enameled badge the *11. U-Flotille*, which was stationed in Bergen, northern Norway. (Private collection)

Enameled badge of the *24. U-Flotille*, which was stationed in Mernel, *Ostpreußen* (East Prussia); today Klaipeda in Lithuania. (Collection of P.-M. Rousseau)

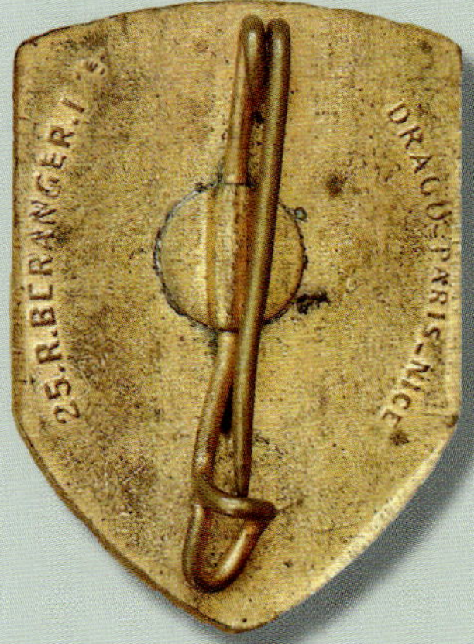

Front and back of an enameled badge of the Lorient *Hafenschutzflottille* (harbor defense flotilla), of French manufacture. (Private collection)

Front and back of the badge of the *1. U-Flotille*, which originated in the pre-war *Weddingen Flottille*. Kiel was its original home base; then the flotilla moved its base to Brest in June 1941, and was disbanded in September 1944 in the same city. This wonderfully worked enamel badge is of French manufacture. (Collection of P.-M. Rousseau)

Leather badge for the *2. Vorpostenflotille*, showing a *Wolfshaken* (wolf's hook) The badge was found in the envelope shown, which an officer of the formation had sent to his family. (Private collection)

Four U 218 crewmembers, wearing their boat's mascot – three fish – on their garrison caps. (Private collection)

White peaked cap of a *Portepee* petty officer with the specially made badge of French manufacture, of an – unfortunately unidentified – *Räumbootsflottille.* The coat of arms of Normandy (two golden leopards on a red shield) on the badge suggests that the formation was deployed there. Note that because of the size of the badge, the cap owner had removed the chinstrap that was probably in the way. (Private collection)

Cap badge of U 66. This badge was originally used by the *"Freikorps Epp"* in the period 1919-1920. It was later adopted by the crew of U 66. (Private collection)

This unusual garrison cap was worn by a crewmember of U 66, which was under the command of the Lorient-based *2. U-Flotille*. The man had not only pinned on the lion's head of U 66 and the flotilla badge, but also rounded it out with the "ensemble" of shields worn with the pith helmet. (Collection of P.-M. Rousseau)

BADGES OF THE 22. U-JAGDFLOTTILLE IN ITALY (1943-45)

The *22. U-Jagdflottille* was deployed to Marseille in December 1942; it was finally disbanded on April 27, 1945 in Genoa. It included thirty-one boats of lower tonnage and motley origin: German, Belgian, French, Dutch, and Italian. The majority of them were converted civilian craft that the Germans – who at that time no longer had the power to do much in the Mediterranean – had turned into warships. Nevertheless, this flotilla successfully fulfilled its mission, namely, protecting the coast and convoys in the western Mediterranean, until the surrender in 1945. Members of this unit wore either the badge of the *22. U-Jagdflottille*, or that of their own boat, on their headgear. We can confirm four different versions of the badge. The style is typical for pieces made during the war in Italy, and the same for all these badges. They are all of painted aluminum, and are exceptionally well made.

Obergefreiter Erwin Kafling, who served aboard UJ 2207, wore this *22. U-Jagdflottille* cap badge in 1944. This *U-Bootjäger*, a 1926 French-built fishing cutter with a displacement of 1,034 tons, was originally named "Cap Nord." In 1942, she was confiscated by the Germans and converted into a German warship. UJ 2207 was sunk near Sestri Levante (Liguria) by American torpedo boats in the night of November 18-19. Erwin Hatting was one of the few survivors of the attack. (Private collection)

Cap badge of SEEROSE R162. The SEEROSE was a *Minenräumboot* (minesweeper) put into service on February 7, 1941 under the command of *Leutnant zur See* Jung. She was scuttled on April 24, 1945 in the port of Genoa. The badge shows a distinctive redhead, dancing, just as God made her, on the water. Above her are the boat's name and number. (Private collection)

Obergefreiter Paul Modrzinski, who served on one of the *Kriegstransporter* (war transport boats) of the *22. U-Jagdflottille*, wore this cap badge during 1944-45. There were a number of cargo boats in the Mediterranean, transporting various kinds of materiel for the different *Kriegsmarine* bases. These armed transports had the abbreviation *KT* before their numbers (KT 8 KT 14, KT 36, KT 43, KT 49, etc.). The badge shows a naked devil holding a trident, riding on a torpedo. Behind him we see a map of Italy and the islands in the Terranean Sea. The devil was originally once painted red, on a blue background with red border – as in the picture to the right. (Private collection)

This *Maat*, likely stationed in the Mediterranean, is wearing the badge of an unfortunately unspecified boat of the formation on his garrison cap. (Private collection)

This badge was used by the crews of the *U-Boote* U 92, U 622, and U 2522. The above example is of local make. (Private collection)

This *U-Boot* officer wears the badge of U 161 on his garrison cap; it shows a Viking ship. U 161 was put into service on July 8, 1941 and sunk off the Brazilian coast on September 27, 1943, on her sixth patrol, with the loss of the entire crew. (Private collection)

Badge for U 777, of local make. (Private collection)

Cap badge for crewmembers of U 73. As with the previous badges, it made by the *U-Boot* men themselves or by the fitters in the *Marine* bases from scrap metal. There are countless copies of badges "made on board," for these, knowledge of original pieces is of course much more difficult. (Private collection)

Erich Topp, the legendary *Kommandant* of U 552, in 1941. In this personally autographed photo portrait, the *Kapitänleutnant* wears on his white peaked cap an enlarged, metal-embossed national emblem, which was intended for the white jacket ... as a national hero, he was certainly able to allow himself this liberty. (Private collection, donated in 1990 by Erich Topp personally)

PEAKED CAP OAK WREATHS

Front and back of a hand-embroidered oak leaf wreath and cockade for officers and *Portepee* petty officers. (Collection of P.-M. Rousseau)

Versions of oak leaf wreaths and cockades for officers and *Portepee* petty officers, made of gold wire thread (left) and celleon (right). (Private collection)

Front and back of an oak leaf wreath with matching metal cockade, stamped from gold colored metal. From 1940, *Marine* officers increasingly wore this style on their peaked caps. Private collection)

Two versions of the cockade: at left, woven; at right, stamped from aluminum. The oak leaf wreaths are both woven. (Private collection)

THE NATIONAL EMBLEM

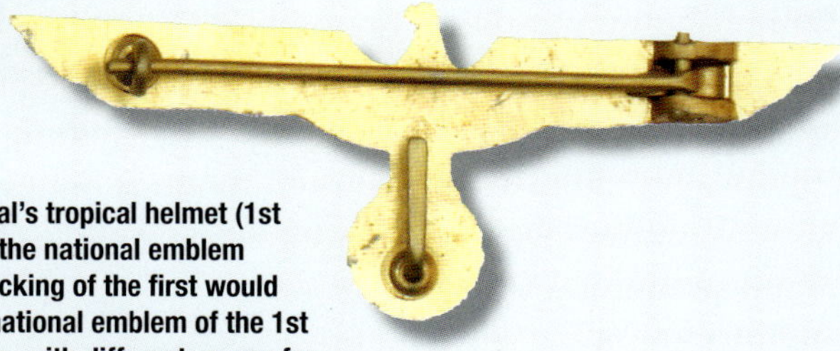

From top to bottom: National emblem for an official's tropical helmet (1st design), in silver metal. Four different versions of the national emblem for white and brown jackets; the navy blue felt backing of the first would certainly be very elegant on a white jacket. Four national emblem of the 1st design for *Maate* and enlisted men's garrison caps, with different means for fastening. (Collection of P.-M. Rousseau)

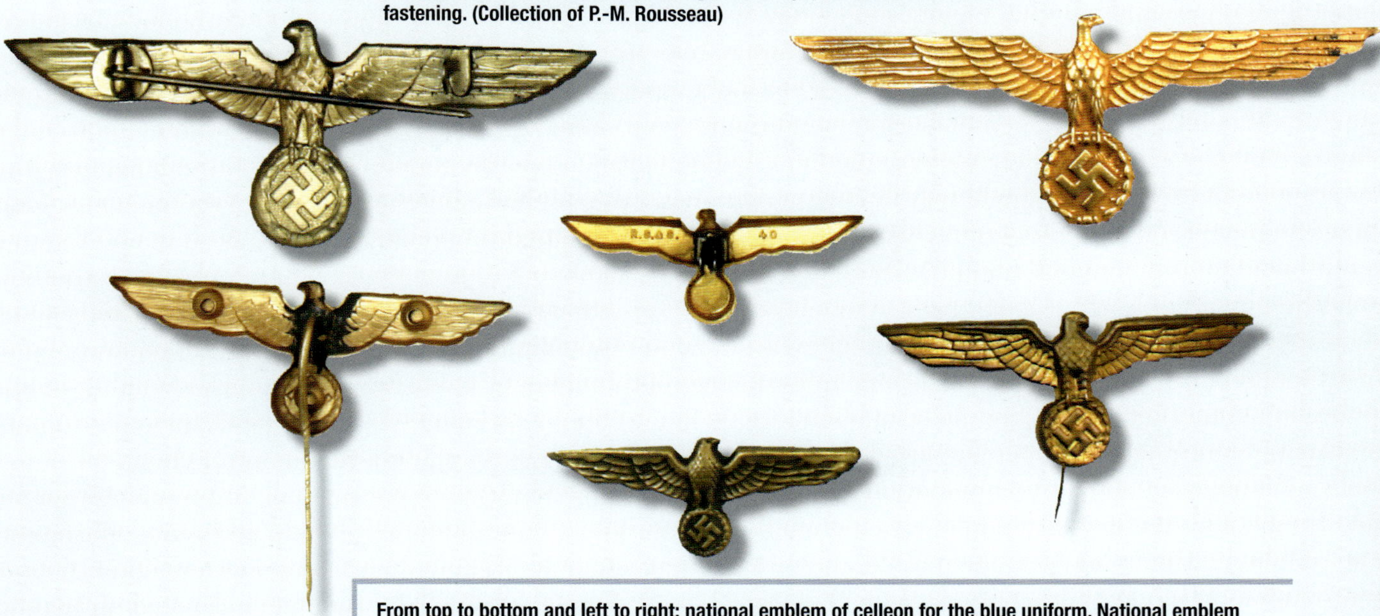

From top to bottom and left to right: national emblem of celleon for the blue uniform. National emblem of celleon for the blue peaked cap (this material will not oxidize, unlike goldwork). Front and back of a goldwork national emblem for the blue uniform. Front and back of a silverwork national emblem for *Marine* officials. (Collection of P.-M. Rousseau)

Front and back of a woven national emblem for the white shirt, for *Maate* and enlisted men. (Private collection)

Differently made versions of national emblem for the blue uniform, in celleon and machine embroidered (Private collection)

Front and back of an embroidered national emblem for the blue uniform (*Maate* and enlisted men). (Private collection)

Woven national emblem for the blue uniform (*Maate* and enlisted men). (Private collection)

Embroidered national emblem for the white uniform (*Maate* and enlisted men). (Private collection)

Front and back of a national emblem of goldwork for the blue peaked cap for officers and *Portepee* petty officers. (Private collection)

Front and back of a garrison cap national emblem for *Maate* and enlisted men. In this second design, eagle and cockade were fastened together. (Collection of P.-M. Rousseau)

Woven national emblem for tropical field tunic (*Maate* and enlisted men). (Private collection)

National emblem for a sports shirt. It measured 25x12-cm, more than twice the size of those for other items of apparel. (Private collection)

This woven tropical uniform national emblem was taken from a field tunic by a French resistance fighter in Marseille in August 1944. Note the triangular backing. (Private collection)

Insignia for superiors (here, petty officers) for the sport suit and shorts; it was sewn on the left side. The officers' insignias also had a yellow cord border around the oval. (Private collection)

This *Matrose*, photographed in 1944 in Marseilles, is wearing a tropical field tunic. It was required to wear the golden national emblem, on a khaki brown backing, on this article of apparel. (Private collection)

Example of the stamped markings on a blue *Marine* uniform. The black stamp of the uniform supply depot ('W' for Wilhelmshaven), gives the date of issue (March 11, 1937) and the size (I). The stitched red muster roll number indicates to which station command the wearer belonged (here: 'N' for North Sea station); next to this is the actual muster roll number (940); below the line is the year of entering service (37) and man's rating, in this case an 'S' for *Seemännisches* Personal (Seaman personnel). The soldier's nametag is sewn on below. (Private collection)

Matrose of a *U-Boot* school in peacetime walking-out uniform, with "monkey jacket" and neckerchief. (Private collection)

The black silk neckerchief was worn by *Maate* and enlisted men with most styles of the blue *Marine* uniform. (Private collection)

Souvenir photograph of an inspection of petty officer candidates, with the permanent and teaching personnel of their training course. The candidates all wear 'middy' shirt collars and neckerchiefs over their blue molton shirts. (Private collection)

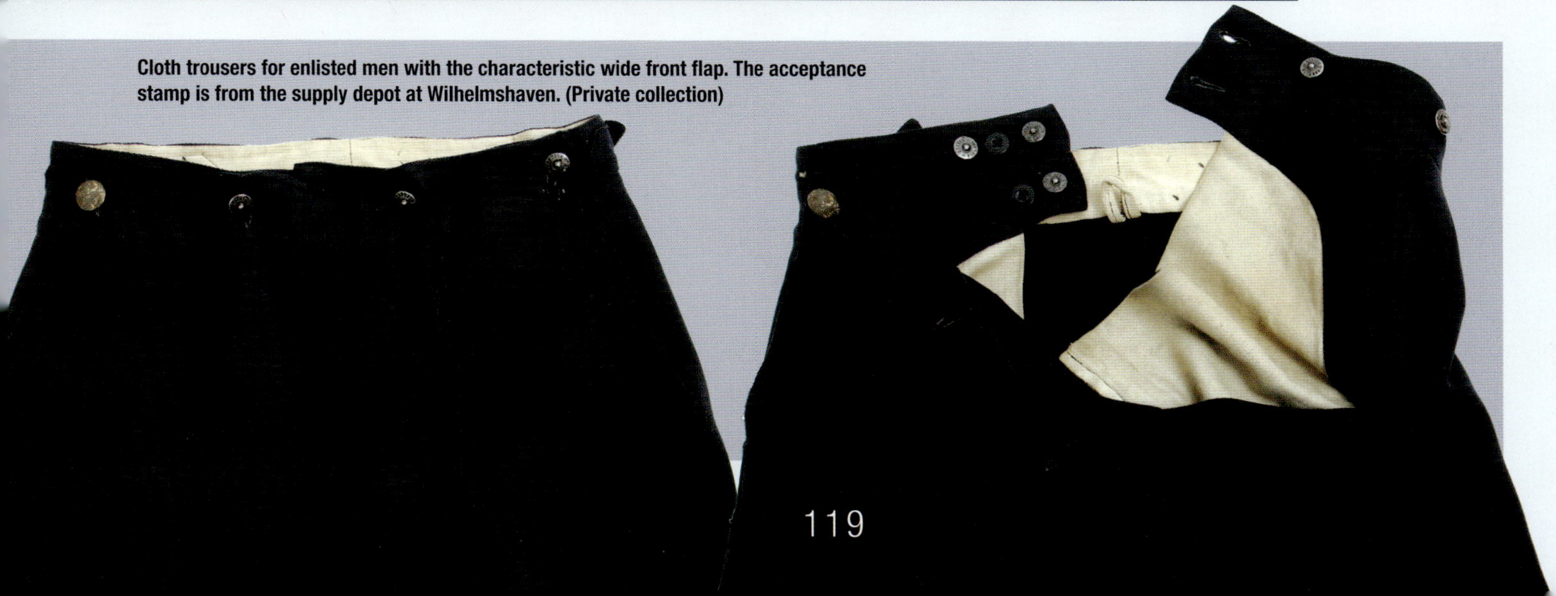

Cloth trousers for enlisted men with the characteristic wide front flap. The acceptance stamp is from the supply depot at Wilhelmshaven. (Private collection)

In front, a white work shirt, behind it a blue cotton molton shirt (for autumn and winter); at the back, white shirt of cotton drill (for the summer months). No national emblem was worn on the work shirt. (Private collection)

White enlisted men's trousers for the summer months, with aluminum buttons. Behind them are blue trousers for winter wear. (Private collection)

Typical souvenir photo of a young seaman, here posing in the white shirt for the summer months. His national emblem is embroidered of blue thread. (Private collection)

Articles of Apparel

The blue shirt in navy blue molton was closely cut and had sleeve cuffs fastened with two black buttons. The rectangular shirt or parade collar was usually worn with this, positioned under the shirt and fastened or tied with long bands, and with it a black silk neckerchief with jacquard woven blue stripes. A machine-embroidered or woven national emblem of golden thread was worn on the right shirt breast, and on the left sleeve, the respective rate, rating, and specific training badges. The blue cloth trousers were made from the same fabric as the shirt. These were "*Schlaghose*" (flared or "bell bottoms") with two side pockets. They had no fly, but had, as for those of almost all the *Marine* forces, a wide flap closure in front, which was buttoned up with four black metal buttons. On the back was a buckle to tighten the pants. Apparel also included a white shirt (with attached shirt collar), worn including during the summer months, often with the white trousers. These differed little from the blue apparel in cut and style.

Parade and dress uniform for a *Signalmaat. Maate* and *Obermaate* wore gold colored sleeve braids on the lower sleeves of their jackets; the rating and rate insignia were worn on the left upper arm. The blue aiguillette (braided cord) on the right breast is a *Marine* decoration for shooting. (Private collection)

For his wedding photo, this *Matrose-Hauptgefreiter* chose the traditional German *Marine* walking-out uniform. For such an occasion, wearing the EK II together with the order ribbon on the uniform was allowed. (Private collection)

A *Kriegsmarine* military band, before marching in a parade in Berlin in 1938. The musicians are wearing parade dress uniforms with "monkey jacket" with the rating insignia for musicians. (Private collection)

After 1939, the jacket meant for the walking-out and parade uniforms, was only worn on command. This front-opening garment with two rows of nine (visible) buttons each, was hooked together with a gold chain. The same sleeve patches were worn on this, as on the shirt. In cold weather, a pea coat (which the servicemen called a "Collani," for the tailors Berger, Collani & Co, who had earlier outfitted the *Kaiserliche Marine*) was worn over the shirt. The pea coat was cut of solid navy blue cloth, with two rows of five each gold anchor buttons on the front, and two straight inset side pockets; it was lined with blue molton. Cornflower blue collar tabs were sewn on the collar points, and, for *Maate* or *Obermaate*, one or two golden braids were also sewn on. The strip of braid around the collar was already mentioned above. The work uniform of white moleskin consisted of a work shirt and work pants, the latter also with button-fastened front flap closing. From 1940 on, petty officers *ohne Portepee* wore only a work jacket of white or gray moleskin. For certain service on board, the crews also wore the "*Takelpäckchen*" ("tackle packaging" or fatigues) of gray canvas, consisting of tackle shirt and pants. The seamen did wear their rank and rating insignia on these clothes, but normally not national emblem. Either the cloth or garrison cap served for headgear. All the previously described apparel was only worn by petty officers *ohne Portepee* and enlisted men.

Work shirt of white moleskin (a heavy, durable cotton fabric) of a *Matrose-Obergefreiter.* The red stripes sewn on the right upper sleeve are the watch badge, indicating to which ship's watch or division the man belonged (here: *Steuerbordwache 5. Division* (Starboard watch 5th division)).

These young sailors are wearing white moleskin work clothes under their life jackets. (Private collection)

This seaman took the opportunity for a nap ... but it hardly looks really comfortable. He is wearing the *"Takelpäckchen"* of gray canvas, worn for daily duties on board. (Private collection)

This young *Maschinen-Obergefreiter* proudly wears all his decorations on his pea coat. In theory, such a large set of decorations as seen here, should only be worn with parade uniform (that is, on jacket or shirt). Such a gross violation of regulations could actually only be done in the photographer's studio. (Private collection)

Pea coat of a *Marineartillerie-Hauptgefreiter*, who wears the specific training badge for *Entfernungsmesser* (range finder) with petty officer training course. According to the fashion taste of the time, the pea coat has been much shortened. (Private collection)

These *Marine* soldiers, who had their picture taken in Italy on March 15, 1942, are wearing their walking-out uniforms with blue enlisted men's cap. (Private collection)

These artistically intertwined initials of the owner, meticulously embroidered by a tailor are found in the lining of a personally owned pea coat. (Collection of P.-M. Rousseau)

In wartime, the pea coat was worn instead of the jacket with the walking-out uniform. From 1943, the latter was also no longer issued. The *U-Boot* war badge on the pea coat of this *Obergefreiter* shows that our happy bridegroom is a *U-Bootmann*. (Private collection)

A group of *Marine* soldiers during an exercise in 1942. They are all wearing the pea coat for the land uniform, with waist belts, carrying straps, and gas masks. (Private collection)

Pea coat of a *Marineartillerie Maat*. Only petty officers *ohne Portepee (Maat and Obermaat)* wore gold braid around the collar. (Collection of P.-M. Rousseau)

Bootsmannsmaat who had specific training as *Waffenleitvormann* (weapons control foreman) (artillery, Flak, coastal). He is wearing the *EK II*, the destroyer war badge, the Fleet war badge, and the SA military insignia on his pea coat. This could also be worn in the summer, in bad weather, with a white cap cover. (Private collection)

A *Maat*, a gunner on the TIRPITZ, together with some of his men alongside one of the huge 38-cm gun barrels. You can see that two of the pea coats, including the petty officer's, have been much shortened by the tailor. (Private collection)

Kriegsmarine Maat with an Italian officer of the *"Regia Marina"* in the port of Messina in 1942. During the war, pea coats were worn with both daytime and walking-out uniform. (Private collection)

An *Obermaat's* pea coat, showing the specific training badge of a torpedo diver. The detail shows the *Obermaat's* collar insignia: golden braid around the collar; two strips of braid on the collar flap. (Private collection)

Nr. 39 - 9. August 1940

....gegen Engeland

DEUTSCHE MARINE-FRONTZEITUNG IN DER BRETAGNE

Unsere Schnellboote sind unverwuestlich

Das Oberkommando der Wehrmacht gab am 8. August bekannt : In der Nacht vom 7. zum 8. August griffen unsere Schnellboote einen stark gesicherten feindlichen Geleitzug an. Trotz heftiger Abwehr durch die begleitenden feindlichen Zerstoerer, durch andere Bewachungsfahrzeuge und durch stark bewaffnete Handelsdampfer selbst, wurden ein Tanker von 8.000 Brt., ein Dampfer von 5.000 Brt. und ein Dampfer von 4.000 Brt. versenkt. Ein kleinerer Tanker wurde in Brand geschossen. Unsere

stellungen bei Manchester und Plymouth mit Bomben belegt. Der Feind flog in der Nacht zum Donnerstag mit einigen Flugzeugen in Nord- und Westdeutschland ein und warf Bomben ohne wesentlichen Schaden anzurichten. Die entstandenen Braende konnten durch Einsatz des Luftschutzes schnell geloescht werden, eine Scheune brannte nieder. Zwei feindliche Flugzeuge wurden abgeschossen.

Am Sehrohr

Die Pause vor der letzten Entscheidung in Europa beschaeftigt sehr stark die politisch interessierten Bevoelkerungskreise in Moskau. Immer wieder hoert man die Frage, warum es denn noch nicht gegen England losgehe, woran dann haeufig die Vermutung geknüpft wird, dass die Deutschen wohl wieder etwas ganz Besonderes in Vorbereitung haetten. Es gibt ein Sprichwort in Russland : « **Der Deutsche hat den Affen erfunden.** » Das soll besagen, dass der Deutsche

The *Marine* front newspaper *"Gegen England"* ("Against England") of August 9, 1940, dedicated a full page to the awarding of the *Ritterkreuz* to *Kapitänleutnant* Otto Kretschmer. His boat's entire crew are wearing captured British "battle dress" khaki uniforms in the photos. (Private collection)

Another picture of the *Ritterkreuz* award to Kretschmer; here you can clearly see that the British jackets are brand new. (Private collection)

A war correspondent in the tunic of the *"U-Boot-Päckchen"* and with his working equipment around his neck. On his lapel he wears a braid chevron, as was often done by petty officers on *U-Boote*. (Private collection)

"U-Boot-Päckchen" ("submarine packaging") of British manufacture. In the French campaign of 1940, large numbers of brand-new British field uniforms fell into German hands, which were then mainly used by *U-Boot* crews. It appears that Otto Kretschmer, *Kommandant* of U 99, was the first to equip his men with these captured uniforms. At the *Ritterkreuz* award ceremony for *Kptlt.* Kretschmer on August 4, 1940, *Großadmiral* Raeder was so well impressed by the U 99 crew's appearance, that he proposed issuing these uniforms to all *U-Boot* crews. This khaki drill British tunic is one taken from captured supplies and worn by German *U-Boot* men. The badges here are from the tropical brown uniform; the buttons are partly German, partly British. (Private collection)

This *U-Boot* petty officer's jacket could also be a British "battle dress." Our man seems to be wearing gold braid around his collar. (Private collection)

These three young *U-Boot* men seem to be wearing tunics of German make without shoulder straps. Both the national emblem and the *Obergefreiter* stripes they are wearing on their tunics have a blue backing. (Private collection)

Kapitänleutnant **Erich Topp in the *U-Boot* tunic. (Private collection)**

U-Boot Kommandanten **Claus Korth *(RK (Ritterkreuz)* on 5/25/41) and Herbert Kuppisch (*RK* on 5/14/41), wearing two different styles of tunics. (Private collection)**

These three *Portepee* petty officers had their picture taken in the German version of the *"U-Boot-Päckchen"* in front of their boat. (Private collection)

The "*U-Boot Päckchen*," (*U-Boot* package or packaging) special clothing for service on board, was introduced for *U-Boote* crews. This included a hip-length tunic of gray to field gray drill and belted trousers of the same material, which sometimes had a large patch pocket on left thigh. The tunic was fastened with five buttons in front and had two breast pockets (initially with a pleat) with pointed pocket flaps. The waistband was buttoned or fastened with a buckle. However, there were also versions that differed somewhat from those described here. Although the national emblem was not always worn on the tunic, officers and *Portepee* petty officers usually wore these on their shoulder boards and straps; *Maate* mostly fastened a metal or braid chevron to their lapels. During the French campaign of 1940, large quantities of British army uniforms fell into the hands of the *Wehrmacht*, and because the British "battle dress" was quite similar in style to the "*U-Boot-Päckchen*," these captured uniforms were issued to *U-Boot* crews and worn mostly as they were. Leather gear was taken on board all *Kriegsmarine* boats and ships and issued as required. There were two jacket patterns, one style for the machinery crew and one for seamen and bridge personnel.

The end of a victorious patrol for this *Kommandant* and two of his officers. The latter are wearing their just-awarded *U-Boot* war badges on their German-made tunics. (Private collection)

This figure shows a *Portepee* petty officer in a similar version of the *"U-Boot-Päckchen."* These uniform parts sometimes varied in cut, kit, and color – as here, the tunic and pants are of different shades of gray. (Collection of *"Musee de la Seconde Guerre mondiale d'Ambleteuse."* Photo: Eric Barbe)

A brown version of the German *U-Boot* tunic. This item has neither a waistband, nor button-up sleeve vents. (Private collection)

The knee-length, two-row buttoned leather jacket (in gray or black) was also very popular with officers. These two subalterns are wearing items that appear to be right out of the supply depot. Only the *Oberleutnant zur See* is wearing shoulder boards on his coat. (Private collection)

This figure of a *Kapitänleutnant* wears the rarely seen rain jacket of gray oilcloth with sleeve stripes painted on corresponding to his rank. (Private collection)

This picture perhaps shows the *Reserve Kapitänleutnant zur See* Karl-Heinz Stephan, *Kommandant* of U 1063. The *Kommandant* and the officer next to him are wearing the leather coat for seafaring personnel; the two men beside them the *U-Boot* tunic. (Private collection)

The first jacket was usually made of black leather, reached down to the pants pockets and had a single row of buttons. The jacket had a low standing collar, one breast pocket on the left and two side pockets, all with rectangular flaps. It was lined with heavy woolen cloth, as was also the style for the seamen. This second style was almost always of gray leather, reached to just above the knee and had two rows of five each of buttons. The jacket had a large turndown collar, two muff pockets at the front, and two side pockets with flaps. This jacket was the most popular with *U-Boot* men and officers. The pants of the two styles barely differed, except in color.

In the winter, and in Arctic waters, men on duty, bridge watch, etc. also wore a navy blue watch coat. This item, of heavy, water-repellent cloth had a wide hood and the shoulders were covered with blue or gray leather.

The seaman's coat was also made of black leather. *Maate* and enlisted men wore no rank insignia on it. (Private collection)

Two styles of leather pants, of gray and black leather. Since no official documents on these items now exist, the background for the introduction of the black and gray leather clothing cannot be traced today. Since these items were for work clothing, they were probably therefore worn equally, as appropriate, by all personnel in sea-going units. (Private collection)

These *Matrosen* are wearing watch coats of heavy, navy blue cloth, issued in cold weather for watch duty on board. The shoulders are reinforced with a patch of dark blue leather. (Private collection)

The navy blue jacket, also known as an "on-board" jacket, was only worn by officers and *Portepee* petty officers. On the front were two rows of buttons, each with five gold anchor buttons, but only the four lowest buttons were fastened. There were two more buttons under the collar lapel. The national emblem was sewn on the right breast, usually hand-embroidered pieces of goldwork or celleon. The rank and rating insignia worn on this piece of clothing have already been discussed above.

Blue cloth trousers, a white over shirt, and a long tie (with the turn-down collar) or bow tie (with the standing collar) were worn with the jacket.

Portepee petty officer of a sea-going unit, in the seaman's jacket, here without shoulder straps. (Private collection)

Leather uniform trousers, of gray or black leather, were sometimes also worn with the *"U-Boot-Päckchen"* tunic, as can be seen on two of these *U-Boot* men. (Private collection)

This charcoal drawing from 1943 shows a *Matrose* armed with an MP40 on guard duty, wearing the *"Lederpäckchen"* ("leather packaging"). (Private collection)

Oberleutnant zur See in gray leather pants aboard a *U-Boot.* (Private collection)

These *Matrosen* of a formation at sea are all wearing the short gray leather jacket for machine operators, showing clearly that this special clothing was not just reserved for *U-Boot* men. (Private collection)

A few encouraging words before the next mission do this *Matrose* in a gray leather jacket a lot of good. (Private collection)

Grey leather jacket for machine operators with short standing collar. On this item, all the anchor buttons are painted gray. (Collection of P.-M. Rousseau)

All the seamen in this picture are wearing the leather jacket for machine operators of gray or black leather. Their buttons are gold-colored. (Private collection)

This *Leutnant zur See* is wearing his shoulder boards on the black version of the short leather jacket. Also here, golden buttons are worn with it. (Private collection)

The buttons on this black leather jacket are of civilian origin. (Collection of P.-M. Rousseau)

Details of the two stamps on the *K-Verband* jacket. (Collection of P.-M. Rousseau)

The *Kleinkampfverbände* (small combat units) *(K-Verband)* were commanded by the *Kriegsmarine Kommandoverband* (command unit); these were manned by combat swimmers, explosive/demolition boats, one-man-torpedoes, and midget *U-Boote*. All *K-Verband* members were hand-picked volunteers. The jacket shown here, with its black leather hood, was designed for drivers of midget *U-Boote*. (Collection of P.-M. Rousseau)

"Oilskins" – black rain jacket of rubberized fabric. (Private collection)

Sailor in rain gear with life jacket worn over it. (Private collection)

Rain pants of rubberized fabric. (Private collection)

Rain pants of rubberized fabric. (Private collection)

These high rubber boots were part of the protective rain gear. (Collection of P.-M. Rousseau)

Acceptance stamp on high rubber boots; issue year is 1944. (Collection of P.-M. Rousseau)

Acceptance stamp on short rubber boots, again with issue year. (Collection of P.-M. Rousseau)

Regulation black rubber boots also served for rain protection. (Collection of P.-M. Rousseau)

These black leather marching boots were lined with felt, to protect against cold and damp. (Private collection)

Black leather lace-up shoes. Heels and soles of footwear worn aboard were strictly not studded with metal tips, to prevent accidents. (Collection of P.-M. Rousseau)

Off-duty members of the Watch enjoying the sun in front of their guardroom. Some of the men are wearing *"Knobelbecher"* ("jackboots"), the usual laced boots. (Private collection)

White shoes were reserved for officers and *Portepee* petty officers, who wore them with the summer walking-out uniform. (Collection of P.-M. Rousseau)

This 1934 dated photo shows a *Matrose* of the Baltic Sea *Schiffsstammdivision* (reception and training unit) in front of his quarters. He is wearing a not quite recognizable armband and a pair of canvas shoes. The new national emblem with the swastika was first worn on the uniform in 1935. (Private collection)

Canvas shoes, leather soled, were worn by petty officers and crew for duty on board, but also inside military installations on land. (Private collection)

Acceptance stamp of the *Marine* uniform supply depot in Wilhelmshaven, dated September 1, 1942. (Private collection)

A ***Stabsobermaschinist's*** **jacket. This item was worn by** ***Portepee*** **petty officers with service, parade, and walking-out dress; the national emblem was the same as for officers. Only the lower four buttons on the right row are for buttoning the jacket; the rest are just for decoration. (Private collection)**

Shoulder strap of a ***Stabsobermaschinist*** **(chief warrant officer machinist).** ***Portepee*** **petty officers wore their rank and rating badges on the shoulder straps, on all articles of apparel. (Private collection)**

Portepee **petty officer joining a formation. He is wearing service dress with jacket and the dagger with** ***Portepee*** **(sword knot.) (Private collection)**

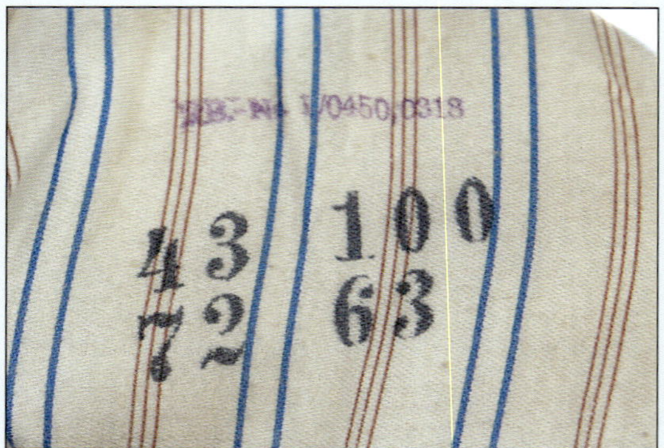

Size stamp on the sleeve lining of a ***Stabsobermaschinist's*** **jacket, and above it the** ***RB*****-No. (*****Reichsbetriebsnummer (Reich*** **company registration number)) of the manufacturer, which was in use around 1942. (Private collection)**

The tropical field tunic resembled that of the *Heer* (Army) in style – four pockets with or without pleats, turndown collar – but was made of the *Kriegsmarine* tropical brown fabric and fastened down the front with four anchor buttons. Tailored pieces, mainly provided for commissioned officers, could vary in features and cut from items issued by the supply depot. On the field tunic were worn only the national emblem (woven onto brown backing or embroidered) and the rank insignia, shoulder boards on brown backing, shoulder straps of tropical fabric with silver rank stars and triangular base patch for enlisted men, also of tropical fabric. Instead of the gold-colored braid band, a cornflower blue facing band was used.

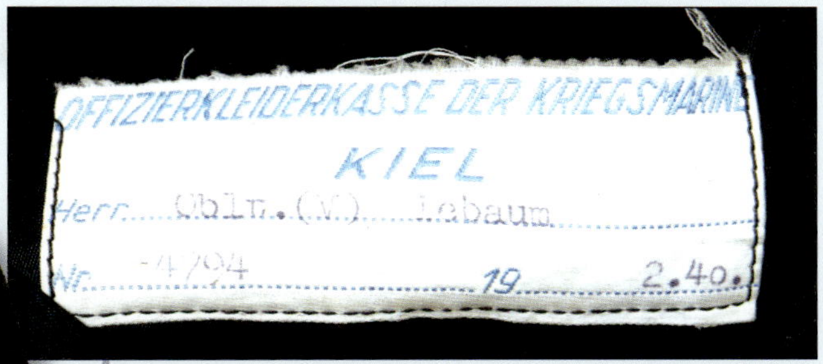

Typical sewn on label of the *Kriegsmarine Offizierkleiderkasse* (officers' clothing account for privately purchasing their uniforms), with the rank, rating, and owner's name noted, including the muster roll number and the date of acceptance. (Private collection)

Jacket of a torpedo technology *Kapitänleutnant.* The gold-embroidered rating badges were attached above the top sleeve stripes. From October 1939, the *EK II* ribbon was to be worn in the top usable buttonhole on the jacket. (Private collection)

This *Korvettenkapitän* had already proven himself in the First World War, as is evident from the so-called 'repetition clasp' for the *EK II*, which he is here wearing on the left breast lapel of his jacket. The fact that he was also was awarded the *EK I* and war decorations for minehunter, *U-Boot* hunter, and security units, indicates that he has certainly been in action in this war. (Private collection)

Winter 1944-45. A *U-Boot Kommandant*, recognizable by the white cover of his peaked cap, *"klönt"* (north German dialect for 'chats') with an older brother officer, before another patrol. The *U-Boot Oberleutnant* is wearing, despite the obviously cold weather, only his jacket with a pullover underneath. (Private collection)

Marine school, Mürwik. The participants in an officers training course had their pictures taken together with the teaching and permanent staff personnel, including *Kapitänleutnant* Werner Töniges (at center with *Ritterkreuz)* a company chief in the 1st Division. The rank insignia of officer candidates *(Fähnriche and Oberfähnriche)* are on their shoulder braids, which they also wore on their jackets, while officers wore sleeve braids. (Private collection)

Regulation jacket for a *Kapitänleutnant.* Our Naval officer had also taken part in the bitter fighting around Narvik, as the corresponding combat badge on his left upper sleeve shows. (Private collection)

Comparison of sleeve stripes of gold thread (left) and of celleon (right). (Private collection)

Size marking shown above the manufacturer's stamp on this officer's jacket. (Private collection)

The following decorations are displayed on the left breast of *Vizeadmiral* Schirlitz' jacket: *Eisernes Kreuz 1. Klasse* with clasp '1939' for *EK I* for 1914, *Kriegsverdienstkreuz* (war order of merit cross) *1. Klasse* with swords, and the commemoration badge for the crews of *Marine* airships (hand-embroidered design). In the First World War, Ernst Schirlitz had served in the *Marine* Airship Division and was shot down in a Zeppelin raid on London in 1916. He spent the rest of the war as a British prisoner of war. (Collection of P.-M. Rousseau)

Tailor's label in Schirlitz' jacket. (Collection of P.-M. Rousseau)

Vizeadmiral Schirlitz on March 11, 1945, the day he received the *Ritterkreuz*. As can be seen, for this occasion, he wore only his most important decorations on his uniform. (Private collection)

Jacket from the estate of *Vizeadmiral* Ernst Schirlitz (1893-1978). Schirlitz was *Festungskommandant* (fortress commander) of La Rochelle from August 20, 1944 until May 9, 1945. He also was awarded the *Ritterkreuz* on March 11, 1945. (Collection of P.-M. Rousseau)

Detail of the national emblem hand-embroidered of goldwork, and the Deutsches Kreuz (German Cross) in gold, also hand-embroidered. (Collection of P.-M. Rousseau)

Manufacturer's label in the vest shown below. (Private collection)

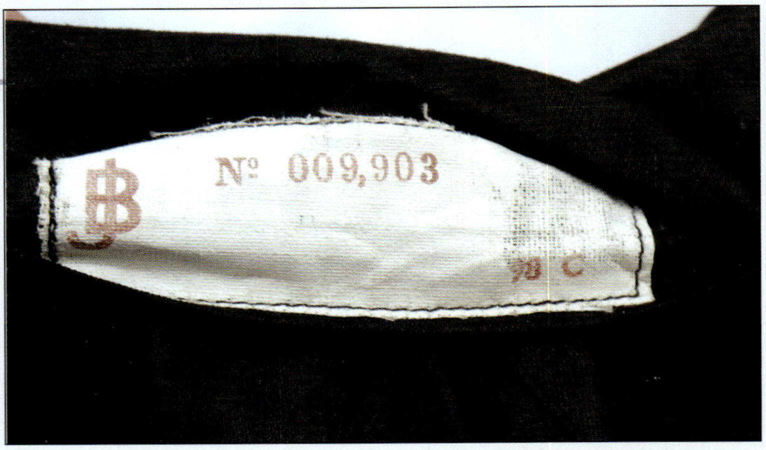

Vest of navy blue cloth for officers and *Portepee* petty officers. (Private collection)

Trouser maker's label. The owner could add rank, name, muster roll number, and acceptance date there. (Private collection)

Blue cloth trousers made of fine material for officers and *Portepee* petty officers. (Private collection)

Tropical field tunic of a *U-Boot Gefreiter*. Aboard the *U-Boote*, dress codes were usually taken quite freely – shown here by the rather colorful checked shirt of civilian origin. (Collection of P.-M. Rousseau)

This *Stabsgefreiter* is wearing on his tropical field tunic a rank chevron on a blue base patch, which was actually not intended for it. (Private collection)

Two petty officers at leisure in an Italian naval base, summer 1942. As you see, national emblems were indeed also on sewn on tropical shirts. (Private collection)

This German petty officer, surrounded by Italian comrades, is not wearing the regulation blue facing on his tropical field tunic, but gold-colored braid – and a blue garrison cap, on top of that. (Private collection)

Tropical field tunic for an *Oberfeldwebel*. Instead of the gold-colored braid, a cornflower blue facing was worn on the brown tropical uniform. (Private collection)

These photos of members of the *21. U-Boot-Jagdflottille* were taken in summer 1942 in Greece. The tropical brown uniform items (shirts, shorts, field tunics and caps) are partially – against regulations – combined with items from the blue uniform. (Private collection)

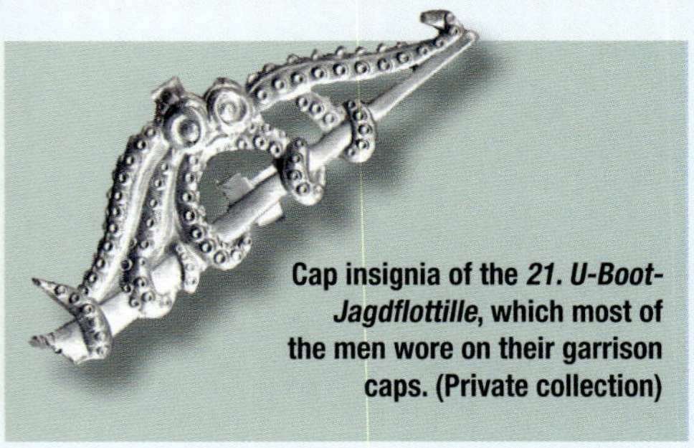

Cap insignia of the *21. U-Boot-Jagdflottille*, which most of the men wore on their garrison caps. (Private collection)

The brown tropical uniform included long and short pants, short- and long-sleeved shirts, as well as peaked and field caps. Officers and *Portepee* petty officers also had a white jacket, which they were allowed to wear with the tropical dress and on certain other occasions. This had one row of buttons, with six (older design) or four (new design) gold anchor buttons, and had four breast and side patch pockets. On it was fastened a removable metal-embossed national emblem, and removable buttons and shoulder boards and straps. White trousers and white shirts were generally worn with the jacket. The coat of dark blue cloth was only worn by officers, *Oberfähnrichen*, and *Fähnrichen*; but with the outbreak of war, this was replaced by the jacket. On the front were two rows of each five buttons, with the top pair of buttons "blind," i.e. not buttoned. The national emblem, epaulettes and shoulder boards, as well as sleeve stripes and rating badges, were worn on the coat.

The *Obermaat* in the foreground is wearing the white working jacket for petty officers. (Private collection)

White jacket of a *Portepee* petty officer. The cut corresponds to the officers' style, but was usually not of the same quality. The item shown here is made of sturdy cotton drill; although the national emblem meets regulations, for this item of apparel, actually gold-colored anchor buttons were required, not gray-painted ones. (Private collection)

Brown jacket of a *Portepee* petty officer. This piece of clothing was very like the tropical field tunic in styling, but was of lighter material. (Private collection)

The petty officer seated at left is wearing a brown jacket with gold-colored metal national emblem. (Private collection)

In this photo we see a handsome selection of parts of the blue uniform: Work shirts of white moleskin, blue vests, a blue shirt with shirt collar, blue jackets, a brown jacket, and a white working jacket. (Private collection)

New-regulation white jacket, with turndown collar. The new design was introduced in 1937. The shoulder boards, braids, and straps, all the buttons, and the national emblem can be removed to make cleaning easier. (Collection of P.-M. Rousseau)

Older-regulation white jacket, with stand-up collar. For this style, introduced already in 1929, the collar was always to be worn fastened; during the war, it was worn less and less. (Collection of P.-M. Rousseau)

The officer in the picture, speaking with several *Marine* women auxiliaries, is wearing the white new regulation jacket. It was expressly prohibited to wear blue trousers with a white jacket, but our man is even also wearing a blue peaked cap. (Private collection)

Cloth coat of a *Kapitänleutnant* and *U-Boot Kommandant.* The coat was to be worn fastened when on duty; however, recipients of *Halsorden* (decorations worn around the neck; here: the *Ritterkreuz*), left the top three buttons unfastened. (Private collection)

The back view of the coat shows the (here) six buttons, for the pleat band and to button the waist belt. (Private collection)

For certain types of dress, officers were required to add a sash, as shown in this picture of parade dress with coat. (Private collection)

This young *Oberleutnant* is showing the manner of wearing *Marine* dagger buckled under the coat, on the so-called coat sling or hanger. (Private collection)

The half-length cloth coat, which resembles the long coat at first glance, had two rows of six buttons each on the front, which were all buttoned (except by *Admirale, Kommodoren*, and recipients of the *Halsorden*). No national emblem was worn, only shoulder boards and straps; no sleeve stripes were worn. *Portepee* petty officers were also allowed to wear this article of apparel.

On land, officers also gladly wore the jackets of gray or black leather, with the service or walking-out uniform. These items were cut similarly to the cloth coat, and also only had shoulder boards.

The raincoat, made of blue, rubberized fabric could be worn by officers and *Portepee* petty officers, in the same situations as the cloth coat, and shoulder boards and straps were buttoned on.

A group of officers in service dress with long coat and sash. (Private collection)

Long coat of a *Kapitän z. See.* This item of officer's apparel was worn with specific uniforms (parade, service, mess or dress, and walking-out uniforms). Shortly after the outbreak of war, the order was given that a jacket should be worn in its place. (Collection of P.-M. Rousseau)

Cape made of waterproof, navy blue fabric. (Private collection)

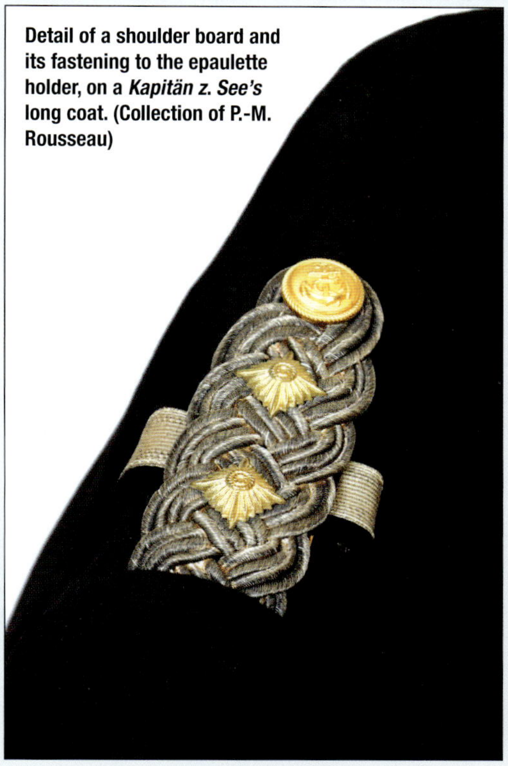

Detail of a shoulder board and its fastening to the epaulette holder, on a *Kapitän z. See's* long coat. (Collection of P.-M. Rousseau)

Oberfähnrich of *Marine* administration in a long coat. With the walking-out uniform, he is wearing his belt buckled over the coat and sword. His rating badge is, as it should be, sewn on the lower left sleeve. (Private collection)

The embroidered mark of the Kiel *Offizierkleiderkasse* (officers' account for private purchase of their uniforms), in the lining of a long coat. (Collection of P.-M. Rousseau)

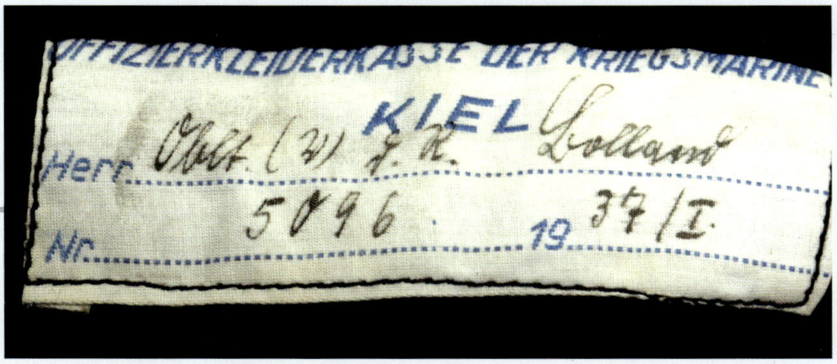

Offizierkleiderkasse label with rank, rating, and name of the owner; below are his muster roll number and the acceptance date. (Collection of P.-M. Rousseau)

The cloak, or "Spaniard," of blue cloth was also reserved for officers. It was lined with silver gray silk or rayon, and fastened with a chain hooked on two gold lion-head buttons. This spectacular item of apparel, in use up to 1940, was worn especially with the mess or ceremonial uniform for special occasions, such as festivities, visits to the opera, etc. We have only briefly listed here the most important items of *Kriegsmarine* apparel. There are a number of areas we cannot go into, such as footwear, sportswear, gloves of all kinds, diving suits, etc. The list could go on, especially if we were to include all the clothing of civilian origin, some of which were worn by *U-Boot* crews.

Front and back of various *Kriegsmarine* anchor buttons. There are different stamps on the back of the buttons, which were made of brass or aluminum, according to maker and year produced. (Private collection)

Buttons were made of glass frit to save valuable raw materials. (Private collection)

Buttons were delivered by the manufacturer in boxes like these; these buttons were painted matte gray, likely to go with the leather jacket. (Private collection)

Kriegsmarine belt buckle for *Maate* and enlisted men, of gold-colored anodized aluminum. This design was manufactured until 1942. (Collection of P.-M. Rousseau)

The *Kriegsmarine* acceptance stamp and the manufacturer's stamp with date appear on the leather tongue. The stamp of the manufacturer 'R.S. & S.' (Richard Sieper & Sohn, Lüdenscheid) is also on the back of the belt buckle. (Collection of P.-M. Rousseau)

Holland, 1942. These two *Matrosen* in walking-out uniform are wearing the bayonet 84/98 on their waist belts, as required in occupied countries. (Private collection)

Kriegsmarine acceptance stamp on a leather belt. (Collection of P.-M. Rousseau)

The buckle back shows the initials of the manufacturer, 'JFS' (Josef Feix & Söhne, Gablonz). (Collection of P.-M. Rousseau)

Blue-gray painted belt buckle for *Maate* and enlisted men. This steel buckle was introduced in 1940 and went with the field-gray uniform. From 1943, this model was generally issued and also worn with the blue uniform. (Collection of P.-M. Rousseau)

Officers wore a sash with various styles of uniform. (Collection of P.-M. Rousseau)

Before the war. *Leutnant z. See* in parade or service dress, and the sash worn with it. (Private collection)

Another *Leutnant z. See* photographed during the war in jacket and sash (and an unusual hat band). (Private collection)

Front and back of the sash buckle. Note the printed stamp of the manufacturer, 'FLL' (Friedrich Linden, Lüdenscheid). (Private collection)

Belts and Sashes

Petty officers *ohne Portepee* and enlisted men wore a belt with certain uniforms; this had an aluminum buckle which differed from the *Heer* model in its golden color. From about 1943, belt buckles were made of sheet steel and increasingly painted field or blue-gray. The waist belt itself was of blackened leather, while a webbing belt was worn with tropical uniforms.

Officers and *Portepee* petty officers usually wore no belt, except perhaps with a land uniform or in occupied regions. Then, they sometimes used an Army officer's waist belt with a two-pronged buckle. The sash worn with certain uniforms, of silver braid with two interwoven black and silver stripes, was reserved for officers and officials of officer rank. The round buckle for the sash was gold colored for officers or silver for officials, and showed a fouled anchor inside a laurel wreath.

Kriegsmarine dagger, with dagger sling for *Marine* officials, identifiable by the silver-colored metal parts. The gilding on the dagger itself has become tarnished gray, which often happened with weapons of later make. (Private collection)

Kriegsmarine dagger with dagger sling, for officers and *Portepee* petty officers. (Private collection)

This *Marine* officer wears the *Marine* sword buckled under his jacket. (Private collection)

Marine sword, with scabbard and sling, for officers and *Portepee* petty officers. (Collection of P.-M. Rousseau)

This *Marine* dagger has an ornamented blade, and its owner also had the insignia of his unit engraved on the dagger scabbard. (Collection of P.-M. Rousseau)

Portepee petty officer with *Marine* dagger. (Private collection)

Portepee petty officer in parade dress on the occasion of his wedding. The Narvik veteran is wearing his *Marine* dagger buckled under, according to regulations. (Private collection)

Kriegsmarine Swords and Daggers

The regulation side arms of the *Kriegsmarine* were the dagger and *Marine* sword. The latter had a gilded hilt or guard, with a lion's head at the top, a white grip with gold wire twisted in the grooves and an anchor on the outer grip plate. The blade was slightly curved and sheathed in a black leather scabbard with gold metal fittings. The sword was worn on the so-called sword sling.

The dagger had a double-edged blade with double grooving and was often furnished with fine etching. The cross guard displayed a fouled anchor, and was, like the hilt with the *Wehrmacht* eagle, of gilt brass. The white grip was of plastic, celluloid-covered wood, or, rarely, of ivory wrapped in gold wire. The gilded sheath was either finely chiseled (a "*Blitzscheide*" or "lightning sheath"), or hammered. The dagger was worn on a so-called dagger sling. Finally, there was the *Kriegsmarine* dagger of honor, which was introduced in 1938 by *Großadmiral* Erich Raeder, and was awarded to only a very small number of recipients (no more than sixteen). The Damascus steel blade had a dedication inscription by Raeder (from 1943, by Dönitz) and the date. The swastika on the gilded knob was set with seventeen small diamonds and the ivory hilt had a gilded oak wreath spiraled around it. The gilded brass scabbard was richly decorated on both sides with oak leaves and anchors, and had, like the ordinary dagger, two brackets and fastener rings. The side arms, which always included the *Portepee* (sword knot) of silver-colored cord, with its "slide" on the cords, and "acorn" ball on the knot, could be worn buckled under (on the under belt) or over (on the over belt) the coat.

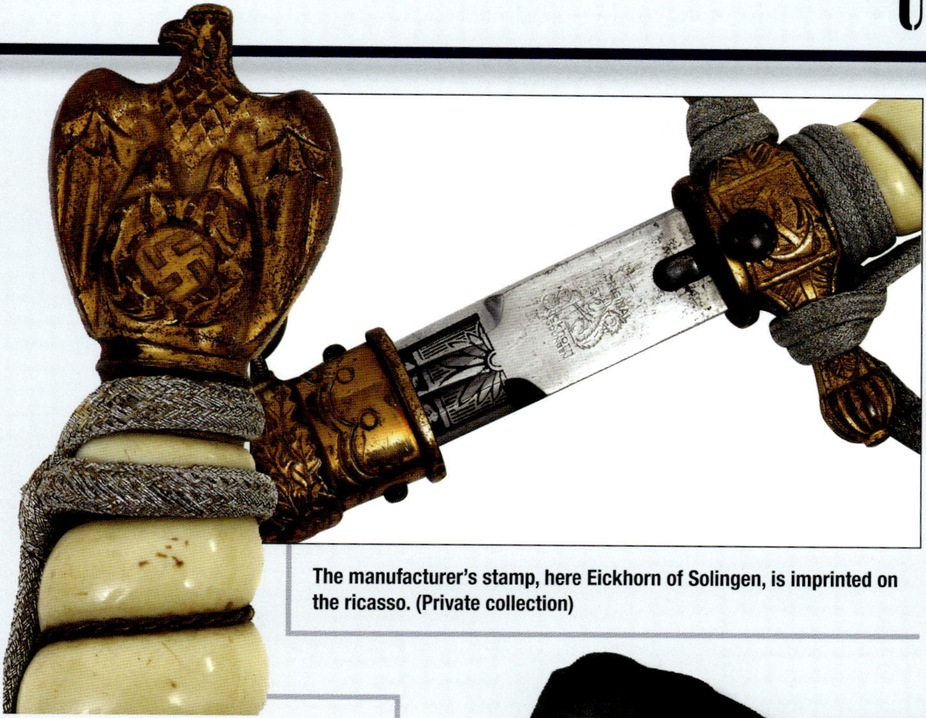

The manufacturer's stamp, here Eickhorn of Solingen, is imprinted on the ricasso. (Private collection)

From 1938, all *Kriegsmarine* daggers were adorned with a hilt with the *Wehrmacht* eagle; prior to that, *Reichsmarine* daggers could also be worn. (Private collection)

Portepee petty officer in walking-out uniform with dagger buckled under. (Private collection)

Marine dagger with dagger sling and belt for buckling outside the coat. The hammered dagger scabbard is somewhat rarer than the so-called *Blitzscheide* (lightning sheath). (Private collection)

Belt for buckling dagger or sword under the coat. Both these side arms were usually word under the outer clothing. (Private collection)

Studio photo of an *Oberfeldwebel*. The style of wearing his *Marine* dagger (under belt and sling), unfortunately, cannot be seen. (Private collection)

DECORATIONS AND CERTIFICATES

To recognize military merit and acts of courage by its soldiers, the Third *Reich* founded countless medals and decorations, as well as combat badges, which, given what was demanded of the victims/casualties, were only a small consolation. The *Kriegsmarine* had their own combat badge; with this, the "*Seewolf*" ("sea wolf") distinguished himself from any "*Etappenhengst*" (*translator's note*: literally, "rear echelon stud or jackass"; "base wallah" or "desk soldier" are among the politer translations) of the administrative services.

THE *U-BOOT* WAR BADGE

Different types of *U-Boot* war badges (metal, gold thread embroidered, and machine embroidered). The badge, founded by *Großadmiral* Raeder on October 13, 1939, was awarded to *U-Boot* men who had proven themselves on two or more patrols. (Collection of P.-M. Rousseau)

Hand-embroidered version of the *U-Boot* war badge. (Private collection)

***U-Boot* war badge of gilded non-ferrous metal, here of French make, in its original box. (Private collection)**

Front and back of a *U-Boot* war badge made by the Schwerin Company in Berlin. (Collection of P.-M. Rousseau)

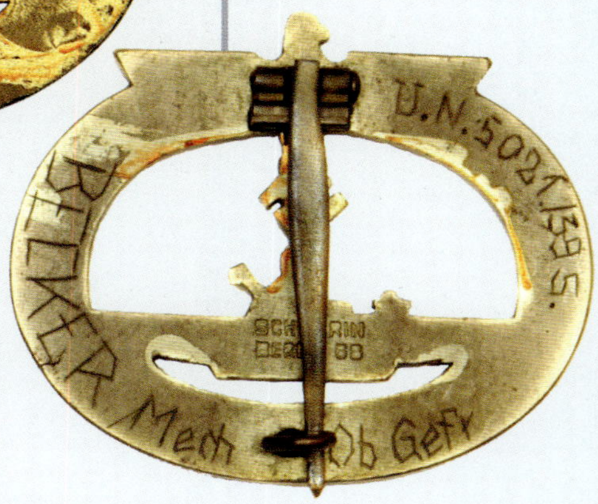

Back of a *U-Boot* war badge engraved with name, rank, and muster roll number of the owner. (Collection of P.-M. Rousseau)

Three examples of smaller versions of the ***U-Boot*** **war badge, which could be worn on civilian clothes. (Collection of P.-M. Rousseau)**

U-Boot **men were actually supposed to shave their beards right after returning from a patrol, but these three appear to be just as proud of them as they are of their** ***U-Boot*** **war badges. (Private collection)**

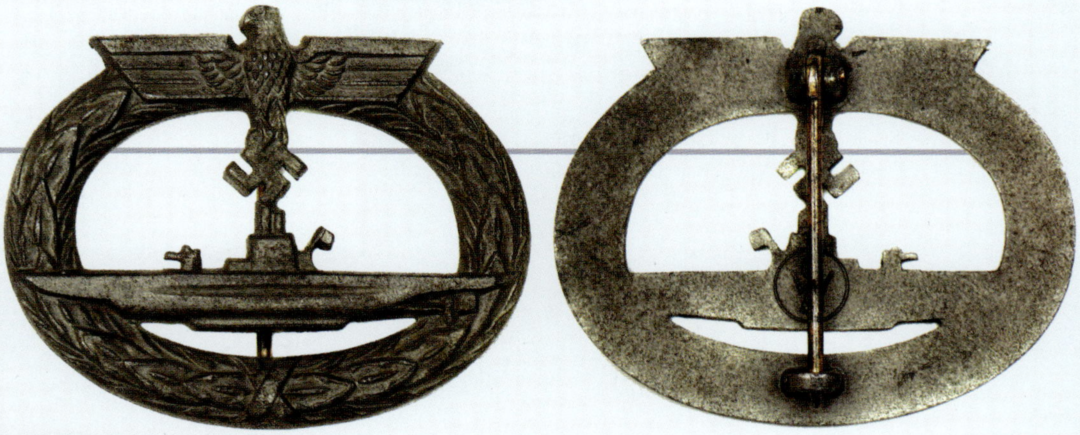

Front and back of a 'GWL' (Gebrüder Wegerhoff, Lüdenscheid)-made ***U-Boot*** **war badge. (Private collection)**

This ***Oberleutnant z. See*** **is wearing an entire row of decorations, including the** ***U-Boot*** **war badge and the very rare** ***U-Boot*** **war front clasp. (Private collection)**

A ***Kapitänleutnant*** **wearing the** ***U-Boot*** **war badge as well as the destroyer war badge. The latter shows that this officer, before or after his tour of duty with the** ***U-Boot*** **forces, must have served in the surface fleet forces. (Private collection)**

Verleihungs-Urkunde.
Auf Grund der Ermächtigung des Oberbefehlshabers der Kriegsmarine verleihe ich dem
Matrosenobergefreiten
(Dienstgrad)
Walter Zabel
(Name)
das
Ubootskriegsabzeichen 1939
Im Felde , den 3. Mai 19 41.
Konteradmiral und Befehlshaber der Unterseeboote
Vize-

U-Boot war badge and the accompanying award certificate (1st design), awarded on May 3, 1941 to *Obergefreiter* Walter Zabel (U 9) and signed by *Konteradmiral* Karl Dönitz. The first certificate design had a border of laurel leaves, while the 2nd design featured geometric figures. (Collection of P.-M. Rousseau)

1.) Certificate for the posthumous award of the *U-Boot* war badge, to the bereaved of *Mechanikermaat* Harald Sebelin. Sebelin, born on February 7, 1920, served on U 280, which was lost on November 16, 1943 southwest of Ireland with the entire fifty-man crew. Note the border of the 2nd design. (Private collection)

2.) The family was also presented with a second certificate, together with the first one. This certificate testified that the serviceman had died a hero for *"Führer, Volk und Vaterland"* ("Leader, people, and fatherland") and was signed by *Admiral* Hans-George von Friedeburg, who became commanding *Admiral* of the *U-Boot* forces since February 1, 1943. (Private collection)

1

Verleihungs-Urkunde
Auf Grund der Ermächtigung des Oberbefehlshabers der Kriegsmarine verleihe ich dem für das Vaterland gefallenen
Mechanikermaaten
(Dienstgrad)
Harald Sebelin
(Name)
als Ehrung für seinen Einsatz
das
Ubootskriegsabzeichen 1939
An Bord , den 25. September 19 44
Admiral
u. Kommandierender Admiral der Unterseeboote

2

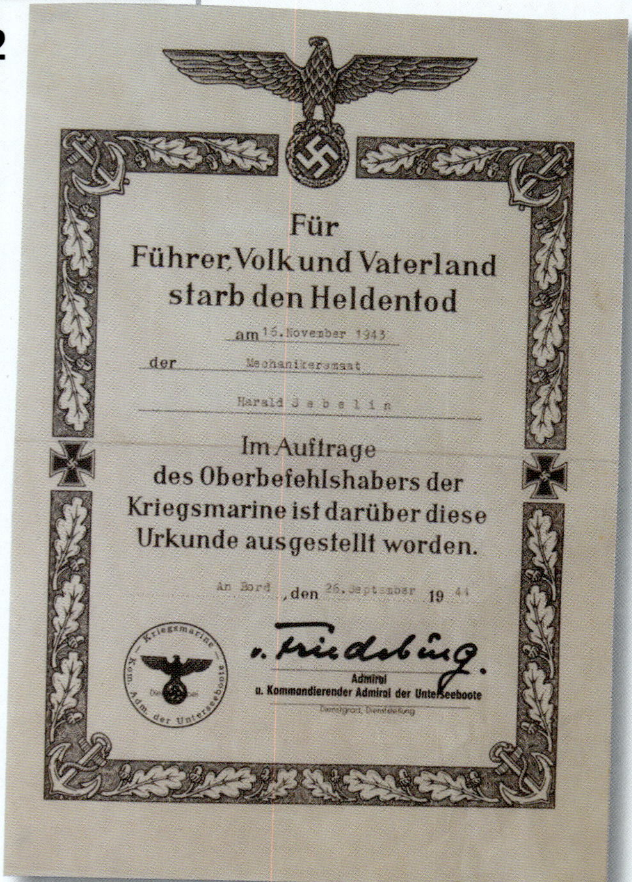
Für
Führer, Volk und Vaterland
starb den Heldentod
am 16. November 1943
der Mechanikermaat
Harald Sebelin
Im Auftrage
des Oberbefehlshabers der Kriegsmarine ist darüber diese Urkunde ausgestellt worden.
An Bord , den 25. September 19 44
Admiral
u. Kommandierender Admiral der Unterseeboote

THE DESTROYER WAR BADGE

Front and back of the destroyer war badge, which was founded on June 4, 1940. It was originally meant for the crewmembers of the destroyers deployed at Narvik, but on August 12, 1940. It was decided that crews of *Schnellboote* could also receive it. In a further postscript of October 22, 1940, the award was eventually extended to torpedo boat crews, who had especially proven themselves in the face of the enemy. (Private collection)

Front and back of a destroyer war badge. This special Schwerin piece was given to a crewmember of the torpedo boat T 25 in August 1943 in Nantes. (Private collection)

This young *Funkgefreiter* (radio operator corporal), who had served on a destroyer or torpedo boat, is wearing the destroyer war badge on his pea coat, showing that he must have taken part in at least three battles. (Private collection)

Embroidered version of the destroyer war badge. This version was relatively rarely worn, because the recipients usually preferred the metal style. (Private collection)

THE WAR BADGE FOR MINEHUNTER, U-BOOT HUNTER, AND SECURITY UNITS

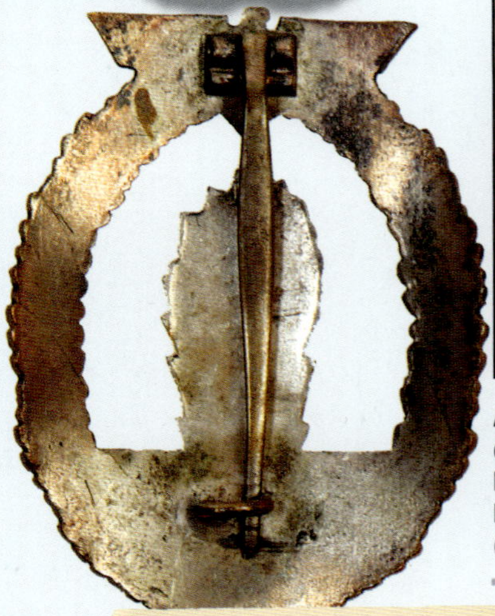

Front and back of the war badge for minehunter, *U-Boot* hunter, and security units, founded on August 31, 1940. Requirements for the award included taking part in three battles or an outstanding single deed. (Collection of P.-M. Rousseau)

A *Signalgefreiter* distinguished with the war badge for minehunter, *U-Boot* hunter, and security units. (Private collection)

This *Leutnant z. See* was still a member of the *Hitlerjugend* (Hitler Youth) not too long ago, as can be seen from the *HJ* achievement badge he is wearing below the minehunter, *U-Boot* hunter, and security units war badge. (Private collection)

1940

Im Namen

des

Oberbefehlshabers

der

Kriegsmarine

verleihe ich

dem Seekadett Wolfgang Dähne

das

Kriegsabzeichen

für

Minensuch-, U-Boots Jagd-

und

Sicherungsverbände

Frankreich, den 1.2.41

Kapitän z. See u. Kommodore
Führer der Minensuchverbände
West

War badge for minehunter, *U-Boot* hunter, and security units and the associated award certificate, issued on February 1, 1941 to *Seekadette* (naval cadet) Wolfgang Dähne. (Collection of P.-M. Rousseau)

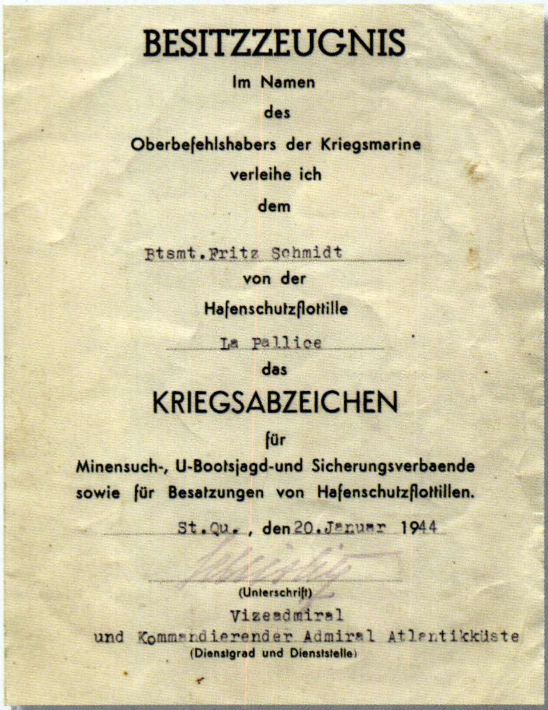

BESITZZEUGNIS

Im Namen

des

Oberbefehlshabers der Kriegsmarine

verleihe ich

dem

Btsmt. Fritz Schmidt

von der

Hafenschutzflottille

La Pallice

das

KRIEGSABZEICHEN

für

Minensuch-, U-Bootsjagd-und Sicherungsverbaende
sowie für Besatzungen von Hafenschutzflottillen.

St.Qu., den 20. Januar 1944

(Unterschrift)

Vizeadmiral
und Kommandierender Admiral Atlantikküste
(Dienstgrad und Dienststelle)

This award certificate, issued in French St. Quentin with the war badge for minehunter, *U-Boot* hunter, and security units, "and for crews of *Hafenschutzflottillen*" ("harbor defense flotillas") bears the signature of *Vizeadmiral* Ernst Schirlitz. (Private collection)

THE WAR BADGE FOR AUXILIARY CRUISERS

Front and back of the war badge for auxiliary cruisers, which was inaugurated on April 24, 1941. One condition for receiving this decoration was service in a successful long-distance operation. The symbolism of the badge, which features a Viking longship sailing over the globe, is especially appropriate. (Private collection)

Three of these officers on an auxiliary cruiser (only eleven of them in total were put into service by the German navy) have been awarded the *EK II* after returning from a successful deployment. They all are wearing the auxiliary cruiser war badge on their jackets. (Private collection)

This *Maat* is wearing the auxiliary cruiser war badge, and the ribbon for the *EK II* on his pea coat. (Private collection)

The wedding picture of the same petty officer, now promoted to *Obermaat.* In this photo, he is wearing, besides his auxiliary cruiser war badge, all the other decorations he received in the meantime, such as the *EK I*, the wound badge in black, and the war badge for minehunter, *U-Boot* hunter, and security units. (Private collection)

THE FLEET WAR BADGE

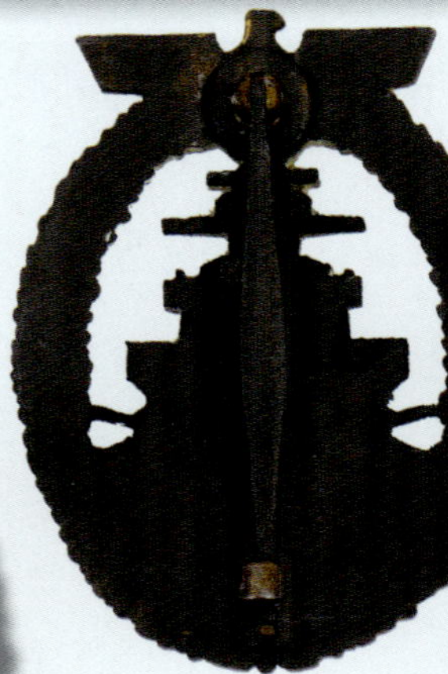

Front and back of the Fleet war badge, founded on May 30, 1941 by *Großadmiral* Raeder, intended for the crews of battleships and cruisers, among others. It could be awarded to a man who had proven himself on one or more war patrols, or fulfilled one of the other special award conditions. (Private collection)

This seaman is wearing the Fleet war badge on the left breast pocket of his tropical shirt and the *EK II* on the pocket flap. (Private collection)

THE *SCHNELLBOOT* WAR BADGE

The 1st design of the *Schnellboot* war badge, here of French make, in its original box. (Private collection)

Front and back of the *Schnellboot* war badge, founded on May 30, 1941. From June 1940 until this badge was founded, *Schnellboot* drivers who had proven themselves were awarded the destroyer war badge. However, given the bravery of the German *Schnellboot* crews, their own war badge was soon introduced. (Private collection)

This *Maat* is wearing not only – much against regulations – a full beard, but also the 1st design of the *Schnellboot* war badge on his pea coat. (Private collection)

The 2nd design of the *Schnellboot* war badge. Since the 1st badge design was not very well received by those who got it, a 2nd design, based on proposals from the front, was introduced in its place on February 15, 1943. (Collection of P.-M. Rousseau)

The young lady in this photo did not serve as a volunteer on a *Schnellboot* – women on board meant bad luck, according to seafaring superstition, and besides, women were not allowed (officially) to serve in the *Wehrmacht* armed forces. She is likely the fiancée of a soldier, and is here wearing his uniform and the attached 2nd design of the *Schnellboot* war badge. (Private collection)

THE MARINE ARTILLERY WAR BADGE

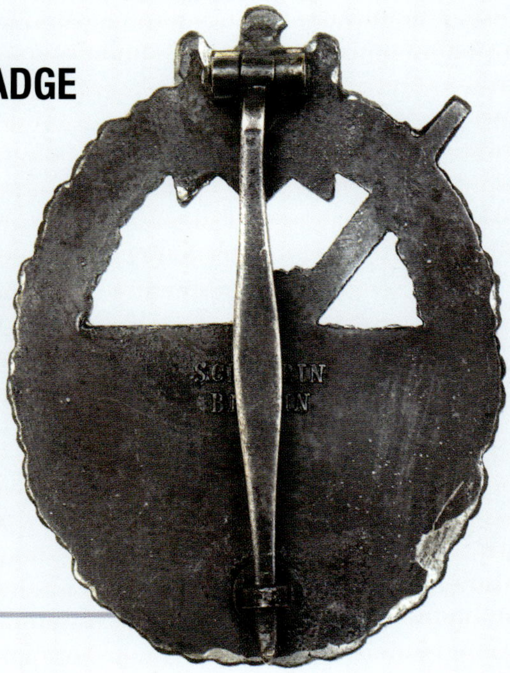

Front and back of the *Marine* artillery war badge, founded on June 24, 1941. It could, among other things, be awarded for firing on enemy aircraft. (Private collection)

Color photo of a *Matrosenobergefreiter*, who is wearing the DRL *(Deutsches Reich)* sports badge and the *Marine* artillery war badge on his blue shirt. (Private collection)

This *Oberfeldwebel* has also been awarded the *Marine* artillery war badge. (Private collection)

Besitzurkunde

Im Auftrage des Oberbefehlshabers der Kriegsmarine

verleihe ich dem

Matrosenobergefreiten
(Dienstgrad)

Paul Modrzinski
(Name)

das Kriegsabzeichen für die Marineartillerie.

O.U. , den 21. September 1944

Vizeadmiral und Befehlshaber des
(Dienstgrad, Dienststellung)
Deutschen Marinekommandos Italien.

Kriegsmarine Deutsches Marinekommando Italien

80847. 3 - 44 - 500

Certificate for the *Marine* artillery war badge, awarded on September 21, 1944 to *Matrosenobergefreiter* Paul Modrzinski. Modrzinski belonged at the time to a *Flak* unit aboard a war transport ship. (Private collection)

Front and back of a *Marine* artillery war badge, of French make. The national emblem is here clearly smaller than on pieces made in Germany, and there is no manufacturer's stamp. (Private collection)

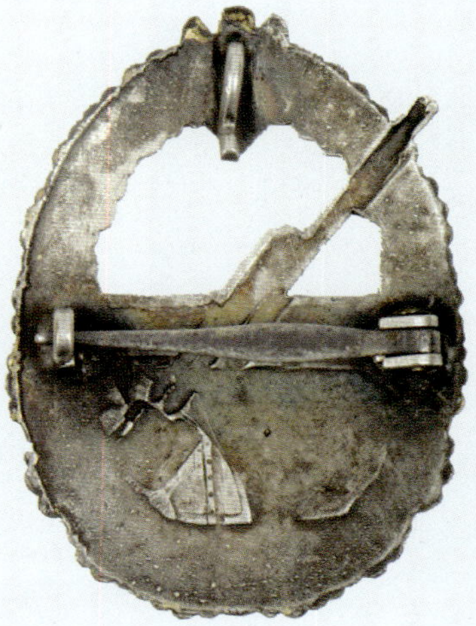

BADGE FOR BLOCKADE RUNNERS

The civilian-dress version of the blockade runners' badge, with attached pin fastener. (Collection of P.-M. Rousseau)

Front and back of the badge for blockade runners. This badge, founded on April 1, 1941, was originally intended for the primarily civilian crews of ocean-going ships sailing under merchant flags, who had, after the outbreak of war, successfully broken through the Allied naval blockade and returned home. (Collection of P.-M. Rousseau)

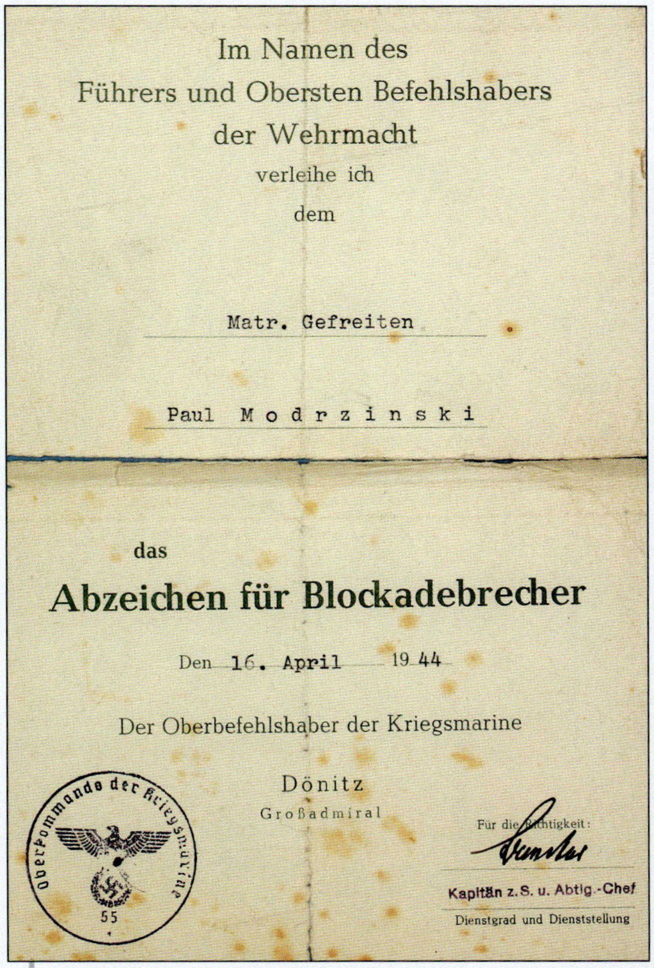

Im Namen des
Führers und Obersten Befehlshabers
der Wehrmacht
verleihe ich
dem

Matr. Gefreiten

Paul Modrzinski

das

Abzeichen für Blockadebrecher

Den 16. April 1944

Der Oberbefehlshaber der Kriegsmarine

Dönitz
Großadmiral

Oberkommando der Kriegsmarine 55

Für die Richtigkeit:

Kapitän z. S. u. Abtlg.-Chef
Dienstgrad und Dienststellung

The *Kriegsmarine Oberbefehlshaber's* certificate for the blockade runner badge awarded to Paul Modrzinski – then still a *Gefreiter* – on April 16, 1944. (Private collection)

This *Gefreiter* wears on his uniform the war badge for minehunter, *U-Boot* hunter, and security units, the DRL sports badge, and the badge for blockade runners. (Private collection)

THE *U-BOOT* NAVAL COMBAT CLASP

Front and back of the *U-Boot* combat clasp in bronze. This new decoration was founded on May 15, 1944 by *Großadmiral* Dönitz in recognition of continuous, strenuous deployment of the men serving on *U-Boote* and their willingness to sacrifice themselves, although by this time there was scarcely any remaining hope for victory. The clasp was manufactured by C. Schwerin in Berlin. (Collection of P.-M. Rousseau)

This subaltern had already served in the Spanish Civil War, as shown the Spanish Cross he is wearing on the right breast of his jacket. His other decorations demonstrate how active he has been since then, as proven by the *U-Boot* combat clasp in bronze on his left breast pocket. (Private collection)

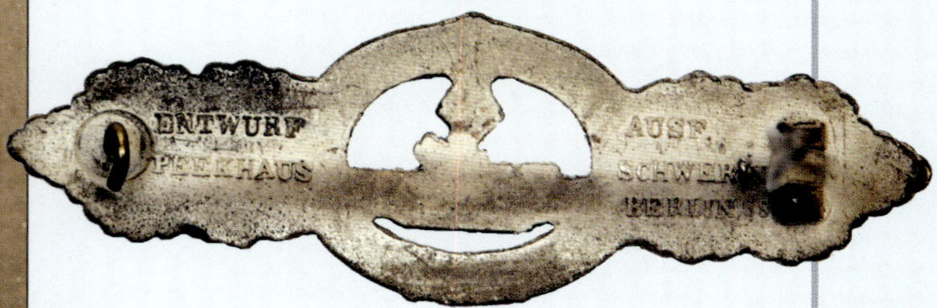

U-Boot combat clasp in silver awarded on November 24, 1944. This decoration had only two grades, bronze and silver – the "golden *U-Boot* combat clasp" is a post-war invention. The silver clasp was also made by C. Schwerin in Berlin. (Collection of P.-M. Rousseau)

Oberleutnant z. See before putting to sea for the next patrol, winter 1944-45. This young *U-Boot Kommandant* appears to be wearing the *U-Boot* combat clasp in silver on his jacket. He has also received the *EK II*, the *U-Boot* war badge and the war badge for minehunter, *U-Boot* hunter, and security units – he had previously served in the surface fleet forces. This photo is an excellent example of a *U-Boot* officer's appearance during the last months of the war. (Private collection)

VERLEIHUNGS-URKUNDE

Auf Grund der Ermächtigung des Oberbefehlshabers der Kriegsmarine verleihe ich dem

Stabsobermaschinisten

H e b e r (Gerhard)

die

U-Boots-Frontspange

in Bronze

Lager Godenstedt/Ha, den 11. 1. 1945

Fregattenkapitän(Ing) und Kommandeur
der 2. Unterseebootsausbildungsabteilung

U-Boot combat clasp in bronze with its accompanying certificate awarded on January 11, 1945 to *Stabsobermaschinist* Gerhard Heber. (Collection of P.-M. Rousseau)

ÄRMELSCHILDER (SLEEVE SHIELDS) AND BANDS AS COMBAT BADGES

THE NARVIK SHIELD

The three *Obergefreiten* in this photo were all in the fighting around Narvik in 1940. They are wearing the appropriate combat badges according to regulations, sewn on the left upper sleeve, above the rating, rate, and specific training insignia. (Private collection)

Front and back of the Narvik shield. This combat badge, established on August 19, 1940, was the first of five officially created and awarded sleeve shields (Cholm, Krim (Crimea), Demjansk (Demyansk) and Kuban). It was awarded to all *Wehrmacht* servicemen who had fought honorably in the landing at Narvik in northern Norway, or in the fighting of the Narvik Group between April 9 and June 9, 1940. Some 8,600 Narvik shields were awarded, 3,700 of them to members of the *Kriegsmarine* and *Handelsmarine*. The *Kriegsmarine* sleeve shields were gold colored on navy blue cloth patches; the *Heer* and *Luftwaffe* versions were silver colored, on field gray or gray-blue backing. (Private collection)

This *Korvettenkapitän* is a former fighter in Spain and a survivor of the battles at Narvik, as can be seen from his Spanish Cross and Narvik shield. (Private collection)

Front and back of the Krim (Crimean) shield. This combat badge, created on July 25, 1942, was awarded to soldiers who took part between September 21, 1941 and July 4, 1942 in the fighting in Crimea. The *Kriegsmarine* version only differed from those of the other *Wehrmacht* branches in its navy blue cloth backing. A number of members of the Italian *Decima Flottiglia MAS*, who operated their *Schnellboote* in the Black Sea during the fighting, were also awarded the Krim shield. (Private collection)

This *Maschinen-Obergefreiter* had earned himself the Krim shield during his deployment in the Black Sea; he is wearing it, according to regulations, above his rate and rating insignia. (Private collection)

THE KRIM SHIELD

The *Ärmelband Afrika* (Africa sleeve band) was created on January 15, 1943 as a combat badge for *Wehrmacht* soldiers who had served honorably for a minimum of six months in North Africa, or for members of sea-going units deployed from fixed bases in Africa. Servicemen who were wounded while serving in Africa and or had caught a disease there, which made them unfit for a further tour of duty in the tropics, were also eligible for this sleeve band. The band shown here is the usual camelhair cloth design, which was also awarded to *Kriegsmarine* members; it was to be worn on the left forearm. There were also irregular Africa sleeve bands on a dark blue background, but which probably came from the *Luftwaffe*. (Private collection)

These five sailors, who had their photo taken in 1944 in Italy, are "old Africa fighters," because they are all wearing the Africa sleeve band on their pea coats. (Private collection)

THE AFRICA SLEEVE BAND

This *Maat* is wearing the Africa sleeve band on his blue pea coat. (Private collection)

LUFTWAFFE TATIGKEITSABZEICHEN (TACTICAL BADGE)

This *Korvettenkapitän* wears his pilot's badge according to regulations, below his *Eisernes Kreuz 1. Klasse* on his jacket. (Private collection)

THE PILOT'S BADGE

The pilot's badge. This *Luftwaffe* tactical badge was indeed quite unusual on the uniform of a *Kriegsmarine* officer, but certainly not unique. Despite Hermann Göring's motto "Everything that flies, is mine," the *Marine* and *Luftwaffe* worked together in the *Seeluftstreitkräften* (naval aviation armed forces). These included not only the aircraft on board the large ships (for reconnaissance and air monitoring), but also the planes for coastal monitoring. Almost all the *Kriegsmarine* officers went through training in the *Luftwaffe*. The pilot's badge they were awarded was identical to the one worn by *Luftwaffe* personnel. (Private collection)

LUFTWAFFE TATIGKEITSABZEICHEN (TACTICAL BADGES)

Luftwaffe observer badge. As with the pilot's badge, the observer badge was also sometimes awarded to those who served in the *Kriegsmarine.* (Private collection)

LUFTWAFFE OBSERVER BADGE

This young *Oberleutnant zur See* has already had plenty of combat experience, as his numerous decorations show. He is wearing on his jacket, besides the *Eisernes Kreuz 1.* and *2. Klasse*, also the *U-Boot* war badge, the *Luftwaffe* observer badge, and the combat clasp for reconnaissance, a *Luftwaffe* combat badge. (Private collection)

COMBAT BADGES FOR *KLEINKAMPFMITTEL* (SMALL BATTLE UNITS)

A German *Kampfschwimmer* (commando frogman) of the *K-Verbände (Kleinkampf* units) showing his equipment to a group of high-ranking officers, including two *Admirale.* The frogman is wearing on his wrist the superb Panerai diver's watch, which had been developed for the Italian comrades of the *Decima Flottiglia* MAS. (Private collection)

First grade combat badge, enlisted men's version (embroidered). (Private collection)

From left to right: Combat badge, 1st grade, a hand-embroidered in gold thread officer's version. Second grade combat badge, machine-embroidered enlisted men's version. Fourth grade combat badge, hand-embroidered officer's version. All the badges shown here, made in 1944-45, appear all to be unworn. (Collection of P.-M. Rousseau)

ÄRMELSCHILDER (SLEEVE BADGES) OF THE *DECIMA MAS* (ITALIAN NAVY 10TH NAVAL ASSAULT UNIT)

Left: sleeve shield (Italian: *scudetto*), of the legendary *Decima MAS Flottiglia* (10th fast attack boat flotilla – the code name for the Italian Navy small battle units) under Prince Junio Valerio Borghese. This sleeve shield, introduced at the end of 1943, was also occasionally awarded to members of the German *Kleinkampfmittelverbände* who had received "training assistance" from their Italian comrades. (Private collection)

Right: Sleeve shield of the *Decima Divisione*. This 10th Division was established in 1944 by the RSI (the post-Mussolini fascist Italian Social Republic) and had a strength of about 25,000 men (frogmen, *Sprengboot* (explosive boat) and midget *U-Boot* drivers, but also infantry, artillery etc.). The shield of the *Decima Divisione* was introduced in December 1944, replacing the previous model, and could also be awarded to members of the German *K-Verbände* who had participated in training courses of these allies across the Alps. (Private collection)

A group of Italian and German frogmen during a break from training in northern Italy, winter 1944-45. A number of the German *"K-Männer"* are wearing the *Decima MAS* shield on the sleeves of their pea coats. (Private collection)

Maat Fritz Tauchnitz in a picture from 1940 (note the unusual beard!). His identification tag meets the regulations which went into effect in 1941, i.e., giving name, muster roll number, and blood type. At the end of 1940, Tauchnitz was seconded to MAA 242 (*Marine* artillery division 242). He fell as a *Feldwebel* on September 29, 1944 at Cap Gris-Nez (Pas-de-Calais) – on the last day of fighting in this sector. (Private collection)

OTHER DECORATIONS

His *Wehrmacht* class service badge (for four-year tour of duty) and medal commemorating October 1, 1938 (the date of the annexation of the Sudetenland) make it clear, how long Fritz Tauchnitz had already been a soldier. (Private collection)

Im Namen
des Führers und Reichskanzlers

verleihe ich

dem Schreibersmaat
(Dienstgrad)

Fritz Tauchnitz
(Vor- und Zuname)

St.-R.-Nr. N. N 1498 / 35 S

Marinenachrichtenoffizier Wilhelmshaven
(Marineteil)

für 4jährige treue Dienste in der Wehrmacht die

Dienstauszeichnung IV. Klasse

Wilhelmshaven, den 1. Juli 1939.

Der 2. Admiral der Nordseestation
von Schrader
Konteradmiral

Für die Richtigkeit

(Dienststempel)

(Name)

Kapitänleutnant
(Dienstgrad und Dienststellung)

und Marinenachrichtenoffizier
Wilhelmshaven.

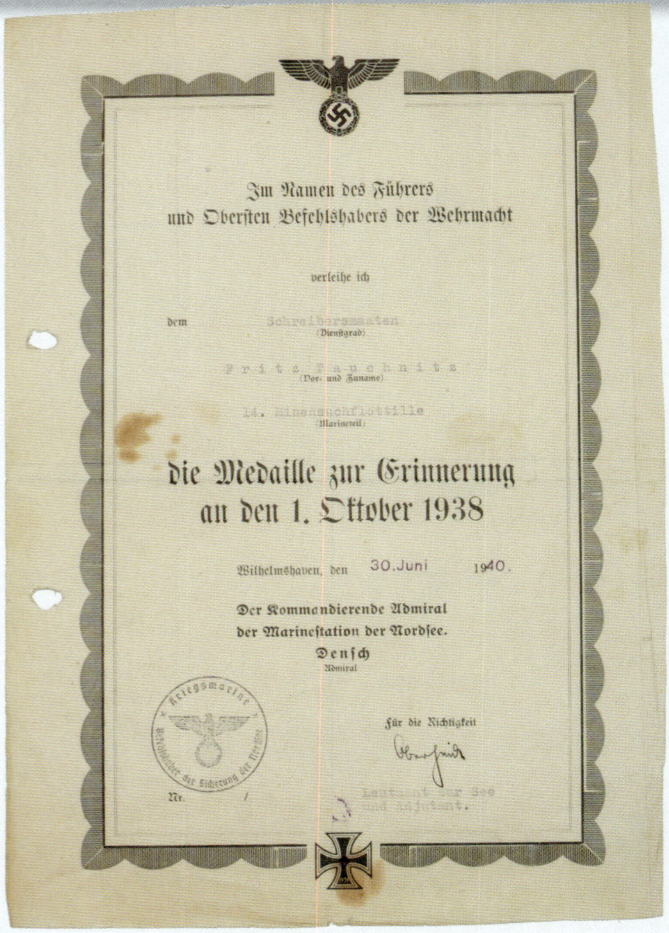

Im Namen des Führers
und Obersten Befehlshabers der Wehrmacht

verleihe ich

dem Schreibersmaaten
(Dienstgrad)

Fritz Tauchnitz
(Vor- und Zuname)

14. Minensuchflottille
(Marineteil)

die Medaille zur Erinnerung
an den 1. Oktober 1938

Wilhelmshaven, den 30.Juni 1940.

Der Kommandierende Admiral
der Marinestation der Nordsee.
Densch
Admiral

Für die Richtigkeit

Nr. /

Leutnant zur See
und Adjutant.

The certificates for the *Wehrmacht* service badges and October 1, 1938 commemorative medal, both awarded to Fritz Tauchnitz. (Private collection)

OTHER DECORATIONS

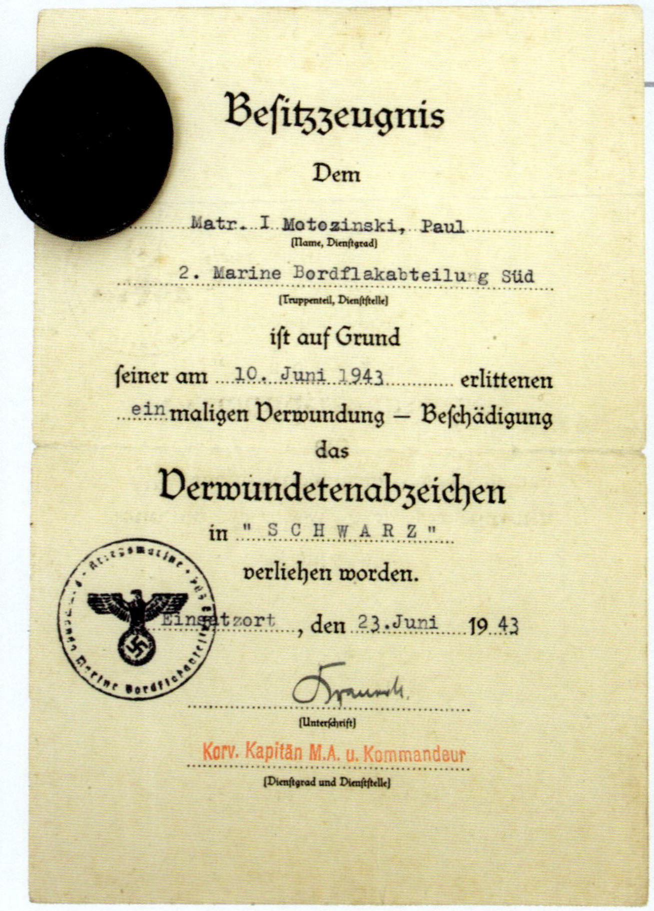

Besitzzeugnis

Dem

Matr. I Motezinski, Paul
(Name, Dienstgrad)

2. Marine Bordflakabteilung Süd
(Truppenteil, Dienststelle)

ist auf Grund

seiner am 10. Juni 1943 erlittenen

ein maligen Verwundung — Beschädigung

das

Verwundetenabzeichen

in " S C H W A R Z "

verliehen worden.

Einsatzort, den 23.Juni 1943

(Unterschrift)

Korv. Kapitän M.A. u. Kommandeur
(Dienstgrad und Dienststelle)

Certificate for a casualty badge in black, showing that it is the third and lowest grade of this war badge. The second grade was of silver and the first of gold. The recipient was the *Matrose* Paul Modrzinski, who served in June 1943 in the 2. *Marine* on-board Flak division South, which was deployed in southern Italy. (Private collection)

This *Maat* has been awarded the *Eisernes Kreuz 2. Klasse* and the wound badge in black. (Private collection)

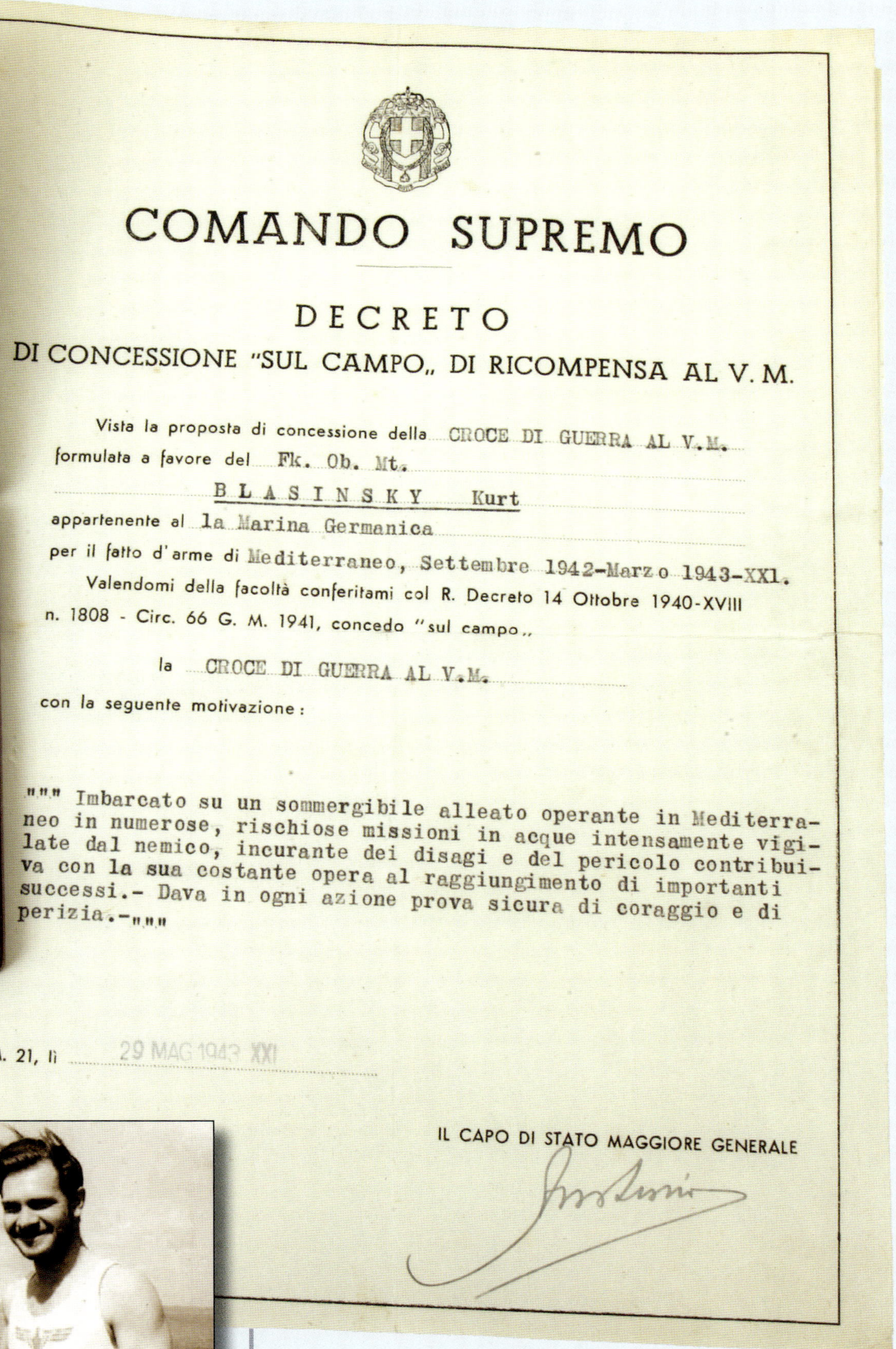

COMANDO SUPREMO

DECRETO

DI CONCESSIONE "SUL CAMPO„ DI RICOMPENSA AL V. M.

Vista la proposta di concessione della CROCE DI GUERRA AL V.M.
formulata a favore del Fk. Ob. Mt.
B L A S I N S K Y Kurt
appartenente al la Marina Germanica
per il fatto d'arme di Mediterraneo, Settembre 1942-Marzo 1943-XXl.
Valendomi della facoltà conferitami col R. Decreto 14 Ottobre 1940-XVIII
n. 1808 - Circ. 66 G. M. 1941, concedo "sul campo„
la CROCE DI GUERRA AL V.M.
con la seguente motivazione:

""" Imbarcato su un sommergibile alleato operante in Mediterraneo in numerose, rischiose missioni in acque intensamente vigilate dal nemico, incurante dei disagi e del pericolo contribuiva con la sua costante opera al raggiungimento di importanti successi.- Dava in ogni azione prova sicura di coraggio e di perizia.-"""

P. M. 21, lì 29 MAG 1943 XXI

IL CAPO DI STATO MAGGIORE GENERALE

Kurt Blasinsky (Private collection)

The Italian War Cross with Swords *("Croce di Guerra al Valor Militare")* and the accompanying award certificate. This decoration was given to *Funkobermaat* Kurt Blasinsky, who was serving at the time on a *U-Boot,* in recognition of his brave service in the Mediterranean from September 1942 to March 1943. (Private collection)

IM NAMEN DES FÜHRERS
U OBERSTEN BEFEHLSHABERS
ER WEHRMACHT
VERLEIHE ICH
DEM

Matr.Ob.Gefr.

Hans Fritsch

DAS
KRIEGSVERDIENSTKREUZ
II. KLASSE
MIT SCHWERTERN

Rouen, DEN 30. Januar 1944

(DIENSTSIEGEL) .Der Kommandierende Admiral Kanalküste

Vizeadmiral.
(DIENSTGRAD UND DIENSTSTELLUNG)

Obergefreiter Hans Fritsch. (Private collection)

Kriegsverdienstkreuz 2. Klasse (War Merit Cross) with swords. The accompanying award certificate was awarded to *Obergefreiter* Hans Fritsch on January 30, 1944 in Rouen. (Private collection)

THE SPANISH CROSS

This young *Oberleutnant zur See* is wearing on the right breast the Spanish Cross – a commemoration of a comparatively straightforward war, in which Germany was on the winning side. (Private collection)

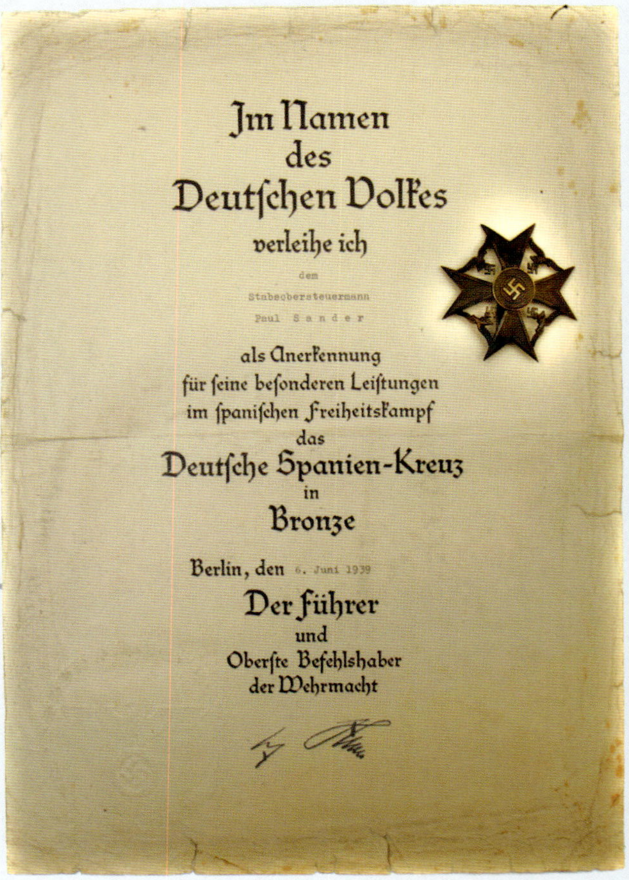

Im Namen
des
Deutschen Volkes
verleihe ich
dem
Stabsobersteuermann
Paul Sander
als Anerkennung
für seine besonderen Leistungen
im spanischen Freiheitskampf
das
Deutsche Spanien-Kreuz
in
Bronze

Berlin, den 6. Juni 1939
Der Führer
und
Oberste Befehlshaber
der Wehrmacht

Spanish Cross in bronze with the award certificate, signed by Adolf Hitler in June 1939. (Collection of P.-M. Rousseau)

Im Namen des Führers
und Obersten Befehlshabers
der Wehrmacht

verleihe ich

dem

Matr.Ob.Gefr.

Hans Fritsch

das

Eiserne Kreuz 2.Klasse

Im Felde, den 19. Juli 1944

Der Kommandierende Admiral
Kanalküste

Vizeadmiral

(Dienstgrad und Dienststellung)

Eisernes Kreuz 2. Klasse and the award certificate issued to *Matrosen-Obergefreiter* Hans Fritsch. The award date of July 19, 1944 and the location, "in the field," indicates that the operational area was Normandy. (Private collection)

DAS EISERNE KREUZ (THE IRON CROSS)

Below left: These two seamen have just been awarded the *Eisernes Kreuz 2. Klasse.* (Private collection)

Bottom: Award certificate for the *Eisernes Kreuz 2. Klasse* with the original signature of *Vizeadmiral* Dönitz. (Collection of P.-M. Rousseau)

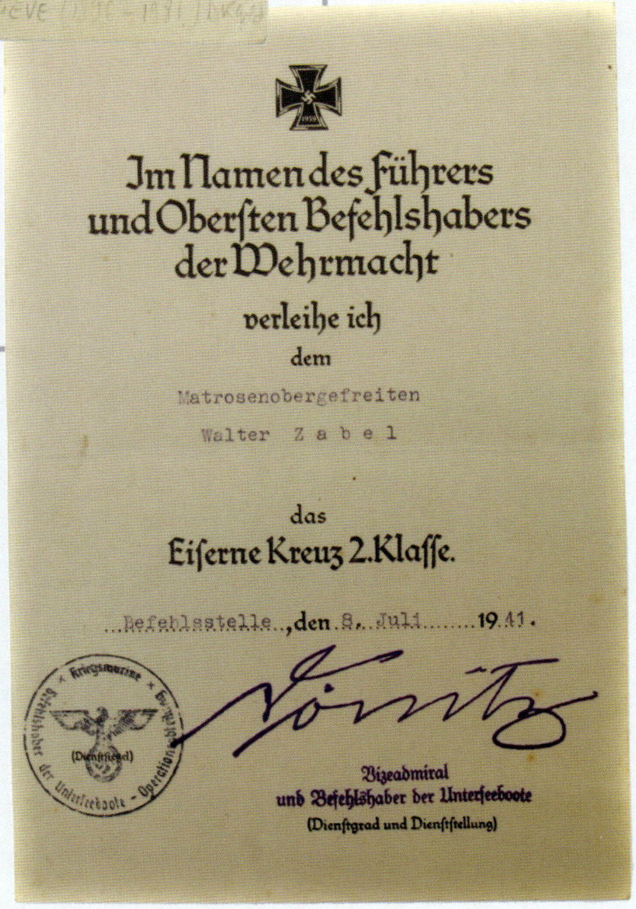

Im Namen des Führers
und Obersten Befehlshabers
der Wehrmacht

verleihe ich

dem

Matrosenobergefreiten

Walter Zabel

das

Eiserne Kreuz 2.Klasse.

Befehlsstelle, den 8. Juli 1941.

Vizeadmiral
und Befehlshaber der Unterseeboote

(Dienstgrad und Dienststellung)

Eisernes Kreuz 1. Klasse and the accompanying award certificate, issued on October 16, 1944 in Italy to *Matrosen-Obergefreiter* Paul Modrzinski. (Private collection)

IM NAMEN DES FÜHRERS
VERLEIHE ICH
DEM

Matrosenobergefreiten

Paul Modrzinski

DAS
EISERNE KREUZ
1. KLASSE

O.U., 16. Oktober 1944

(DIENSTSIEGEL)

Vizeadmiral
und Befehlshaber des
Deutschen Marinekommandos Italien.

(DIENSTGRAD UND DIENSTSTELLUNG)

DAS EISERNE KREUZ (THE IRON CROSS)

The *U-Boot* man at right, a *Maschinen-Obergefreiter*, is wearing a whole set of decorations, in this photo from winter 1944-45, including the *U-Boot* combat clasp, and both classes of the *Eisernes Kreuz*. (Private collection)

IM NAMEN DES FÜHRERS
VERLEIHE ICH
DEM

Bootsmannsmaaten

Walter Zabel

DAS DEUTSCHE KREUZ
IN GOLD

BERLIN, DEN 23. Mai 1944.

DER OBERBEFEHLSHABER
DER KRIEGSMARINE

Großadmiral.

Front and back of the *Deutsches Kreuz* (German Cross) in gold, mounted with four solid rivets, thus a piece of later make (two rivets are here covered by the pin). The digit '1' on the outer side of the pin refers to Deschler & Sohn in Munich as maker of this order. (Collection of P.-M. Rousseau)

THE DEUTSCHES KREUZ (GERMAN CROSS)

Gold *Deutsches Kreuz* in original case and the accompanying award certificate, which was signed by *Großadmiral* Dönitz on May 23, 1944. (Collection of P.-M. Rousseau)

Front and back of an embroidered *Deutsches Kreuz*. From the end of October 1944, only the cloth version was to be generally handed out, to save material, but this was not always followed. (Collection of P.-M. Rousseau)

Presentation of the *Deutsches Kreuz* in gold to Kapitänleutnant Hermann Lamby, Kommandant of U 437, on April 19, 1944. (Collection of P.-M. Rousseau)

The Mediterranean region, summer 1944. A staff officer striding in front of a *Kriegsmarine* formation. On the right breast pocket of his white jacket, he has pinned the *Deutsches Kreuz* in gold. (Collection of P.-M. Rousseau)

THE *KRIEGSMARINE EHRENTAFEL-SPANGE* (HONOR ROLL CLASP)

The *Ehrentafel-Spange* (honor roll clasp) of the *Kriegsmarine* was founded in May 1944 for the *Marine* servicemen who were named to the *Kriegsmarine* "honor roll," but had not been awarded the *Ritterkreuz*, the *Eisernes Kreuz*, or the *Deutsches Kreuz* in gold. This decoration was only awarded twenty-four (other sources say twenty-nine) times. (Collection of P.-M. Rousseau)

The *Ritterkreuz* of the *Eisernes Kreuz* in its original presentation case and a *U-Boot* war badge. The *Ritterkreuz* was the most esteemed and prestigious decoration of the Third Reich. (Collection of P.-M. Rousseau)

THE *RITTERKREUZ DES EISERNEN KREUZ* (KNIGHT'S CROSS OF THE IRON CROSS)

Four first-class *U-Boot Kommandanten* who were awarded the *Ritterkreuz*, from top to bottom and from left to right: Reinhard Hardegen, *RK* on 1/23/42, and oak leaf cluster on 4/23/42. Robert Gysae, *RK* on 12/31/41, oak leaf cluster on 5/31/43. Günther Prien, *RK* on 10/18/39, oak leaf cluster on 10/20/40. Heinrich Bleichrodt, *RK* on 10/24/40, oak leaf cluster on 9/29/42. (Private collection)

Below: A baptismal certificate signed personally by "Neptune," for the "crossing the line" ceremony, given to a sailor on the battleship SCHLESIEN in 1937 for his first equator crossing. (Collection of P.-M. Rousseau)

Above and below: The stoker Heinz Fraatz, who also served aboard the battleship SCHLESIEN, got two certificates after his equatorial baptism on November 23, 1936. (Private collection)

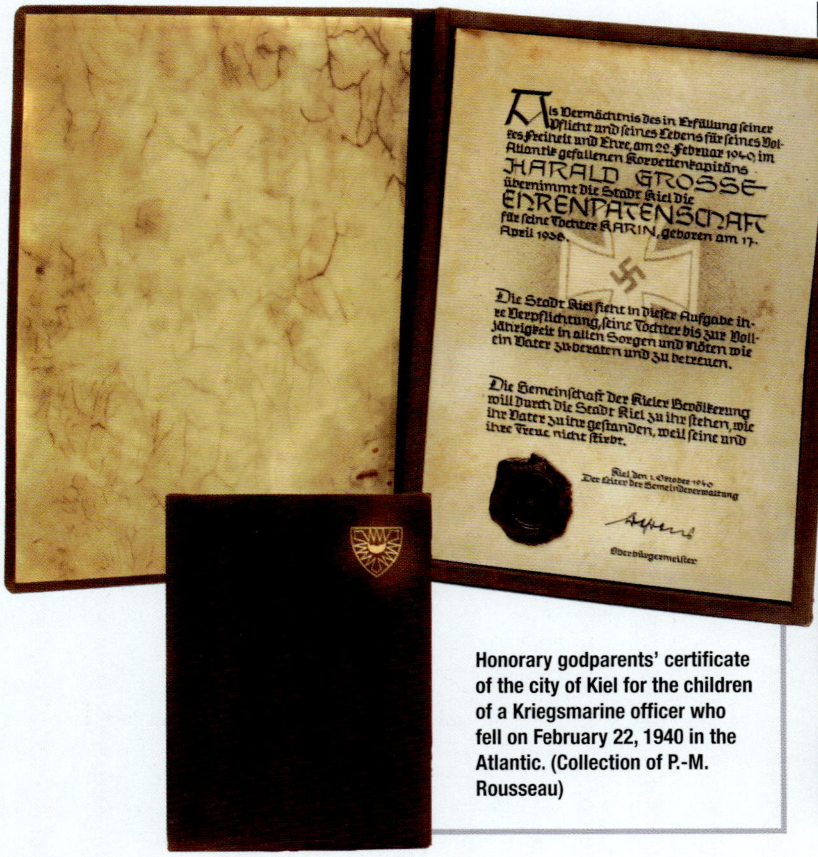
Als Vermächtnis des in Erfüllung seiner
Pflicht und seines Lebens für seines Vol-
kes Freiheit und Ehre, am 22. Februar 1940 im
Atlantik gefallenen Korvettenkapitäns
HARALD GROSSE
übernimmt die Stadt Kiel die
EHRENPATENSCHAFT
für seine Tochter KARIN, geboren am 17.
April 1938.

Die Stadt Kiel sieht in dieser Aufgabe ih-
re Verpflichtung, seine Tochter bis zur Voll-
jährigkeit in allen Sorgen und Nöten wie
ein Vater zu beraten und zu betreuen.

Die Gemeinschaft der Kieler Bevölkerung
will durch die Stadt Kiel zu ihr stehen, wie
ihr Vater zu ihr gestanden, weil seine und
ihre Treue nicht stirbt.

Kiel den 1. Oktober 1940
Der Leiter der Gemeindeverwaltung

Oberbürgermeister

Honorary godparents' certificate of the city of Kiel for the children of a Kriegsmarine officer who fell on February 22, 1940 in the Atlantic. (Collection of P.-M. Rousseau)

The so-called equatorial baptism is an age-old seaman's custom, followed by all the Navies of the world. Even the German U-Boot crews did not escape it, even in war. Kapitänleutnant Asmus Nicolai Clausen (RK on 3/13/42) here in conversation with the sea god Neptune. (Private collection)

Taufschein

Wir Neptun,
Herr aller Meere,
Seen, Flüsse und Teiche,
Beherrscher aller Nixen, Quallen, Seehunde
und Fische, Freund und Helfer aller wackeren
Seeleute, vollzogen an Bord von U – 108
heute die

ÄQUATORTAUFE

an dem Mtr.Ob.Gfr. Zabel

Wir befehlen allen uns untertänigen Meereshoheiten,
den vom Schmutz der nördlichen Halbkugel gereinigten
Täufling hinfüro ungehindert die Linie passieren zu lassen

Meeresgott

Atlantischer Ozean, 32° westl. Länge, den 16.9.1941

Another equator baptismal certificate, dated September 1941, this time for a U-Boot man who served on U 108. (Collection of P.-M. Rousseau)

DOCUMENTS AND IDENTITY TAGS

Every serviceman kept his *Soldbuch* (identification and pay book) with him during his entire active service. His *Wehrpass* (military service record), however, was held by the soldier's unit during his tour of duty.

Soldbuch of a petty officer of a sea-going unit. The _Soldbuch_ contained the first and last names of the owner, all his promotions, ID number, blood type, immunizations, all his transfers, a notation of pieces of clothing and equipment issued, and decorations awarded. All _Wehrmacht_ personnel, including General officers, had to keep this document with them at all times. Soldiers travelling alone, such as on leave, had to present the document to the military police at checkpoints. (Private collection)

Soldbuch **and identification tag of a *U-Boot* man who served aboard U 233 or S 75. On the back of his "dog tags," Heinz Wolf had the emblem of his boat riveted, which was not exactly according to regulations. (Collection of P.-M. Rousseau)**

Soldbuch
zugleich Personalausweis
Nr. 67
für
den Matr.
(Dienstgrad)
(Besoldungsgruppe)
befördert: zum:
ab
ab
ab
ab
ab
Gerhard Klinowski
(Vor- und Zuname)
Beschriftung und Nummer der Erkennungsmarke N. 491/41 S
Blutgruppe A
Gasmaskengröße 2
Marine-Stammrollen-Nr. N 491/41 S
Stamm-Marineteil 2 Ad. N
1

The *Soldbuch* made it possible to follow the (service) movements of the soldiers. His periods of leave were also entered. The three identity cards shown, which grant entry to certain cities and ports, were only valid with the *Soldbuch*. (Collection of P.-M. Rousseau)

Beurlaubungen
(ausgenommen Standort- und Sonntagsurlaub)
1. vom 25.8. bis 29.8. nach Allenstein
Grund:
den 23.8.41.
Leutnant zur See
(Unterschrift des Disziplinarvorgesetzten)
2. vom 4.11. bis nach Allenstein
Grund:
den 4.11.41.
3. vom bis nach
Grund:
den
Ob. Strm. R.O.A.
4. vom 23.8. bis 6.9.42 nach
Grund:
den
36
5. vom 19.8. bis 26.8.42 nach
Grund:
den 18. Aug. 42
Leutnant z. S. und Gruppenführer
6. vom bis nach Allenstein
Grund: Sonderurlaub (Todesfall)
3. Dezember 1942
und Gruppenführer
7. vom bis nach Allenstein
Grund:
den
Leutnant z. S. und Gruppenführer
8. vom 6.9. bis nach
Grund:
den
Leutnant z. S. und Gruppenführer
37

2. Sicherungsdivision Prf. Nr 78E
Ausweis
(gültig bis 30 SEP. 1943)
Dieser Ausweis ist nur gültig in Verbindung mit einem Truppen-, Personalausweis oder Soldbuch.
Der Mtr. Ob. Gfr. Klinowski
Dienststelle
von der Feldpostnummer M 00012
ist berechtigt, sämtliche Häfen im Bereich von St. Malo bis Hoek v. Holland von und an Bord auf dem kürzesten Wege an Sonn- und Werktagen zu betreten.
Bemerkungen: Den Anweisungen der Wachmannschaften ist Folge zu leisten.
Ausgestellt am 1. JULI 1943
Unterschrift und Dienstgrad
Leutnant zur See und Gruppenführer

LE HAVRE den 16. Mai 1944
AUSWEIS Nr 12 246.
SOLDBUCH-Nr 67.
Der Mtr. Obgefr. Klinowski, Gerhard
ist berechtigt, das abgesperrte Hafengebiet zu betreten.
Grund dienstlich
Der Ausweis gilt vom 16.5. 1944 bis 16.8. 1944
Der Ausweis hat nur Gültigkeit in Verbindung mit einem Lichtbild-Ausweis.
DER HAFENKOMMANDANT - Le Havre
I. A.

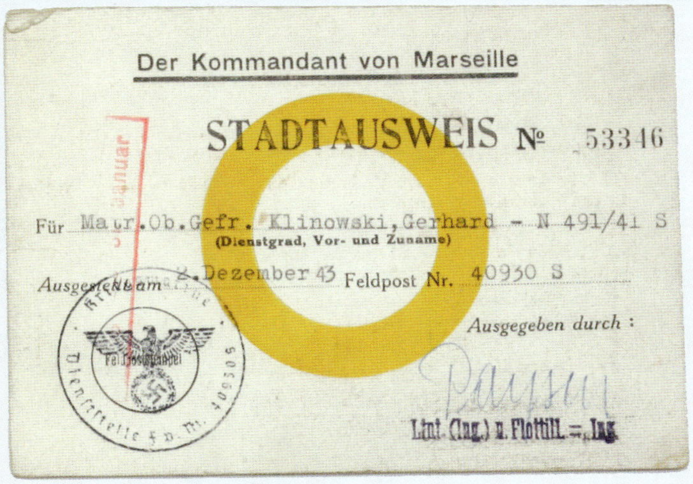
Der Kommandant von Marseille
STADTAUSWEIS № 53346
Für Matr.Ob.Gefr. Klinowski,Gerhard - N 491/41 S
(Dienstgrad, Vor- und Zuname)
Ausgestellt am 2.Dezember 43 Feldpost Nr. 40930 S
Ausgegeben durch :
Lnt. (Ing.) u. Flottill. - Ing.

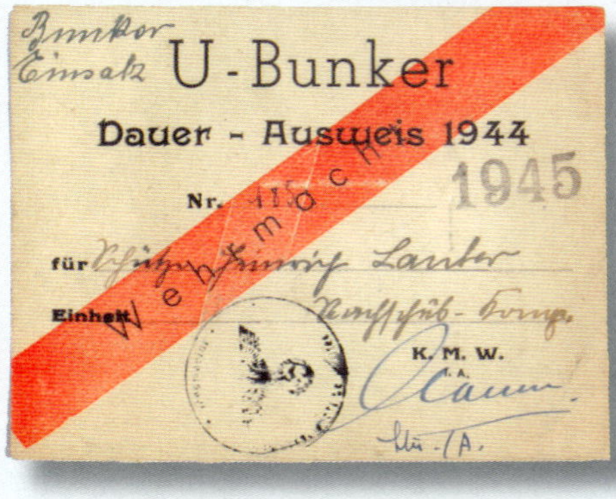

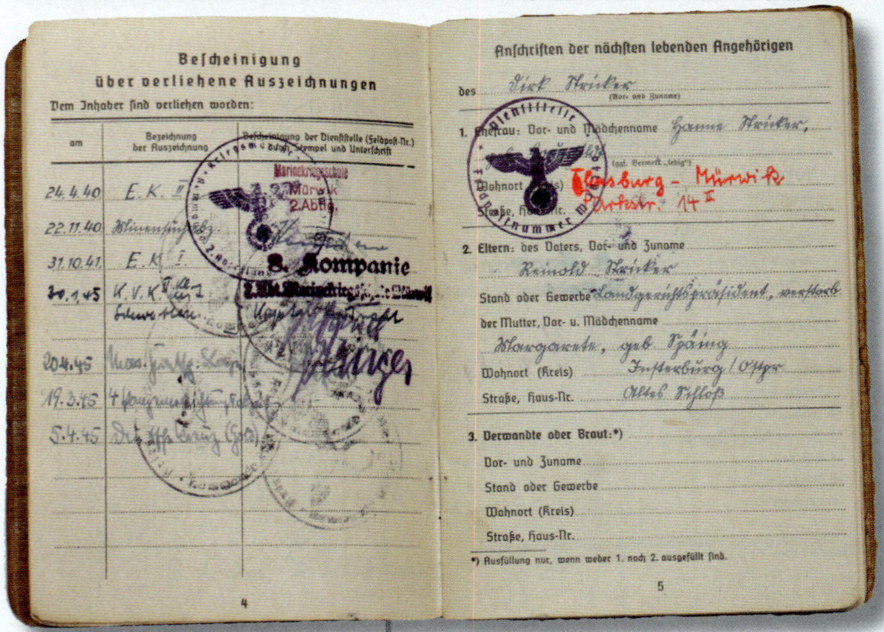

The *Soldbuch* was the same for officers, petty officers and enlisted men alike. Our *Kapitänleutnant's* decorations, according to the entries in his *Soldbuch*, included both classes of the *Eisernes Kreuz*. (Collection of P.-M. Rousseau)

Soldbuch and two more identity cards of a *Marine-Artillerist* deployed at the *K.M.W. (Kriegsmarinewerft* (*Kriegsmarine* dockyard) at La Pallice. (Private collection)

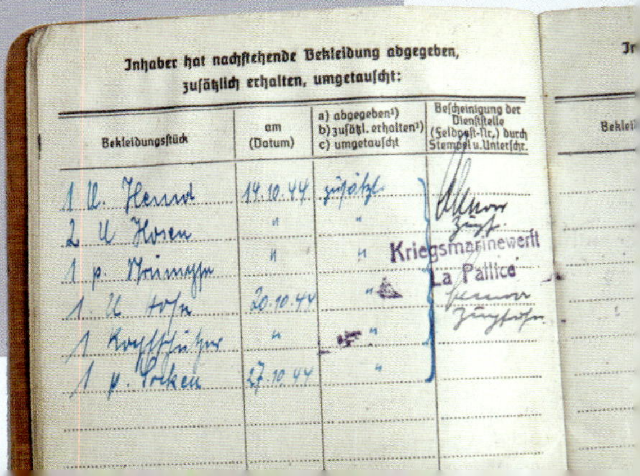

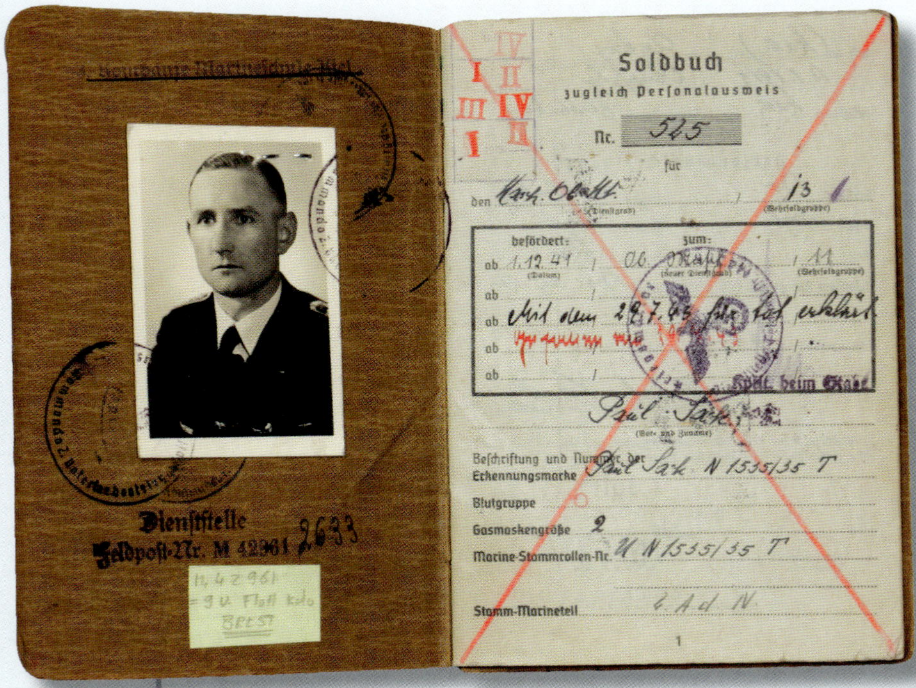

When a soldier fell in action, his *Soldbuch* was marked 'void' by red crosses. This naval officer served at the end in the *9. U-Flotille*, based in Brest. (Collection of P.-M. Rousseau)

The *Wehrpass* (military service record), which recorded the bearer's entire military career, was kept by his unit during his active service. There were three different *Wehrpass* types. The earliest (issued between 1935-37) displays on its front cover the *"Wehrmacht* eagle" (with drooping wings) and below this the word *'Wehrpass'* in *Fraktur* (Gothic) script. In the rectangular box below was stamped the soldier's *Wehrmacht* branch. The second type (issued between 1937-42), displayed the national emblem with outstretched wings. The final type (between 1942-45) differed from its predecessors in that the word *'Wehrpass'* was printed in Latin script. (Collection of P.-M. Rousseau)

When a soldier fell, it was also noted in his *Wehrpass* – in this case also with a stamp. The "closed" document was then given to the bereaved. (Collection of P.-M. Rousseau)

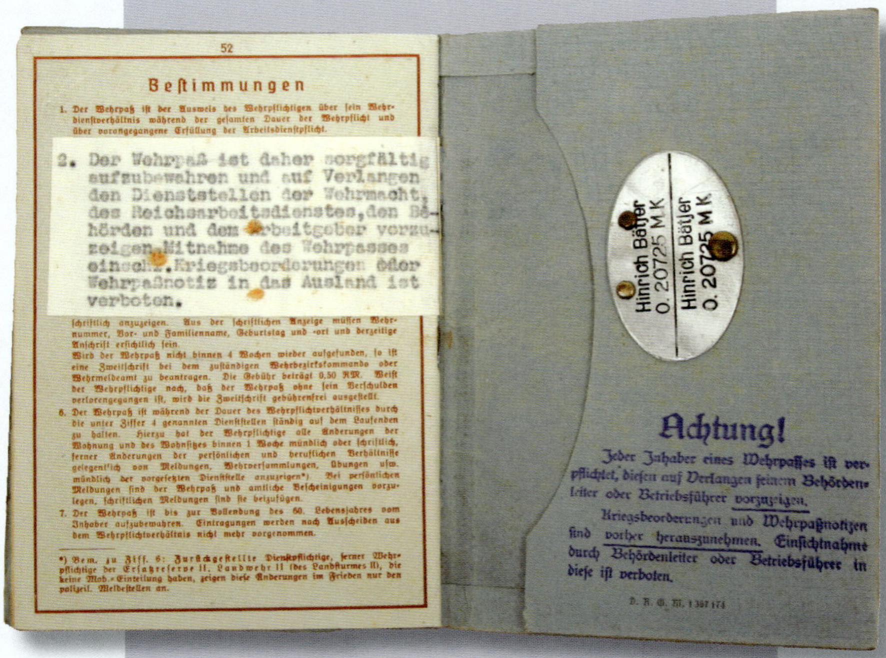

Wehrpass of the first type with its protective case. At the back, the soldier's identity tag is also fastened inside the pass. (Private collection)

Photo identity card of a worker, who worked for the *Kriegsmarine* in the oil depot at Achim (southeast of Bremen). (Private collection)

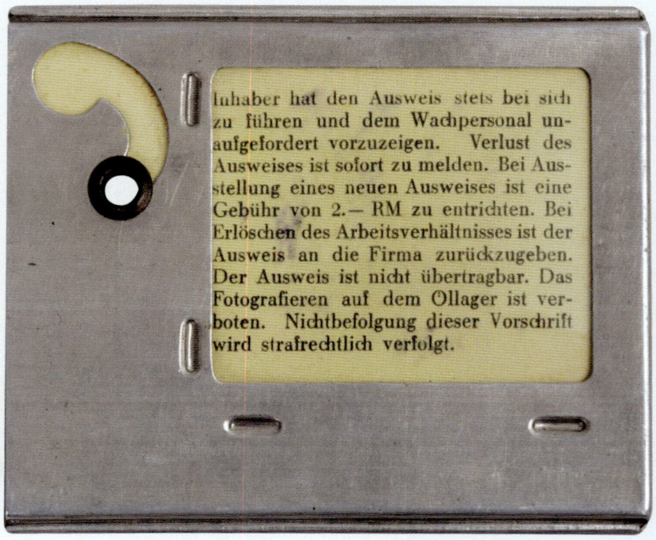

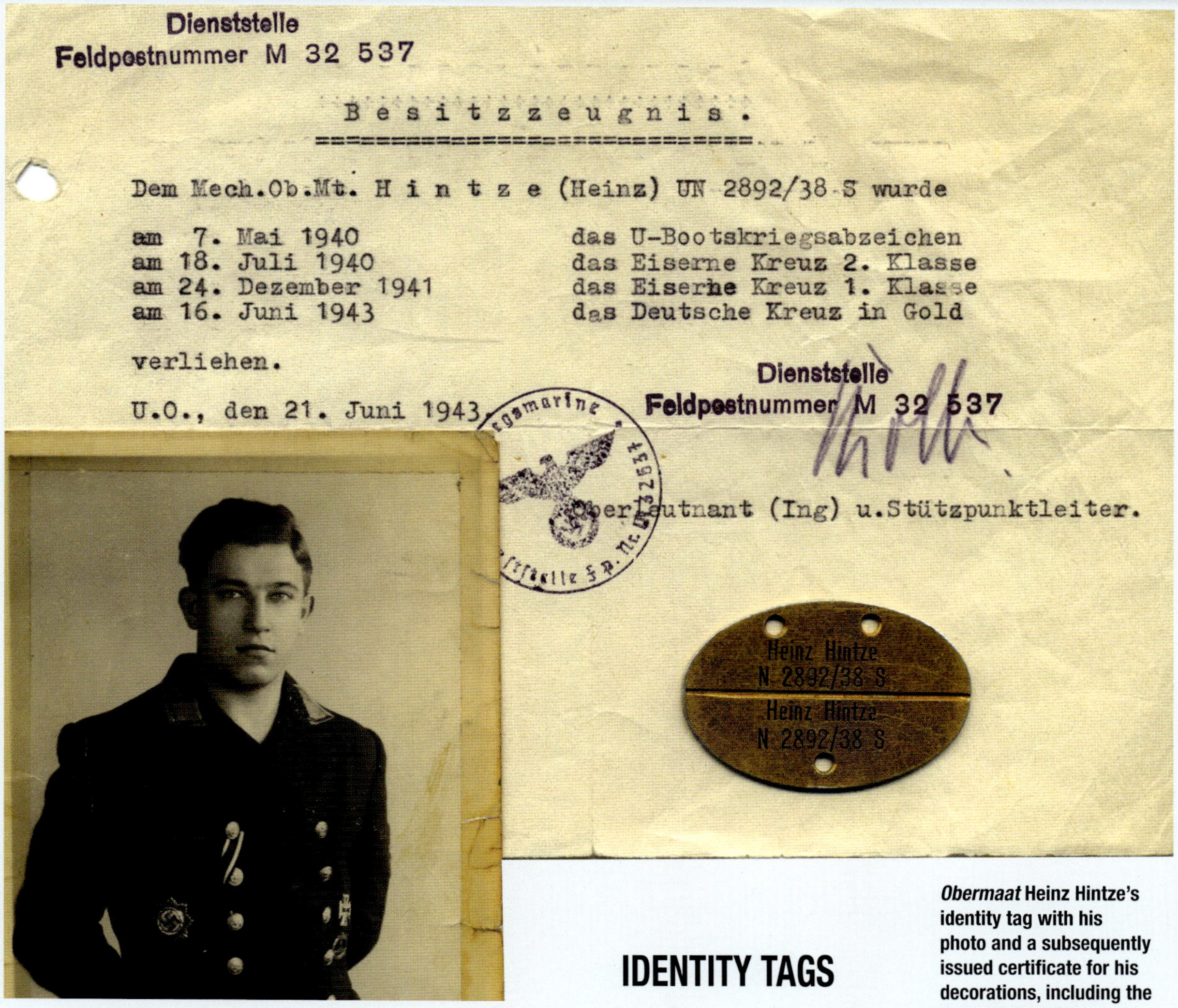

Dienststelle
Feldpostnummer M 32 537

Besitzzeugnis.

Dem Mech.Ob.Mt. Hintze (Heinz) UN 2892/38 S wurde

am 7. Mai 1940 das U-Bootskriegsabzeichen
am 18. Juli 1940 das Eiserne Kreuz 2. Klasse
am 24. Dezember 1941 das Eiserne Kreuz 1. Klasse
am 16. Juni 1943 das Deutsche Kreuz in Gold

verliehen.

U.O., den 21. Juni 1943.

Dienststelle
Feldpostnummer M 32 537

Oberleutnant (Ing) u.Stützpunktleiter.

Obermaat Heinz Hintze's identity tag with his photo and a subsequently issued certificate for his decorations, including the *Deutsches Kreuz* in gold. (Private collection)

IDENTITY TAGS

Identity tags for petty officers and enlisted men, made of aluminum bronze (top) or anodized aluminum (bottom): The first line gives the soldier's first and last name. In the second line, the muster roll number was imprinted, which began with the letter 'N' or 'O '(depending on belonging to the Marine station "North Sea" in Wilhelmshaven or the Marine station *"Ostsee"* ("Baltic") in Kiel); this was followed by the man's serial number within the year he entered service, and then, usually after a slash, the year itself (without '19'). Next came the rating ID – until 1941, these were repeatedly altered – in the form of one or two letters, such as: 'S' - seaman rating, 'T' - technical rating, 'M' - mobilization recruitment, 'K'- naval artillery or military driver rating. From 1942, the word *'Kriegsmarine'* was imprinted, rather than the name, and the blood group was added. Volunteers from the East (Balts, Ukrainians, Caucasians, Galicians) wore ID tags with the inscription *'Kriegsmarine Ostlegionär'* ('Eastern legionnaire') on one side and their first and last name and number on the other. (Private collection)

Identification tag for an employee or worker of the *Kriegsmarine* duty station in Bordeaux, who worked in the *U-Boot* base there. There were also some civilian personnel who worked at the *Kriegsmarine* shipyards in occupied areas, who were known as the *Wehrmachtgefolge* (*"Wehrmacht* auxiliaries or attendants"). (Private collection)

THE *KRIEGSMARINE* SHIPYARDS

The Western shipyard achievement badge. This badge was introduced for workers in the *Kriegsmarine* shipyards in the West, and was awarded "in recognition of exemplary performance and leadership." The badge was worn on the jacket or coat lapel. At least three versions of this badge are known. (Private collection)

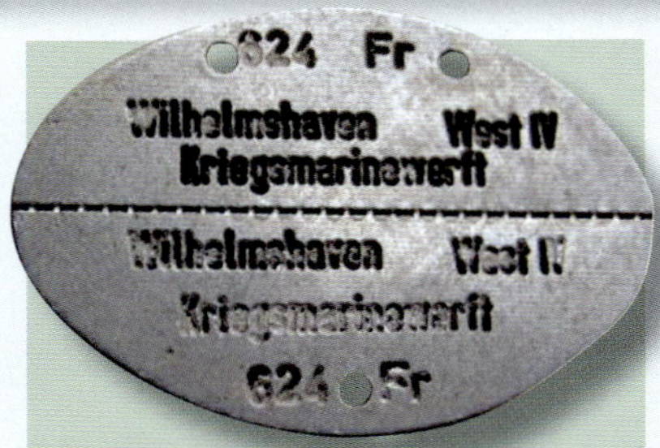

ID tag of a worker at the *Kriegsmarine* shipyard in Wilhelmshaven. (Private collection)

ID tag of another civilian who worked at the *Kriegsmarine* arsenal in Bordeaux. (Private collection)

Different service badges for civilian personnel who worked in the *Kriegsmarine U-Boot* bunker at La Rochelle-La Pallice. (Collection of P.-M. Rousseau)

Identification tag of a woman *Kriegsmarine* auxiliary, appointed in 1943. (Private collection)

Identification tag of an ordnance officer, who belonged to the "Crew 1940." (Private collection)

Aufenthalts - Genehmigung

FESTUNG LA ROCHELLE

Ausweis № 4719

für Jean Paul Marie

wohnhaft in La Flotte

Strasse und Haus-Nr. rue de l'electricité 6

Kennkarte Nr. 394 Gemeinde La Flotte

Der Festungskommandant
I. A.

Kaptlin. (M.A.) Ltn. (A.M.D.)

Residence permit for a French employee at the fortress of La Rochelle. (Private collection)

ID tag of an engineering officer, who had joined the *Marine* already in 1924. (Private collection)

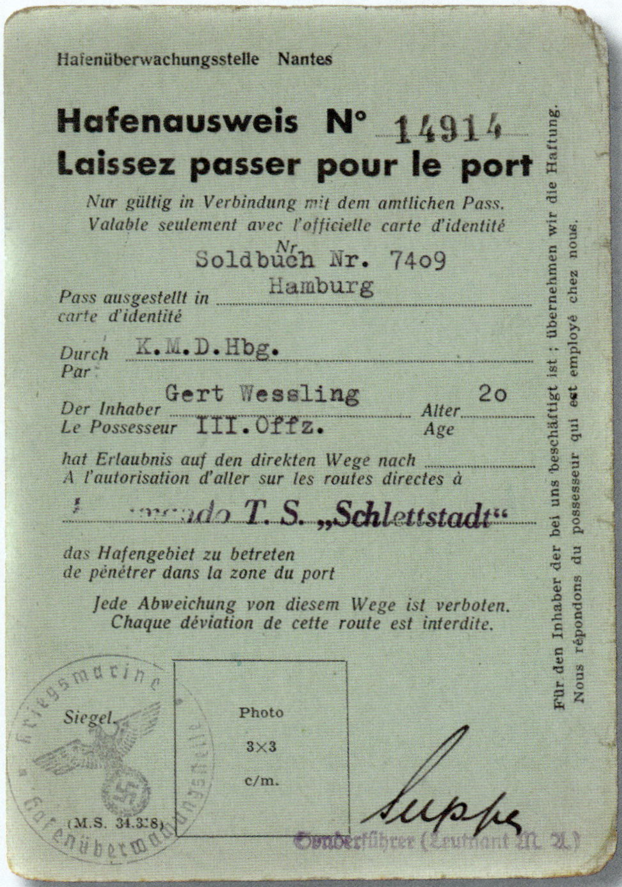
Hafenüberwachungsstelle Nantes

Hafenausweis N° 14914
Laissez passer pour le port

Nur gültig in Verbindung mit dem amtlichen Pass.
Valable seulement avec l'officielle carte d'identité

Soldbuch Nr. 7409
Pass ausgestellt in / carte d'identité: Hamburg
Durch / Par: K.M.D.Hbg.
Der Inhaber / Le Possesseur: Gert Wessling, III.Offz.
Alter / Age: 20
hat Erlaubnis auf den direkten Wege nach
A l'autorisation d'aller sur les routes directes à
T. S. „Schlettstadt"
das Hafengebiet zu betreten
de pénétrer dans la zone du port
Jede Abweichung von diesem Wege ist verboten.
Chaque déviation de cette route est interdite.

Siegel.
Photo 3×3 c/m.
(M.S. 34.3.8)

Für den Inhaber der bei uns beschäftigt ist; übernehmen wir die Haftung.
Nous répondons du posseseur qui est employé chez nous.

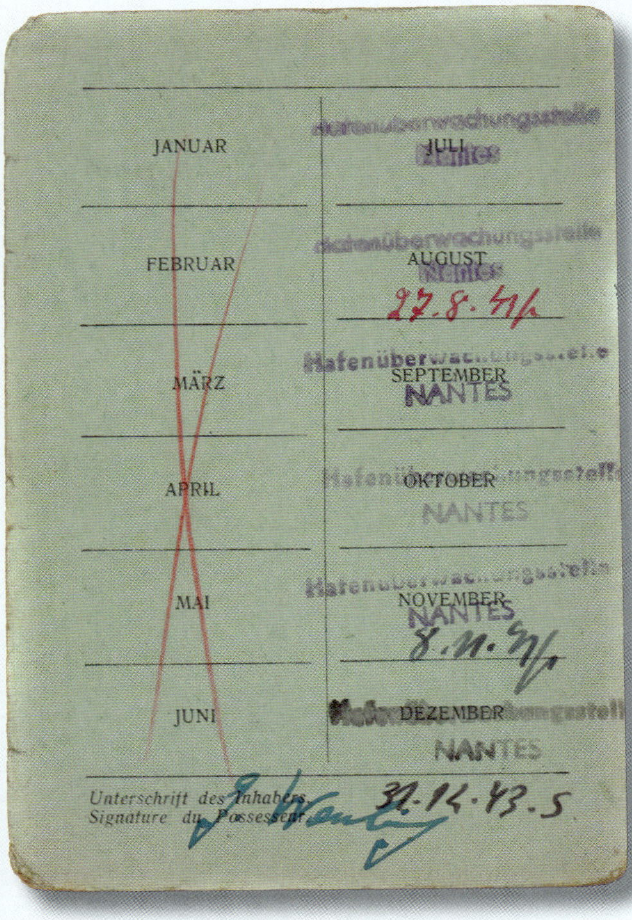
JANUAR | JULI
FEBRUAR | AUGUST 27.8.41
MÄRZ | SEPTEMBER NANTES
APRIL | OKTOBER NANTES
MAI | NOVEMBER NANTES 8.11.41
JUNI | DEZEMBER NANTES 31.12.43.5
Unterschrift des Inhabers
Signature du Possesseur

Harbor identity card for the port in Nantes, issued to a Hamburg German worker for the K.M.D. (*Kriegsmarine Dienststelle* (duty station). (Private collection)

STERBEBILDER (DEATH CARDS)

Zum Gedenken im Gebete
an
Georg Ehm
Schneidermeisterssohn von Reichersdorf
Sig.-Obergefreiter 22. U.-Jagdflottille
gestorben am 26. April 1945
im Kriegslazarett 4/561 Gardone/Italien
im 20. Lebensjahr.
R. I. P.
O Herr, gib ihm die ewige Ruhe und das ewige Licht leuchte ihm! Laß ihn ruhen in Frieden! Amen.
Mein Jesus, Barmherzigkeit! (300 Tage Ablaß)
Vater, in Deine Hände empfehle ich meinen Geist. (500 Tage Ablaß.)
Trausnitz-Druckerei, Landshut

Ein guter Sohn nahm Abschied
Vom lieben Elternhaus;
Ihn rief die Pflicht zu kämpfen
Bis zum letzten Lebenshauch.
O guter Sohn und Bruder,
Dein Abschied fiel uns schwer
Nun seh'n wir uns
In diesem Leben nimmermehr.

Death card of an *Obergefreiter* of the *22. U-Jagdflottille*, who died of his wounds on April 26, 1945, at just twenty years old, in a military hospital at Lake Garda in northern Italy. (Private collection)

Zum frommen Andenken
im Gebete
an unseren lieben Sohn und Bruder
Franz Xaver Untersteger
Landwirtssohn von Forstkastl
Matrose auf dem Schlachtschiff „Bismarck"
welcher am 27. Mai 1941 im 19. Lebensjahre den Heldentod fürs Vaterland erlitten hat.
Mein Jesus, Barmherzigkeit!
Gebr. Geiselberger, Altötting

Death card of a sailor on the BISMARCK, who died when the battleship sank on May 27, 1941. (Private collection)

Gebets-Andenken
an Gefreiten
Xaver Pritzl
von Frahels
welcher am 5. September 1943
im Alter von 19½ Jahren
bei einem schweren Kanonengefecht
in Südfrankreich
den Heldentod starb.

Ob wir den Ort, an dem du starbst,
Wohl jemals sehen werden?
Fern der Heimat ruht dein Leib
In kalter fremder Erden.
Nicht durften wir zum letztenmal
Die liebe Hand dir drücken,
Nicht deinen Grabeshügel still
Mit Liebesrosen schmücken.

Ludwig Lembergers Nachf., Lam.

Er ruhe in Frieden!

Death card of a *Gefreiter* who fell on September 5, 1943 in a battle in southern France. (Private collection)

Zum Gedenken
an den
Leutnant zur See
K. Gerhard Schwaiger
Inh. des E. K. I, II, U-Bootabz. mit Spange
geb. am 4. 11. 1922 in Göggingen
gefallen am 20. 8. 1944 im Kanal
Höhe von Le Havre

Mein Jesus Barmherzigkeit!
Hlgst. Herz Jesu ich vertraue auf Dich!

Death card of an officer. The twenty-one-year-old *Leutnant zur See* was lost with his *U-Boot* in the English Channel, on August 20, 1944. (Private collection)

Der Georg Jakstadt
(Vor- und Zuname)
erhält die Erlaubnis, nach Ablegung der Prüfung ein
Kraftfahrzeug mit Antrieb durch
der Klasse == 2 == zu führen.
Paris, den 30 ten April 1941
Kommandierender Admiral in Frankreich.
(Stempel) im Auftrage
Liste Nr 208/194.1
Freg. Kapitän (Ing.)
Nach bestandener Prüfung ausgehändigt
Paris, den 30 ten April 1941
Der Wehrmacht-Kraftfahr-Sachverständige
Liste Nr 208/1941
(Stempel)
Eigenhändige Unterschrift des Inhabers:

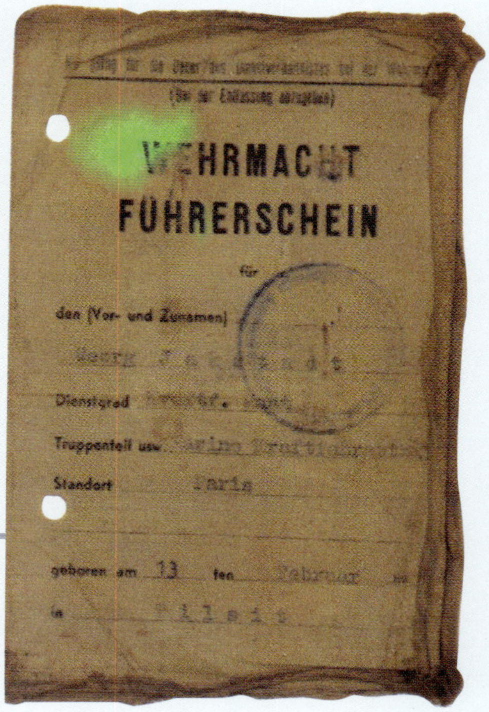

WEHRMACHT
FÜHRERSCHEIN
für
den (Vor- und Zunamen) Georg Jakstadt
Dienstgrad
Truppenteil usw.
Standort Paris
geboren am 13 ten Februar
in Tilsit

This *Wehrmacht* driver's license for a petty officer was issued in 1941 in Paris. (Private collection)

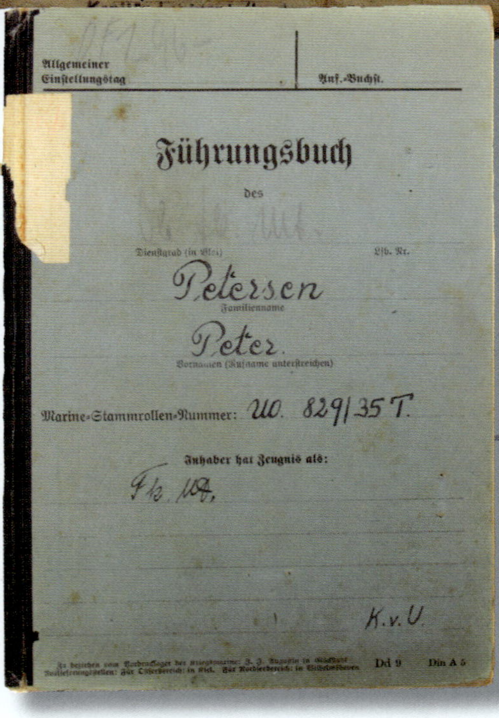

Allgemeiner Einstellungstag
Anf.-Buchst.
Führungsbuch
des
Dienstgrad (in Blei)
Lfd. Nr.
Petersen
Familienname
Peter
Vornamen (Rufname unterstreichen)
Marine-Stammrollen-Nummer: UO. 829/35 T.
Inhaber hat Zeugnis als:
K.v.U.
Dd 9 Din A 5

Kriegsmarine Führungsbuch (conduct book). This document was used by the troop recruitment division for every serviceman up to *Oberfähnrich*, and contained all of his appointments, promotions, punishments, leave, time at sea outside home waters, and all personal changes (e.g. marriage, birth of a child, etc.). In addition, training and decorations as well as medical examinations were to be listed in the conduct book. (Collection of P.-M. Rousseau)

Portepee petty officers with various items of equipment (watch, Morse lamp, binoculars, and inflatable life jacket. (Photographic reenactments – Private collection)

Signal lamps, also known as Morse lamps, *("Klappbuchse"* in slang ("collapsible/folding jacks")), were to be found on all *Kriegsmarine* ships. The large lever on its left side served for optical transmission of the short and long Morse characters. (Private collection)

Die Kriegsmarine

HEFT 23

BERLIN · ERSTES DEZ.-HEFT 1942
HEFTPREIS 25 PFENNIG FREI HAUS

DEUTSCHE MARINE-ZEITUNG

HERAUSGEGEBEN MIT UNTERSTÜTZUNG DES OBER-KOMMANDOS DER KRIEGSMARINE

Funkspruch des Führerbootes an den Verband

Foto: PK Name nicht angegeben, PBZ

The cover picture of this magazine *"Die Kriegsmarine,"* shows a signalman sending a message with a Morse lamp. (Private collection)

It is astounding how many pieces of equipment there are, which display a *Kriegsmarine* acceptance stamp. These included the most varied nautical instruments, ship fittings, optical devices of all kinds, and so forth. The suppliers were both from the German *Reich* and the occupied regions.

The goods available in the canteen were also extremely diverse, and the canteen offerings varied according to the region where the soldiers were quartered. These offerings included commemorative plates, beer mugs, cigarette cases, wooden models of ships and *U-Boots*, wall plaques bearing the name of the military base or unit, and so forth.

Christmas time gave the military superiors a good opportunity to give their men presents, to express their appreciation – such as books with a personal dedication from the formation leader.

There are two different manufacturer's labels, with serial number and other information, on this 20-cm *Marine Einheits-Scheinwerfer* (standard signal lamp), *ESw 20*, as the Morse lamp was officially called. (Private collection)

A *Maat* signalling in Morse code. Note the power cable needed to operate the *"Klappbuchse."* (Private collection)

BINOCULARS

Marine **binoculars 7x50, short pre-war model. The letter 'N' indicates that the glasses belonged to the North Sea station. (Private collection)**

Portraits of two *U-Boot* men equipped with the short 7x50 *Marine* binoculars. (Private collection)

A *Leutnant z. See* scans the horizon with 7x50 binoculars. (Private collection)

7x50 binoculars, long model, with black leather case and rubber covers. The manufacturer's code 'beh' was used by Ernst Leitz GmbH (Inc.) in Wetzlar. (Collection of P.-M. Rousseau)

Marine binoculars 7x50 with leather case. The stamp markings are those of the *Kriegsmarine*, and here we again see the 'N' of the North Sea station. The mark 'H.W.O.' on the case show that these glasses were intended for the Second *Wachoffizier* (Watch Officer). (Collection of P.-M. Rousseau)

Several binoculars are lined up ready at hand on the bridge of a *U-Boot*, just before she puts to sea for the next patrol. Note the rubber cases (for protection against spray). (Collection of P.-M. Rousseau)

This model of the *U-Boot* binoculars 7x50 was made especially for *U-Boot* crews by the Carl Zeiss company in Jena between 1943 and 1945. (Collection of P.-M. Rousseau)

This *Schnellboot* crewman is clocking the timing of a just-fired torpedo with his stopwatch. Around his neck hang *Marine* binoculars 7x50 with rubber spray protectors. (Private collection)

A *U-Boot Kommandant* on the bridge of his boat. His glasses are also protected by a coating of hard rubber. (Private collection)

Two views from the bridge of a *U-Boot*, where we can see, besides the *U-Boot* glasses, a so-called *UZO (U-Boot Zieloptik* (target optical sight) – used for targeting when shooting on the surface). (Private collection)

10x80 *Doppelfernrohr* (service binoculars or periscope binocular) with case. The manufacturer of this piece, used for targeting ships, was the Optische Präzisions-Werke GmbH (Precision Optical Works) in Warsaw. (Private collection)

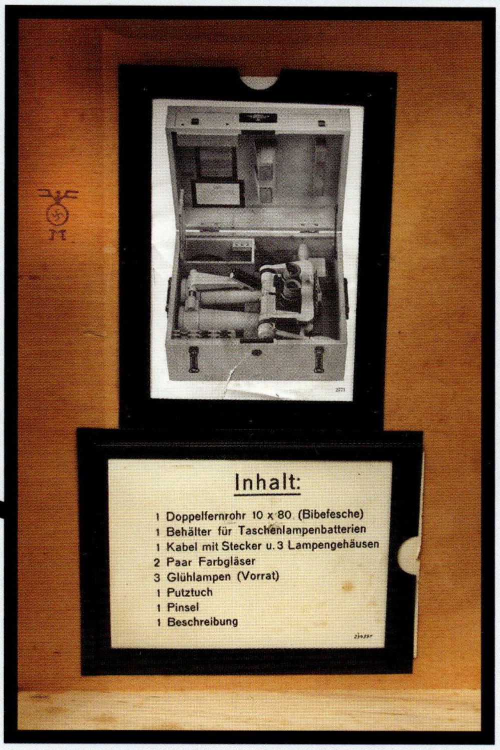

Standard *Trommelsextant* (drum sextant) (manufactured by the C. Plath company) with its accompanying wooden case; in the lid is the inspection certificate. There are *Kriegsmarine* acceptance stamps on both the sextant and its case, both with the same number. (Collection of P.-M. Rousseau)

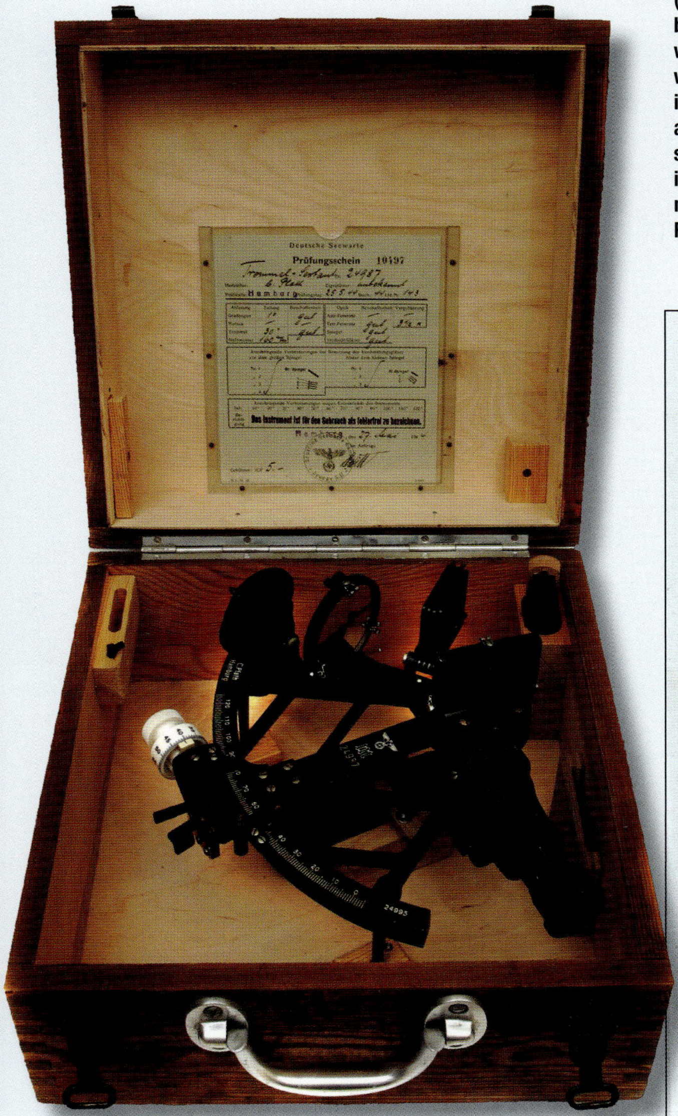

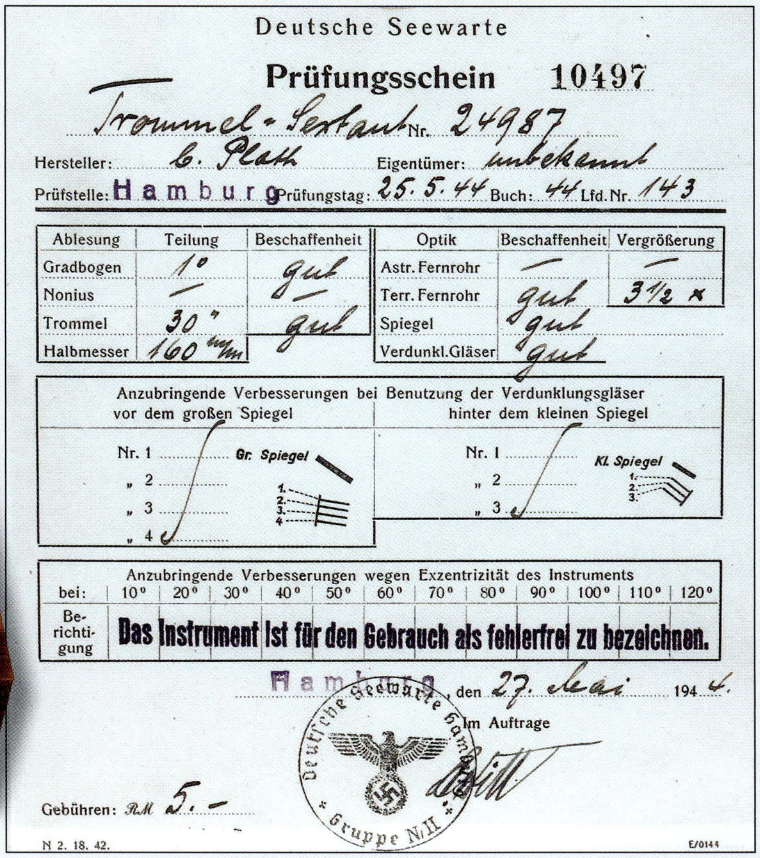

Deutsche Seewarte

Prüfungsschein 10497

Trommel-Sextant Nr. 24987

Hersteller: C. Plath Eigentümer: unbekannt

Prüfstelle: Hamburg Prüfungstag: 25.5.44 Buch: 44 Lfd. Nr. 143

Ablesung	Teilung	Beschaffenheit	Optik	Beschaffenheit	Vergrößerung
Gradbogen	1°	gut	Astr. Fernrohr	—	—
Nonius	—	—	Terr. Fernrohr	gut	3½ x
Trommel	30″	gut	Spiegel	gut	
Halbmesser	160 mm		Verdunkl. Gläser	gut	

Anzubringende Verbesserungen bei Benutzung der Verdunklungsgläser

vor dem großen Spiegel		hinter dem kleinen Spiegel	
Nr. 1	Gr. Spiegel	Nr. 1	Kl. Spiegel
„ 2		„ 2	
„ 3		„ 3	
„ 4			

Anzubringende Verbesserungen wegen Exzentrizität des Instruments

bei:	10°	20°	30°	40°	50°	60°	70°	80°	90°	100°	110°	120°
Berichtigung	Das Instrument ist für den Gebrauch als fehlerfrei zu bezeichnen.											

Hamburg, den 27. Mai 1944.

Im Auftrage

Deutsche Seewarte Hamburg Gruppe N.II

Gebühren: RM 5.—

N 2. 18. 42. E/0144

U-Boot men being trained on the Dräger diving lung. The purpose was to enable them to get out of a submerged *U-Boot*. (Private collection)

LIFE JACKETS

This figure of a *U-Boot* man is wearing one of the *Kriegsmarine's* simplest life vest models. (Private collection)

Sailors of a sea-going unit with the simple type lifejackets. The colors ranged from gray-beige to black. (Private collection)

Front and back of a *Kriegsmarine* inflatable life jacket. It was inflated using a gas cartridge; the shoulder section could be inflated more by using the mouthpiece. (Collection of P.-M. Rousseau)

Here, the life jacket shown above, worn for a rescue drill. (Private collection)

Kommandant of a Schnellboot **or** ***Räumboot*** **wearning an inflatable life jacket. (Private collection)**

Figure of a *Leutnant zur See* with a simplified version of the inflatable life jacket. (Private collection)

These *Portepee* petty officers are wearing two different versions of the inflatable life jacket. (Private collection)

Backless inflatable life jacket. Only the straps cross the back in this model. (Collection of P.-M. Rousseau)

A *U-Boot* man wearing the inflatable life jacket shown above on the deck of his boat. (Private collection)

At first glance, this picture appears to show a member of the *Kriegsmarine*, but actually this serviceman belongs to the *Luftwaffe Seenotdienst* (Air Force naval emergency service), which was deployed to identify naval emergencies and rescue downed aircrews and shipwrecked sailors. On his left forearm we can see the appropriate tactical service badge. His kapok life jacket is the *Luftwaffe* model, with device number 10-76. (Private collection)

Luftwaffe tactical badge for seamen. The badge, inaugurated in 1936, was worn by crews of the air traffic control and *Flugbetriebsboote* (flight operations rescue boats) of this branch of the *Wehrmacht*. (Private collection)

Figure of a *U-Boot* man with a *Luftwaffe* inflatable life jacket, which were occasionally also found in the *Kriegsmarine*. (Private collection)

This figure of a *Matrose* is wearing a *Luftwaffe* kapok life jacket. (Private collection)

Marine wall clocks were found on almost all *Kriegsmarine* ships and boats. All models, large and small, bore the usual acceptance stamp of this *Wehrmacht* branch. (Private collection)

Smaller diameter (9.5-cm) wall clock, manufactured by Junghans. This model was found on smaller ships and also aboard *U-Boote*. (Private collection)

Version of the small *Marine* wall clock with the inscription *'Kriegsmarine.'* (Private collection)

Marine chronometer made by the company A. Lange & Söhne. (Collection of P.-M. Rousseau)

Below: Torpedo-stopwatch with the usual three-second revolution. The acceptance stamp is on the case back. (Collection of P.-M. Rousseau)

Above: *Kriegsmarine* observation watch with the corresponding acceptance stamp. This piece was made by Junghans. (Collection of P.-M. Rousseau)

Service wristwatches were issued to servicemen during their tour of duty. They were of both German and Swiss make. (Private collection)

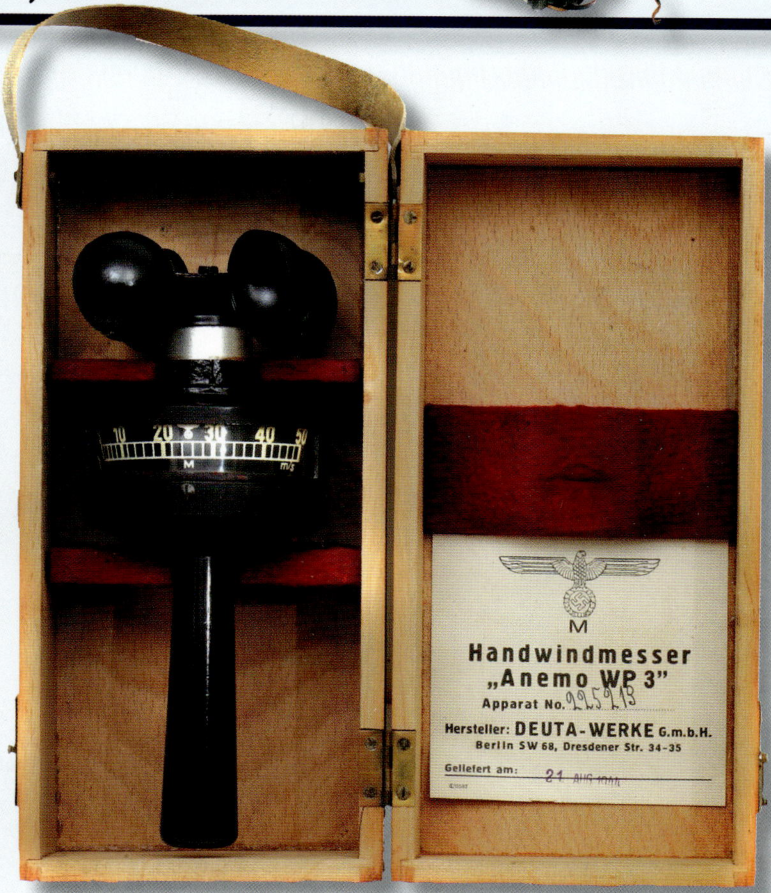

Hand-held wind gauge in its original wooden case. (Collection of P.-M. Rousseau)

NAVIGATION DEVICES

The celestial globe was used for roughly setting sextant measurements. (Collection of P.-M. Rousseau)

Double goniometer in its original wooden case; this detail shows the nameplate with acceptance stamp, manufacturer's code, and factory number. (Collection of P.-M. Rousseau)

This *Kriegsmarine* nameplate was found at Saint-Nazaire. The C. Plath company of Hamburg, whose logo we see here, manufactured nautical instruments. (Private collection)

Opposite: Marine nautical chart for the area of Lorient and the accompanying navigation instruments (protractor, marine compass, parallel ruler, and pencils). (Collection of P.-M. Rousseau)

BISKAYA BUCHT
KÜSTE VON FRANKREICH
LORIENT UND PORT-LOUIS
EINFAHRTEN UND REEDEN
MASSSTAB 1:10000
HÖHEN UND TIEFEN IN METERN
Allgemeine Erläuterung und Zeichenerklärung für die S.B.-Karten:
Wracks
KRIEGSMARINE

This *U-Boot* man checks the indicators on the control panel while submerging. (Private collection)

Radio devices like this were found aboard most *Kriegsmarine* ships. (Collection of P.-M. Rousseau)

Manometer for checking engine pressure. (Collection of P.-M. Rousseau)

Headphones with *Kriegsmarine* stamp markings. (Private collection)

U-Boot radio operator sending a Morse signal. (Private collection)

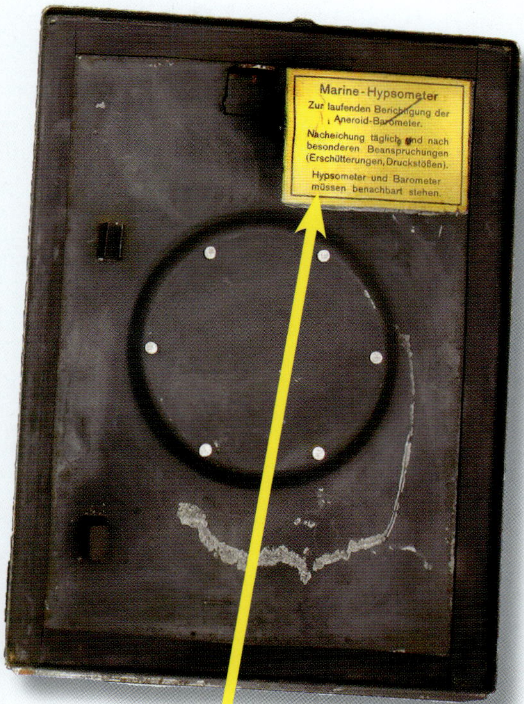

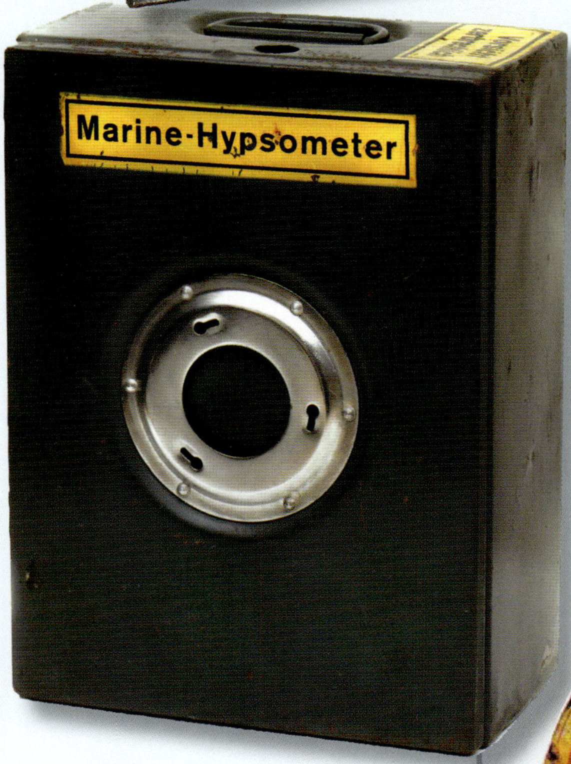

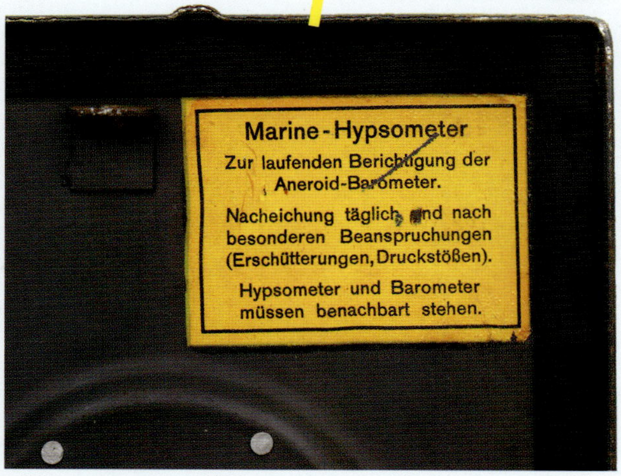

Marine hypsometer, which measured the diving depth based on the water temperature. (Collection of P.-M. Rousseau)

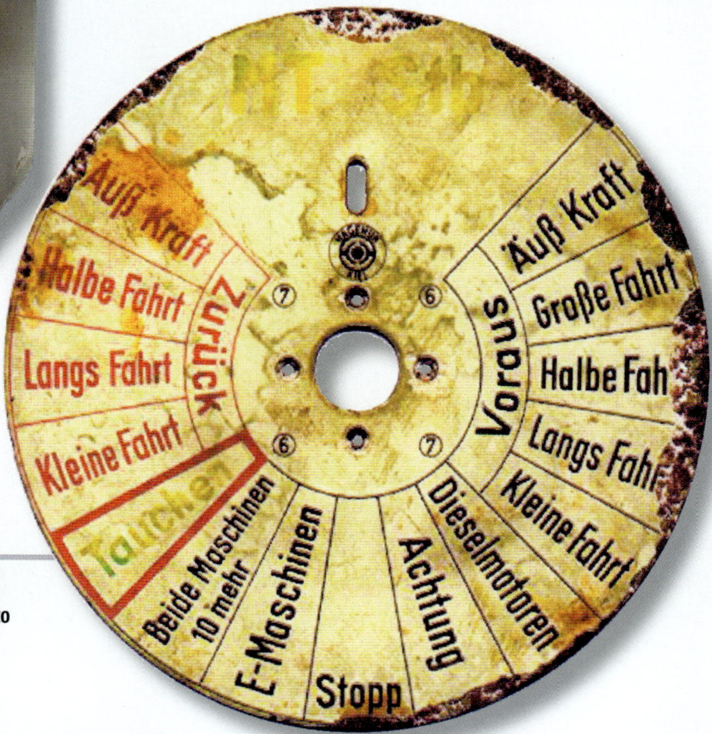

Engine room telegraph display. This device was used to transfer engine commands from the control room to the engine room. (Private collection)

Hand plane, with manufacturer's marks and acceptance stamp, as was used for repairs. (Private collection)

Diving knife. (Private collection)

Gyroscopic steering mechanism for torpedoes (here for training), this was used to set the pendulum lateral control of the "Aal" ("eel," slang for torpedo). (Collection of P.-M. Rousseau)

Two different *Kriegsmarine* lamps. The *Marine* also had its suppliers, which produced the thousands of different pieces of equipment necessary for the war machine to function. (Collection of P.-M. Rousseau)

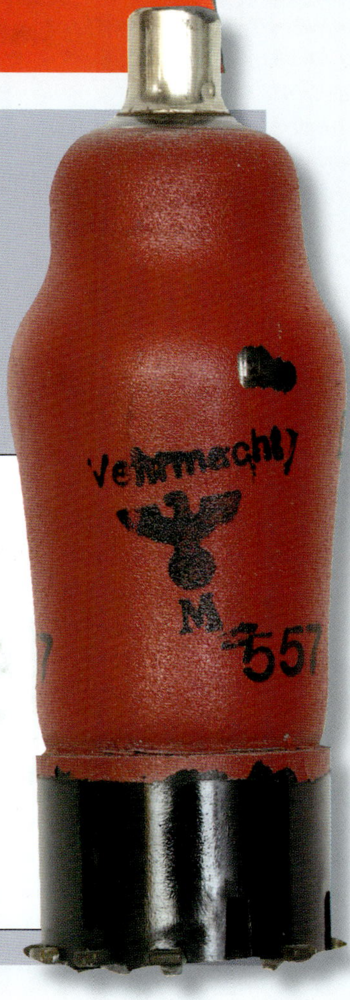

The most varied possible oilcans were used in the equipment and repair shops, as well as on *Kriegsmarine* ships and boats. Of course every item was numbered and stamped. (Private collection)

***Kriegsmarine* butchers in white work clothes. (Private collection)**

This canister was on board *U-Boot* U 385; its insignia and identification are engraved on the top. (Private collection)

Cooking oil canister, needed for food preparation on board. (Private collection)

Canister of fruit syrup, also for food preparation on board. (Collection of P.-M. Rousseau)

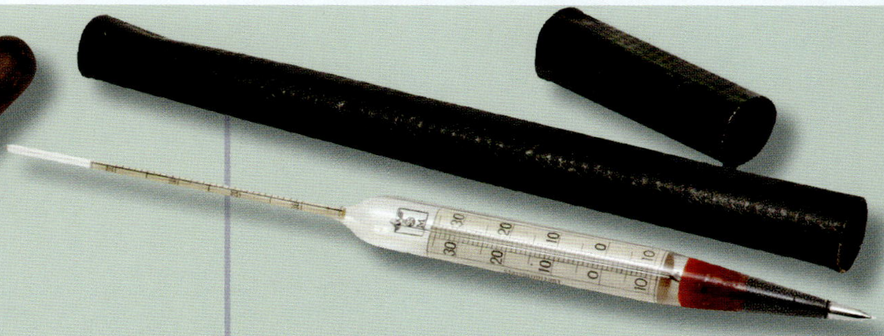

Hydrometer (with built-in thermometer) for measuring the acid density of batteries. (Collection of P.-M. Rousseau)

Powder thermometer. (Private collection)

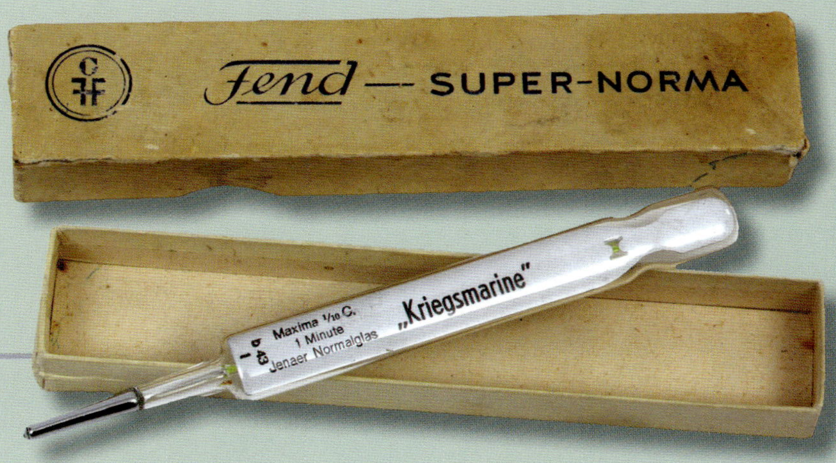

Kriegsmarine fever thermometer in original case. (Private collection)

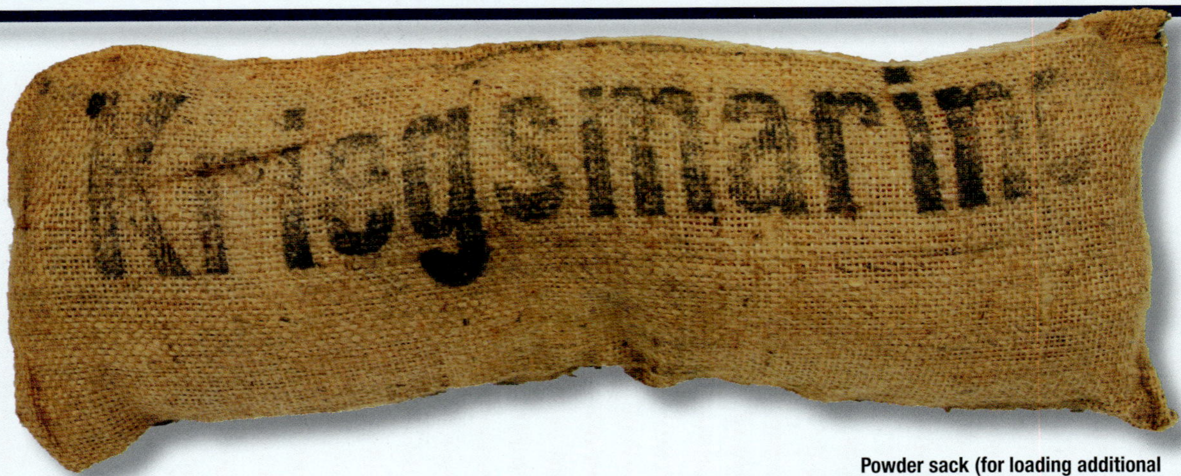

Powder sack (for loading additional supplies) with the *Kriegsmarine* stamp. (Private collection)

Boatswain's pipe. (Collection of P.-M. Rousseau)

For protection against sea water: Metal container for an 8.8-cm grenade cartridge. (Collection of P.-M. Rousseau)

Portepee petty officer "piping aboard" with the boatwain's pipe. This was how important visitors were greeted as they came aboard or went ashore. (Private collection)

Enameled sign plates like these, which identified the various pipes, etc. in the engine rooms, were found aboard the large warships. (Collection of P.-M. Rousseau)

Stamp markings of the Wilhelmshaven *Marineverpflegungsamt* (Naval supply depot) on a food sack (for potatoes, vegetables, etc.). (Private collection)

Dish towel and napkin with *Kriegsmarine* stamps. (Collection of P.-M. Rousseau)

Dish towel with stamp of the *Marine* base at Lorient. (Private collection)

Dish towels with the inscription *'Kriegsmarine.'* The colors and pattern varied depending on the manufacturer. (Private collection)

"Smutjes" (slang for cooks) in work clothes. The man at left has a *'Kriegsmarine'* dishtowel tied around his waist. (Private collection)

Kriegsmarine **service issue wool blanket. (Private collection)**

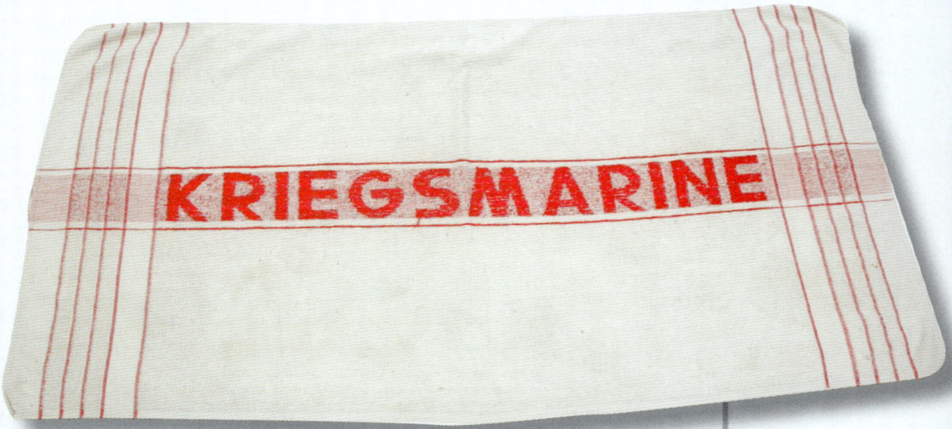

Hand towel with jacquard woven lettering *'Kriegsmarine.'* (Private collection)

Kriegsmarine **duffel bag (also called a "sea bag"). (Private collection)**

Other examples of *Marine* woolen blankets. The top one is in the earliest pattern issued, from 1935. (Private collection)

After arriving by rail, these sailors prepare to march into their quarters. Their duffel bags, containing all the serviceman's worldly goods, can be easily recognized. (Private collection)

Gray painted gas mask case. Gas masks were issued to all *Marine* personnel. For sea-going units, the cases, originally painted field-gray, were often repainted, usually with ship's gray camouflage color. (Private collection)

Gas masks and their cases. The nametag of the owner sewn on the mask band. (Private collection)

Waterproof document holders like these were used aboard ships. (Collection of P.-M. Rousseau)

Both deep sea divers are carrying a diving knife at the hip. (Private collection)

Bronze *Kriegsmarine* diving knife. (Private collection)

We can see the acceptance stamp on this diving knife. The knife was screwed into the round case, which was sealed with a rubber ring. (Private collection)

This framed wall plaque shows an artfully made *Kriegsmarine* battleship. (Collection of P.-M. Rousseau)

CANTEEN GOODS

Paperweight with a model torpedo and *U-Boot* war badge. (Collection of P.-M. Rousseau)

Servicemen could buy wall plaques like these in the canteen. Those here are from several *U-Flotillen.* (Collection of P.-M. Rousseau)

Wall plaque for the *U-Boote* U 437 and U 3029; both had elephants as mascots – and both were commanded by *Kptlt.* Hermann Lamby. (Collection of P.-M. Rousseau)

Wall plaque commemorating a tour of duty in Saint-Nazaire. (Private collection)

Carved wood model of a boat of the *29. U-Flotille*, which had its base in Toulon in 1943. (Private collection)

Enameled wall plaque of the *2. U-Flotille*, which was probably relocated to Lorient in 1941. (Collection of P.-M. Rousseau)

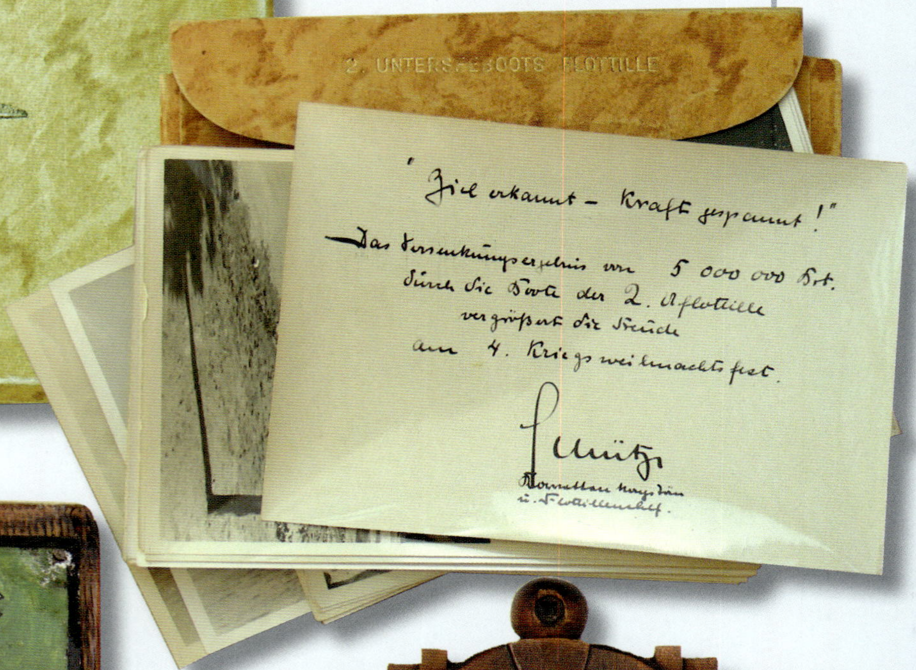

Jewelry case with commemorative photos of the *2. U-Flottille*, compiled for the fourth winter of the war (1942). (Private collection)

A wall plaque commemorating time spent in Brest is from 1944. (Private collection)

This wooden wall plaque is also from Brest and commemorates a minesweeper flotilla stationed there. (Private collection)

Commemorative plaque for the 1941 *"Kriegsmarine* Sports Festival" held in the Netherlands. (Private collection)

Carton for sweets with the symbol of the *1. U-Flottille* in Brest. (Private collection)

Commemorative wooden plate, possibly of the hospital ship KONSTANZ. (Collection of P.-M. Rousseau)

This platter was for sale in the canteens of the *2. U-Flotille*. It was made by the faience maker Henriot in Quimper, Brittany. (Private collection)

The Henriot company in Quimper also made this commemorative plate for Christmas 1942, intended for the servicemen of the duty station of the *Marinebefehlshaber* in western France. (Private collection)

Again, a commemorative plate for the wartime Christmas of 1941, and sold in the *2. U-Flotille* canteen. Also made by the Henriot company. (Private collection)

This commemorative plate, also made by Henriot, comes from one of the *Kriegsmarine* canteens in Brittany. (Private collection)

Ashtray for servicemen in a *Stammkompanie* (reception and training unit) of a landing flotilla stationed in Italy. (Private collection)

Christmas 1941. Commemorative plate for the *Marine* harbor unit in Rotterdam, Holland. (Collection P.-M. Rousseau)

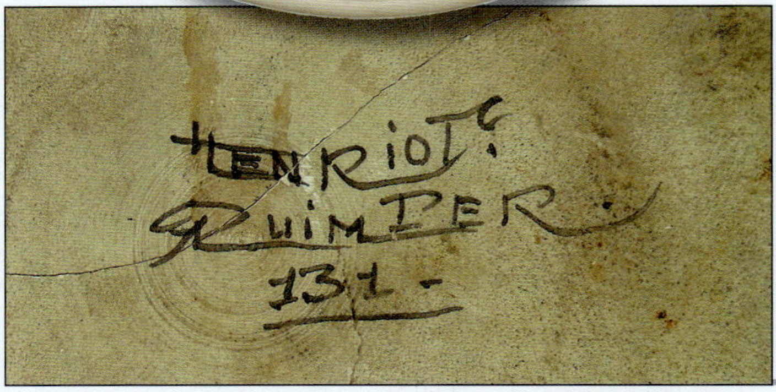

Faience tile, sold in the canteen of the Saint-Nazaire-based *6. U-Flotille.* This piece also comes from the Henriot factory in Quimper. (Private collection)

These two commemorative plates were made in 1943 for Christmas festivities for the *Marinegruppenkommando West* (Naval Group Command West), based since August 1940 in Paris. They represent "typical" Parisian street scenes. (Private collection)

Two members of the administration, legal, and supply rating who are stationed in Paris, celebrate living like "God in France" with a huge cigar. One can assume that the *Marine* personnel stationed in Paris were regarded with some amount of envy by their comrades in the sea-going units even the *U-Boot* forces. (Private collection)

Cigar box made of root wood (with contents). This exquisite Christmas present of the *Marinegruppenkommando West* for 1943 was probably only given to a select group. At the time, the *MGK West* was commanded by *Admiral* Theodore Krancke. (Private collection)

Here the multi-sided version of the *MGK West* plate, with the same designs. (Private collection)

Packs of cigarettes like these could also be bought in *Wehrmacht* canteens. (Private collection)

Whoever succeeded in getting hold of a special leave pass for entering greater Paris, as this group of *Marine* servicemen did, also wanted the typical souvenir photo in front of the Eiffel Tower. (Private collection)

Silver-plated decorative cup with the symbol of *U-Boot* U 553. (Collection of P.-M. Rousseau)

Silver cigarette box to commemorate the commissioning of U 553 on December 23, 1940. (Collection P.-M. Rousseau)

Such a silver cup was presented by the city of Kiel to every crewmember of U 47, for their victory in Scapa Flow. (Collection of P.-M. Rousseau)

Silver-plated decorative cup of the *6. U-Flotille* in Saint-Nazaire. (Private collection)

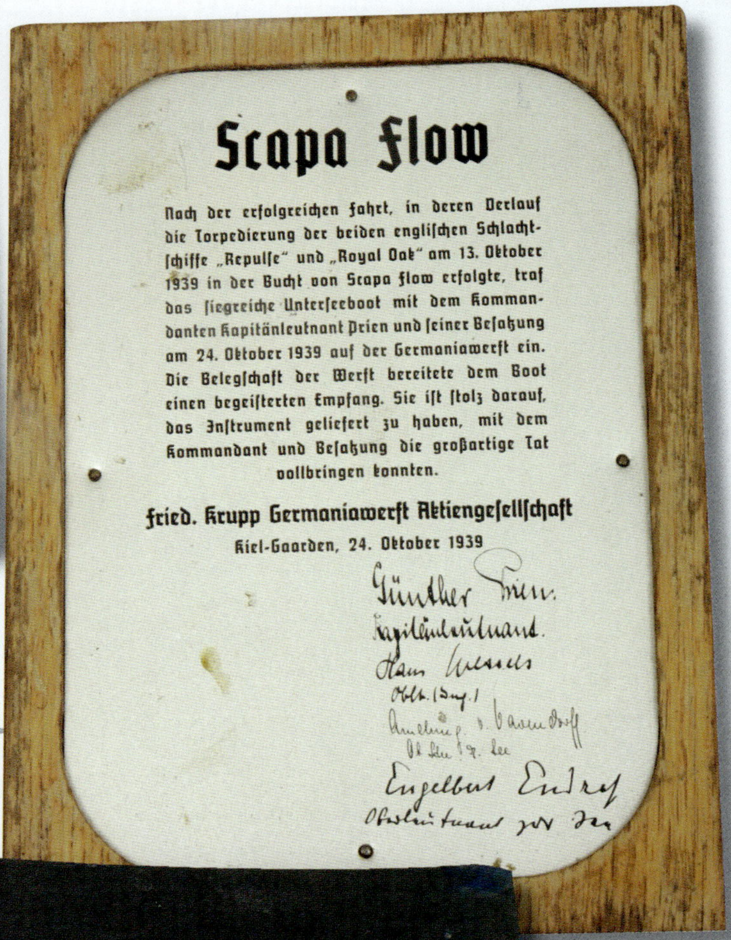

The victorious crew of U 47 under Günther Prien thanked the workforce of the Germania shipyard for their contribution to the success of the *U-Boot* war with this keepsake: An earpiece used during the successful raid on Scapa Flow. (Collection of P.-M. Rousseau)

Photo albums and wall plaques for the Paris-based *Marinekraftfahrabteilung* (motor transport unit) in memory of the years 1940-41. (Private collection)

Photo albums commemorating time in service. These could be bought in the *Kriegsmarine* canteens in various styles; here we see only a small selection. (Collection of P.-M. Rousseau and private)

This pre-war souvenir photo shows two crewmembers of the light cruiser LEIPZIG. (Private collection)

Front and back of a *Kriegsmarine* event badge of pressed cardboard. Such small pinned-on badges were sold to the civilian population, and the proceeds benefitted the aid funds for the respective squadrons, etc. (Private collection)

This peaked cap was for a child's uniform and was quite popular in the Third *Reich*. (Private collection)

This *Obergefreiter*, who is wearing the war badge for minehunter, *U-Boot* hunter, and security units on his pea coat, seems to be living out *"das Kind im Manne"* ("in every true man a child is hiding"), in this souvenir photo from a studio. (Private collection)

Kriegsmarine songbook. (Private collection)

Such humorous postcards were very popular among *Kriegsmarine* soldiers. (Private collection)

Propaganda postcard with *Marine* theme for "Postage Stamp Day." (Private collection)

Color propaganda postcard with the portrait of *Kapitänleutnant* Prien (by Wolfgang Willrich). (Private collection)

This propaganda postcard promotes the men of the *Kriegsmarine*. (Private collection)

The famous "periscope photo" shows Erich Topp in the control room of his U 552. The German *Reich* postal service issued a special stamp with this design in 1944. (Private collection)

Off the African coast, 1941. Photos of a war correspondent taken by one of his comrades. (Private collection)

6+4
GROSSDEUTSCHES REICH
Gläser
Farb-
Ausbauteil
-10°
Erich Topp

The two most-read *Kriegsmarine* newspapers: *"Gegen Engeland"* ("Against England") and *"Die Kriegsmarine."* (Private collection)

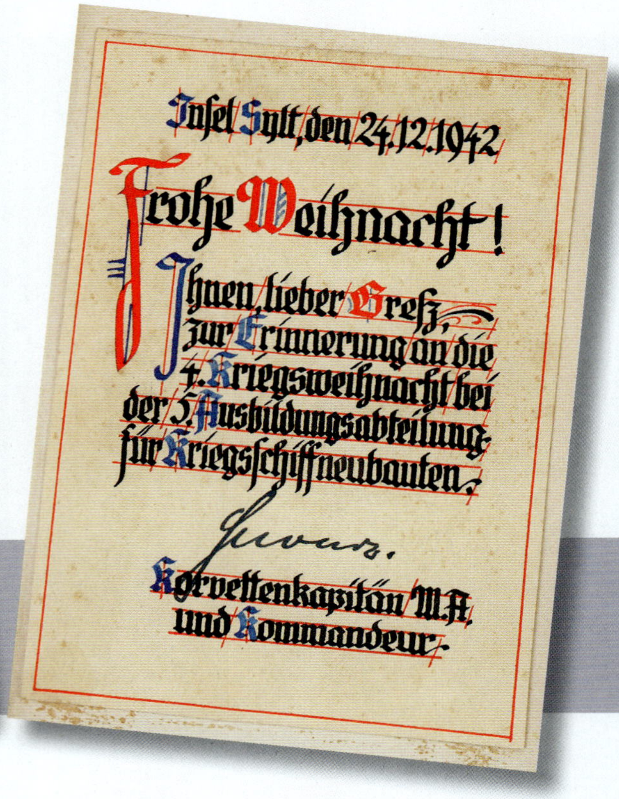

Razor blade packets with *Marine* theme. (Private collection)

Brochures like this were to recruit volunteers for service in the *Kriegsmarine*. (Private collection)

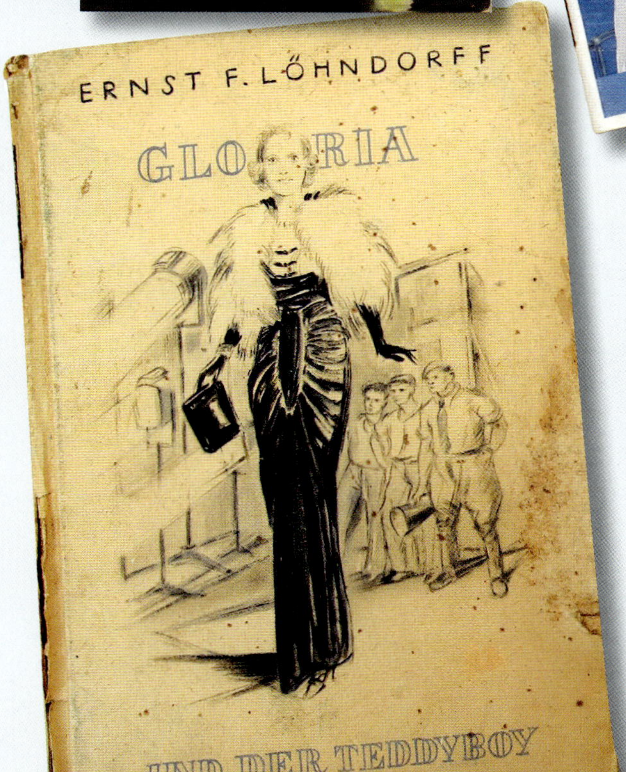

Above and opposite page: For Christmas, the *Kriegsmarine* formation and unit leaders often took the opportunity to express their appreciation to their men with greeting cards or with books or other gifts. (Private collection)

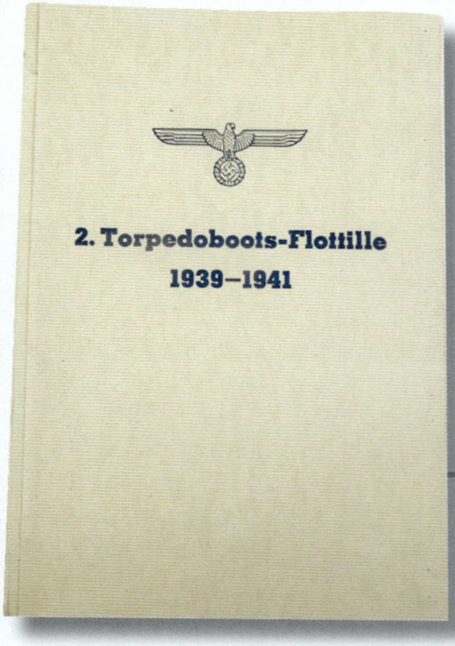

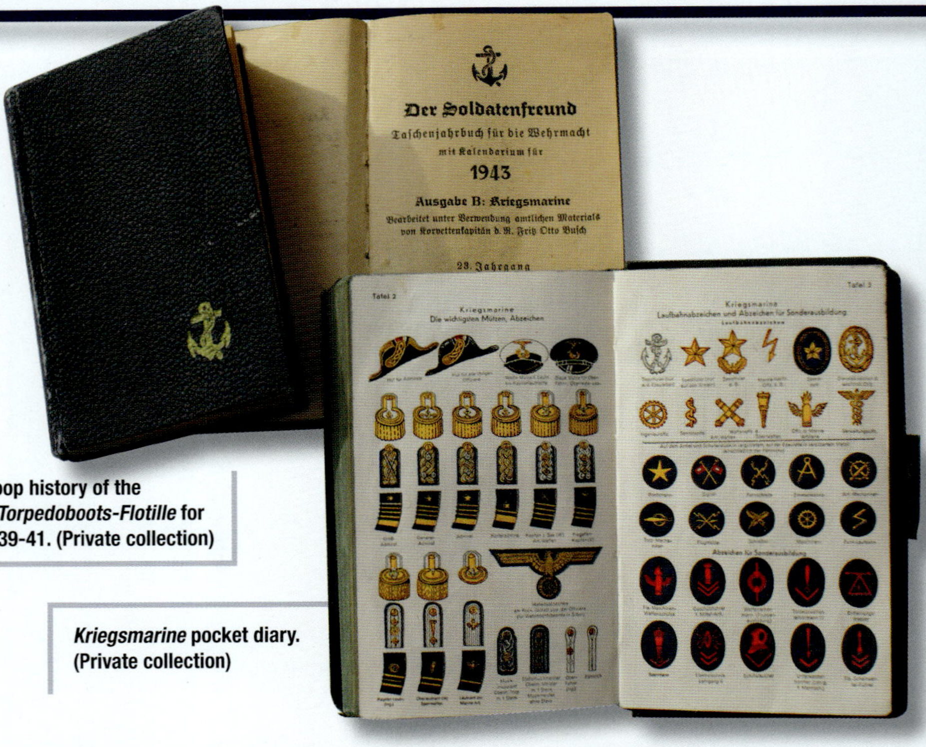

Troop history of the *2. Torpedoboots-Flotille* for 1939-41. (Private collection)

Kriegsmarine pocket diary. (Private collection)

German *Marine* calendar for 1942. (Private collection)

Kriegsmarine yearbook for 1937. (Private collection)

A *Kriegsmarine* primer on uniforms. (Private collection)

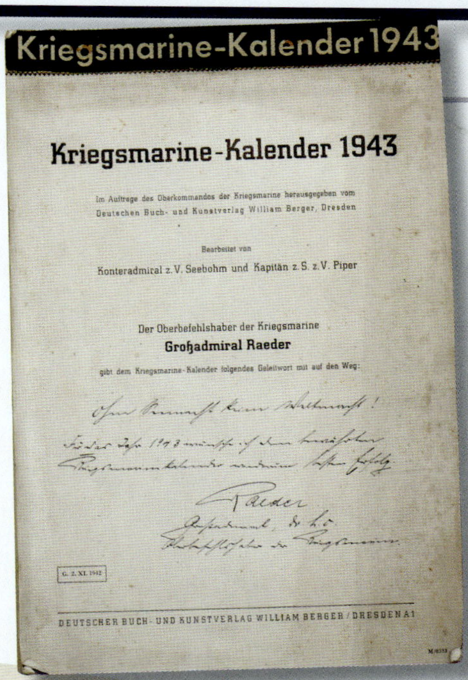

Still another *Kriegsmarine* calendar, this one for 1943. (Private collection)

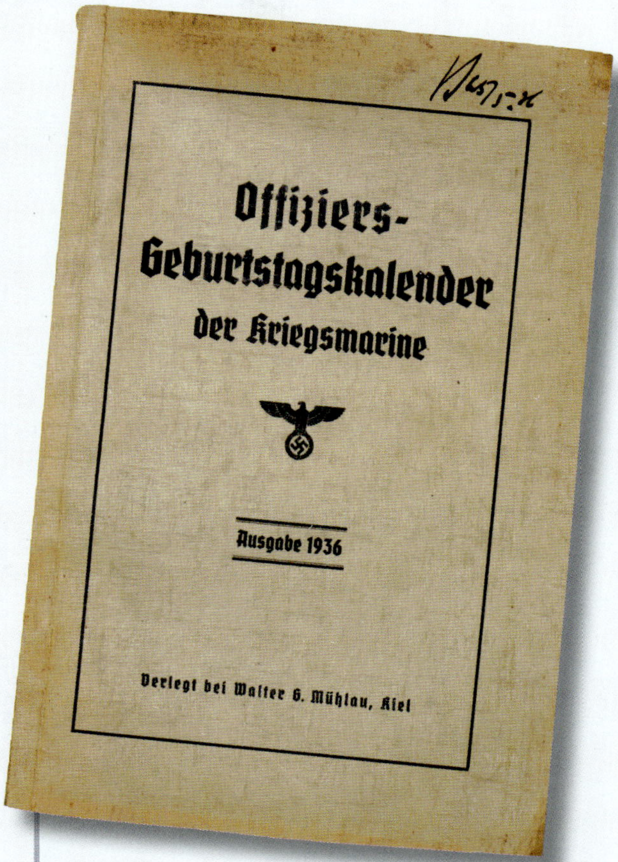

Officer's birthday calendars like this (here for 1936) were published as recently as 1939. (Private collection)

Kriegsmarine promotional brochure for French volunteers, who served, for example, as shipyard police or soldiers. (Private collection)

"The present times demand the liberation of the seas" – This propaganda poster was to recruit French volunteers for the *Kriegsmarine*. (Private collection)

Instruction book "The Signalman" from 1934 is aimed to recruit for the *Kriegsmarine*. (Private collection)

THE *MARINE* OFFICIALS (MARINEBEAMTEN)

Peaked cap with white cover of a *Marine* official of officer rank. For officials, all insignia were silver-colored; in place of the chin strap, they wore a also silver-colored cord trim on their peaked caps. (Private collection)

Marine Senior Paymaster (rank equivalent to *Oberleutnant)* in coat and peaked cap. *Marine* officials wore no embroidered visor decoration. (Private collection)

Marine Paymaster (rank equivalent to *Leutnant)* in jacket and buckled under *Marine* dagger. (Private collection) (Private collection)

These *Wehrmacht* officials were *Marine* personnel with combatant status (personnel of the regular fighting forces) and undertook many tasks within the *Kriegsmarine*, especially in administration, technical services, and the judiciary. Most officials wore uniforms, which, however, differed from those of the *Kriegsmarine* servicemen, in that on the officials' uniforms, all insignia were silver- rather than gold-colored. This was true for national emblems, sleeve stripes, cap borders, or buttons, as well as for the metal fittings for the sash, etc. They also wore special rating badges and the facings on their shoulder boards and straps were in their rating colors. And, at long last, we should here briefly mention the Catholic and Protestant *Marine* clergy, who, although they had no combatant status, nevertheless played an important role for the servicemen.

Garrison cap of a *Marine* official of officer rank. This headgear was manufactured by A. Soldner of Rothenburg ob der Tauber. (Private collection)

Sash clasp, front and back view. The silver color of the clasp shows that it belonged to a *Marine* official of officer rank. The manufacturer code 'FLL' stands for Fredrich Linden of Lüdenscheid. (Private collection)

A *Marine* chaplain speaking the last words over the coffins of *Marine* servicemen who had fallen in Greece. (Private collection)

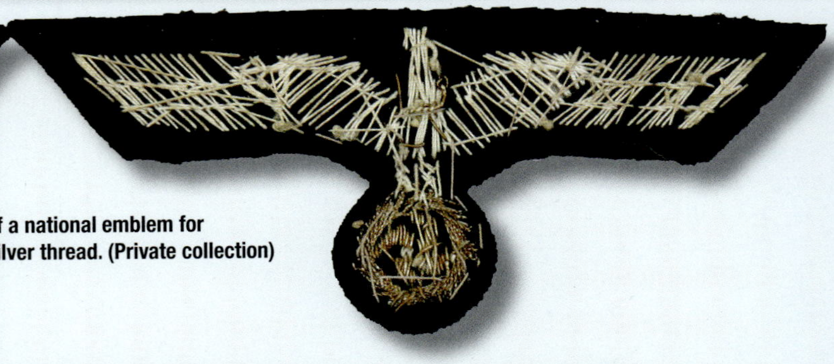

Front and back of a national emblem for officer-rank officials of silver thread. (Private collection)

Small selection of rating badges for *Marine* officials of officer rank (left to right): Justice official of the *Gehobenen Dienstes auf Kriegsdauer* (Elevated service for the duration of the war) (recognizable by the silver-colored border); Technical official of the *Höheren Dienst* (Higher service) (three triangles), Administrative Official of the *Höheren Dienst* (three chevrons); a *Marine* college teacher (two rosettes, i.e., *Gehobener Dienst* (Elevated service)). (Private collection)

Version of the national emblem for officials of officer rank of silver thread. (Private collection)

Another version of a hand-embroidered national emblem for officer-rank officials. (Private collection)

Shoulder boards of an official of petty officer rank *(Oberfeldwebel* rank) in the design from 1940. (Private collection)

Marine chaplain collar tab: left, the 1943 design; right, the design for the longest-serving *Marine* deans, introduced in 1942. (Private collection)

This is how the second prize for the *Reich Marine-SA (Sturmabteilung)* competition looked; it was held in Kiel in 1939. (Collection of P.-M. Rousseau)

Collar patch of a *Marine SA*-man from the *Sturm 7* (company) of *Standarte 5* (regiment) and the anchor pin used during 1938-39 by the *Marine SA*. (Private collection)

Portrait photo of a *Marine SA* man in brown shirt, wearing the first style of the *Marine SA* peaked cap. (Private collection)

THE *MARINE* SA

The first detachment of the *Marine SA* was founded in Hamburg in 1930. It was not long until there were *Marine SA* (*Sturmabteilung*) units, the "party soldiers" of the Nazi Party, in all German port cities. The *Marine SA*'s job was to give pre-military, Navy-specific training to members of this paramilitary Nazi organization. During the war, many *Marine SA* members did military service in the *Kriegsmarine*, but without having any great influence on this conservative-traditional *Wehrmacht* branch which – at least initially – was not very receptive to Germany's new political policy.

HJ (HITLER YOUTH) *MARINE* AUXILIARY

Male adolescents between fourteen and eighteen were required from 1939 to serve in the *Hitler Jugend (HJ)*. Especially in northern Germany, many of them served in the *Marine-HJ*, where they were trained to serve aboard war and merchant ships. From 1943, German youth, many of them barely fifteen years old, had to serve as war auxiliaries, so that *Marinehelfer der HJ* (HY Navy aides) were also deployed in civilian *Flak* units. Besides their *Hitler Jugend* uniforms, they wore a blue or field-gray *Marine* uniform, but (rather) with *HJ* armband; on their left forearm they wore a sleeve band with the inscription '*Marine helfer*' (Navy aide) sewn on it.
Their *Marinehelfer* ID cards had a stamp identifying them as members of the *Kriegsmarine* with combatant status.

HJ Hauptscharführer (master sergeant) in summer service dress with the armband and sheath knife of his organization. (Private collection)

HJ Marinehelfer **in blue pea coat. On the left sleeve he wears the *"Marinehelfer"* sleeve band, above it – contrary to regulations and also in the wrong place – the rating badge of the *Marine* artillery and at top the *HJ* district triangle. (Private collection)**

Comrade unit leader of the *Marine-HJ*. The band on his cloth cap indicates that he is from Kahla in Thuringia, where the *HJ 94* had its home. (Private collection)

A *Marine-HJ* member piping on board, on a training sailing ship. (Private collection)

Also this *HJ Marinehelfer* is wearing the blue pea coat with *"Marinehelfer"* sleeve band. He wears the blue *Kriegsmarine* garrison cap as headgear. (Private collection)

Garrison cap worn by sub-leaders of the *Wasserschutzpolizei (WSP)* (Water Police) until mid-1941 and by the *Marine Küstenpolizei (MFP)* (Coastal Police) until 1945. (Private collection)

Front and back of the police national emblem for the peaked cap, and sleeve bands of the *Marine-Küstenpolizei.* (Private collection)

THE MARINE KÜSTENPOLIZEI (COASTAL POLICE)

Marine-Küstenpolizei gorget. It was inspired by the Army piece, especially that for the *Feldgendarmerie* (military police). (Private collection)

At left rear is sitting a special leader *(MKP Leutnant)*, wearing the jacket of the Naval uniform required since July 1941. The police sleeve patch is on his left sleeve, and he is wearing the *Kriegsmarine* national emblem on his chest. (Private collection)

The unit members were recruited from the ranks of the Water Police; however, they were no longer subordinate to the police, but rather to the *Kriegsmarine*. Their primary task was, initially, policing and security for shipping and the port facilities in the occupied countries. Soon, however, their police duties were extended, and they also had to contribute to military defense. Until well into 1941, the *MKP* continued to wear the uniform of the Water Police, but with the gold-colored national emblem of the *Kriegsmarine*. Only at this time, was the *MKP* ordered to wear the uniform of the *Kriegsmarine*, but with the national emblem of the *Ordnungspolizei* (Order Police) on the upper left sleeve of their jackets. A cornflower blue armband was also added, with the words *'Marine-Küstenpolizei'* in gold *Fraktur.* Their gorgets also bore the same inscription (these gorgets were modeled on the *Heer* (Army) military police's gorget). Sub-leaders fastened this on the left breast of their uniforms with a long pin while on duty – earning them the additional name of the "*blauer Kettenhunde*" ("blue watch dogs").

Front and back of the service brooch for *Kriegsmarine* women auxiliary members (up to and including sub-leader). (Private collection)

Women *Marine* auxiliary members wearing blouse and trousers of their service protective clothing. (Private collection)

Woman *Marine* aide in service dress, with blue cap and gray suit jacket, on which she wears the armband inscribed *'Marinehelferin.'* Note also the service brooch on the tie. (Private collection)

THE *MARINEHELFERINNEN* (*MARINE* WOMEN'S AUXILIARY)

Portrait photo of a woman aide. (Private collection)

Service brooch for a leader. In this version, the rim was wider and decorated. (Private collection)

Such promotional brochures were to recruit volunteers. (Private collection)

To free soldiers for combat duty, German women and girls were used in various *Kriegsmarine* services from 1940, initially as volunteers, but later they were conscripted. They took over duties in the typing pool, the news service, and later also on *Flak* searchlights. The *Marinehelferinnen* service was established in 1942. Their uniforms consisted at first of service dress and protective clothing, which included a service tunic, suit jacket and skirt, cap, protective clothing or service blouse. On this, they wore their rank badge as well as the round service brooch (in two styles) and a dark blue armband with the gold inscription '*Marinehelferin*.'

The war is over and the heroes of yesterday found themselves behind barbed wire. This photo shows *Ritterkreuz* recipient Fritz Breithaupt (center) with two fellow officers. They had to remove the national emblem from their uniforms, but they proudly continue to wear their decorations. (Private collection)

This war prisoner *Oberleutnant z. See* also had to remove the national emblem of the German *Reich* from his uniform, even though he was allowed to wear his decorations – so far. (Private collection)

THE PRISONERS OF WAR

Ausweis
Certificate

Die durch das nebenstehende Lichtbild dargestellte
The person presented by the added photograph
Person ist
Hermann Lamby
geb. am 30. 12. 1915 in Bentheim
born on the at
und wohnt in BENTHEIM, Bahnhofstrasse 15
living at
BENTHEIM, den 6. September 1945.
Gültig bis 7. September 1946.
DER BÜRGERMEISTER
THE MAYOR

Gültigkeit verlängert bis zum 22. August 1947.
Bentheim, den 23. August 1946.
Der Bürgermeister
Im Auftrage:

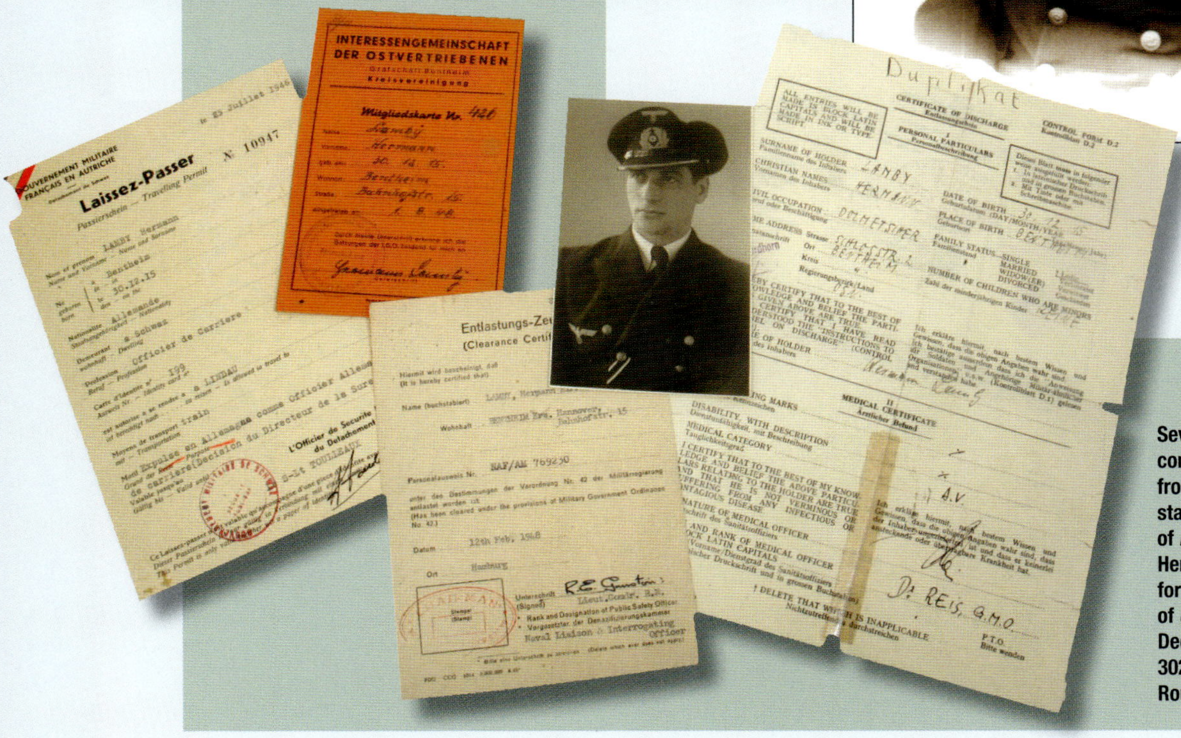

INTERESSENGEMEINSCHAFT DER OSTVERTRIEBENEN

Laissez-Passer N. 10947

Entlastungs-Zeugnis (Clearance Certificate)

CERTIFICATE OF DISCHARGE

Duplikat

Several documents concerning release from prisoner of war status from the estate of *Kapitänleutnant* Hermann Lamby, the former *Kommandant* of *U-Boot* U 437 (until December 1942) and U 3029. (Collection of P.-M. Rousseau)

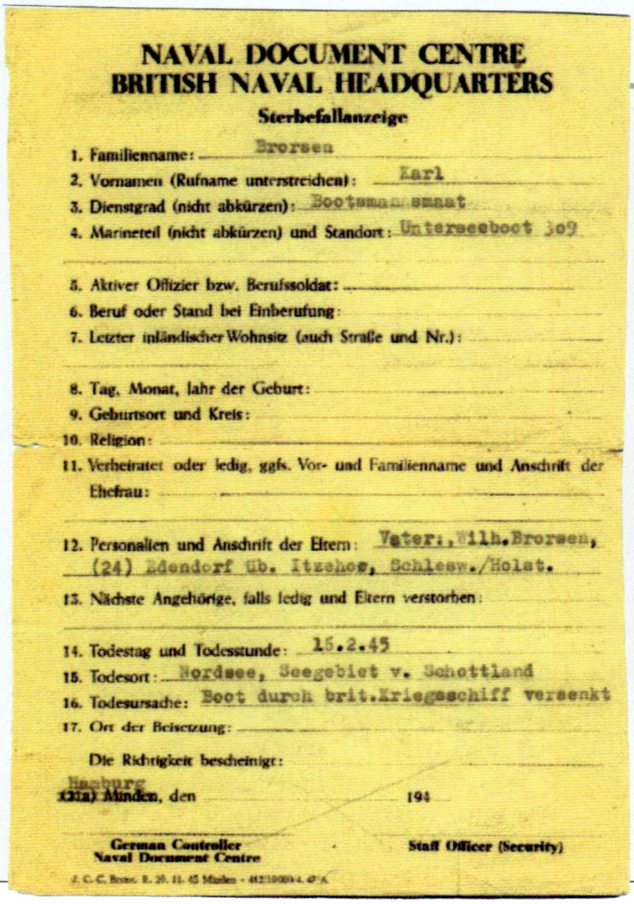

NAVAL DOCUMENT CENTRE
BRITISH NAVAL HEADQUARTERS

Sterbefallanzeige

1. Familienname: Brorsen
2. Vornamen (Rufname unterstreichen): Karl
3. Dienstgrad (nicht abkürzen): Bootsmannsmaat
4. Marineteil (nicht abkürzen) und Standort: Unterseeboot 309
5. Aktiver Offizier bzw. Berufssoldat:
6. Beruf oder Stand bei Einberufung:
7. Letzter inländischer Wohnsitz (auch Straße und Nr.):
8. Tag, Monat, Jahr der Geburt:
9. Geburtsort und Kreis:
10. Religion:
11. Verheiratet oder ledig, ggfs. Vor- und Familienname und Anschrift der Ehefrau:
12. Personalien und Anschrift der Eltern: Vater: Wilh. Brorsen, (24) Edendorf üb. Itzehoe, Schlesw./Holst.
13. Nächste Angehörige, falls ledig und Eltern verstorben:
14. Todestag und Todesstunde: 16.2.45
15. Todesort: Nordsee, Seegebiet v. Schottland
16. Todesursache: Boot durch brit. Kriegsschiff versenkt
17. Ort der Beisetzung:

Die Richtigkeit bescheinigt:

Hamburg
(21a) Minden, den 194

German Controller
Naval Document Centre

Staff Officer (Security)

Death certificate for a German *U-Boot* man, issued by the British Royal Navy. (Private collection)

Home-made birthday card for a former member of the *6. Artillerieträger-Flottille* (artillery barge flotilla), who celebrated his 30th birthday on April 5, 1945 in the POW camp "Camp Aliceville" (Alabama, USA). There were more than 6,000 German prisoners of war in this camp. (Private collection)

The former *Kommandant* of U 130 and *Ritterkreuz* recipient *Kapitän z. See* Ernst Kais (seated, center) with fellow officers of all *Wehrmacht* branches in a POW camp near Lorient in 1945. Note the original footwear! (Private collection)

- Ailsby, Christopher: ***A Collector's Guide to The Kriegsmarine.*** *Ian Allan Publishing, 2007.*
- Alaluquétas, Jacques: ***U-Boot Richtung Mittelatlantik.*** *Loki Verlag, 1978.*
- Angolia, John R. and Schlicht, Adolf: ***Die deutsche Wehrmacht. Uniformierung and Ausrüstung 1933-1945. Vol. 2: Die Kriegsmarine.*** *Motorbuch Verlag, 1995.*
- Angolia, John R. and Schlicht, Adolf: ***Die Kriegsmarine. Uniforms & Traditions (3 Volumes).*** *James Bender Publishing, 1991.*
- Beaver, Paul: ***E-boats and Coastal Craft.*** *PSL, 1980.*
- Blocksdorf, Helmut: ***Das Kommando der Kleinkampfverbände der Kriegsmarine.*** *Motorbuch Verlag, 2003.*
- Braeuer, Luc: ***La base sous-marine de St Nazaire.*** *Luc Braeuer, 2001.*
- Braeuer, Luc: ***U-boote Saint-Nazaire.*** *Luc Braeuer, 2006.*
- Chazette, Alain and Reberac, Fabien: ***Kriegsmarine, Mer du Nord, Atlantique 1940-1945.*** *Éditions Heimdal, 1997.*
- Dallies-Labourdette, Jean-Philippe: ***S-boote. Les vedettes rapides de la Kriegsmarine.*** *Histoire et Collections, 2003.*
- Dallies-Labourdette, Jean-Philippe: ***U-boote.*** *Histoire et Collections, 1996.*
- Fock, Harald: ***Schnellboote. (3 Volumes).*** *Koehlers Verlagsgesellschaft, 1973-74.*
- Gamelin, Paul: ***Les bases sous-marines allemandes de l'Atlantique et leurs defenses 1940-1945.*** *Éditions des Paludiers, 1981.*
- Dönitz, Karl: ***Zehn Jahre und zwanzig Tage. Erinnerungen 1935-1945.*** *Bernard & Graefe, 1997.*
- Högel, Georg: Embleme, ***Wappen, Malings deutscher U-Boote 1939-1945.*** *Koehlers Verlagsgesellschaft, 1987.*
- Kemnade, Friedrich: ***Die Afrika-Flottille.*** *Motorbuch Verlag Stuttgart, 1978.*
- Krellenberg, Manfred: ***U-Boot-Jagd im Mittelmeer. Der Einsatz der 22. U-Jagdflottille.*** *E.S. Mittler & Sohn, 2003.*
- ***Les Flottes de combat.*** *Volumes 1936, 1940-1942, and 1944-1945.*
- Littlejohn, David: ***The SA 1921-1945: Hitler's Stormtroopers.*** *Osprey Publishing, 1996.*
- Mallmann-Showell, Jak P.: ***German Navy Handbook 1939-1945.*** *Sutton Publishing, 2002.*
- Mallmann-Showell, Jak P.: ***Das Buch der deutschen Kriegsmarine 1935-1945.*** *Motorbuch Verlag, 1991.*
- Mayen, Jan: ***Alerte... vedettes rapides.*** *Les Presses de la Cite, 1962.*
- Meyer, Hubert: ***Entre marins. Rochefort – La Rochelle – Royan (1944-1945).*** *Robert Laffont, 1966.*
- ***Nauticus.*** *Volumes 1938, 1939, 1940, 1941, 1942, 1943.*
- Prien, Günther: ***Mein Weg nach Scapa Flow.*** *Deutscher Verlag Berlin, 1940.*
- Rivier, Horst: ***Die Mützenbänder der deutschen Reichsmarine and der Marine des III. Reiches 1920-1945.*** *Self-published by the author, 1980.*
- Rohwer, Jürgen: ***U-Boote. Eine Chronik in Bildern.*** *Gerhard Stalling Verlag, 1962.*
- Rössler, Eberhard: ***Geschichte des deutschen U-Bootbaus.*** *J.F. Lehmanns Verlag, 1975-*
- Rössler, Eberhard: ***The U-Boat: The Evolution and Technical History of German Submarines.*** *Arms and Armour Press, 1981.*
- Rüge, Friedrich: ***In vier Marinen.*** *Bernard & Graefe, 1979.*
- Schepke, Joachim: ***U-Boot-Fahrer von heute.*** *Deutscher Verlag Berlin, 1940.*
- ***Taschenbuch der Kriegsflotten 1941-1942 and 1943-1945.*** *Weyers.*
- von Gartzen, Wirich: ***Die Flottille. Außergewöhnlicher Seekrieg deutscher Mittelmeer-Torpedoboote.*** *Koehlers Verlagsgesellschaft, 1982.*
- Williamson, Gordon: ***German Seaman 1939-45.*** *Osprey Publishing 2001.*
- Williamson, Gordon: ***Torpedo los!*** *R. James Bender Publishing, 2006.*
- Williamson, Gordon: ***U-Boat Crews 1914-45.*** *Osprey Publishing, 1995.*

Journals: ***Gazette des Uniformes; Marine-Arsenal; Marines Magazines; Militaria Magazine (France); Militaria Magazin (Germany); Navires et Histoire, 39-45 Magazine, War Set.***

CHRONOLOGY OF IMPORTANT EVENTS FOR THE GERMAN *KRIEGSMARINE*

January 18, 1871	Founding of the German *Reich* in the Hall of Mirrors, Versailles
1872	**Founding of the *Kaiserliche Marine***
November 1, 1914	Naval battle of Coronel
December 8, 1914	Naval battle of the Falkland Islands
May 31, 1916	Naval battle of Jutland
October 31, 1918	Beginning of the Kiel sailors' mutiny
November 11, 1918	Armistice of Compiegne
November 18, 1918	Internment of the *Kaiserliche Marine* High Seas Fleet at Scapa Flow
April 6, 1919	**Founding of the provisional *Reichsmarine***
June 21, 1919	Scuttling of the *Kaiserliche Marine* High Seas Fleet at Scapa Flow
June 28, 1919	Signing of the Versailles Treaty
November 12, 1921	Beginning of the Washington Naval Conference to end the naval arms race
March 31, 1921	**Founding of the *Reichsmarine***
February 6, 1922	Signing of the Washington Naval Treaty
August 17, 1923	Ratification of the Treaty
April 22, 1930	Beginning of the London Naval Conference
February 2, 1932	Beginning of the Geneva Disarmament Conference
May 1, 1933	Commissioning of the pocket battleship DEUTSCHLAND
October 14, 1933	The German *Reich* refused to participate further in the Geneva Conference
November 15, 1933	The DEUTSCHLAND renamed the LÜTZOW
November 12, 1934	Commissioning of the pocket battleship ADMIRAL SCHEER
1935	*Admiral* Erich Raeder became *Oberbefehlshaber* of the German *Marine.*
March 16, 1935	The German *Reich* introduced universal conscription, openly violating the Treaty of Versailles
May 31, 1935	**Founding of the *Kriegsmarine***
June 18, 1935	Signing of the Anglo-German Naval Agreement
1936	Erich Raeder promoted to *Kriegsmarine Oberbefehlshaber* and *Generaladmiral*
January 6, 1936	Commissioning of the pocket battleship ADMIRAL GRAF SPEE
January 15, 1936	Japan left the London Naval Conference of 1936
March 25, 1936	France, Britain, and the United States signed the Second London Naval Treaty
July 17, 1937	Germany and England signed a bilateral naval agreement
May 21, 1938	Commissioning of the battleship GNEISENAU
1939	*Generaladmiral* Raeder promoted to *Großadmiral*
January 7, 1939	Commissioning of the battleship SCHARNHORST
April 28, 1939	The German *Reich* renounced the Anglo-German Naval Agreements of 1935 and 1937
April 29, 1939	Commissioning of the heavy cruiser ADMIRAL HIPPER
September 3, 1939	**Great Britain, followed by France, declared war on the German *Reich***
September 1939	Beginning of the Battle of the Atlantic, initially primarily as a *U-Boot* war
September 20, 1939	Commissioning of the heavy cruiser BLÜCHER
October 1939	Karl Dönitz, as *Befehlshaber* of the *U-Boote* forces, promoted to *Konteradmiral*
December 13, 1939	Naval battle off the Rio de la Plata
December 17, 1939	Scuttling of the GRAF SPEE off Montevideo
April 7-12, 1940	Occupation of Norway in *Unternehmen "Weserübung"*
August 1, 1940	Commissioning of the heavy cruiser PRINZ EUGEN
August 24, 1940	Commissioning of the battleship BISMARCK
February 25, 1941	Commissioning of the battleship TIRPITZ
May 22 -27, 1941	Naval battle of the Denmark Strait – sinking of the BISMARK
January 30, 1943	Karl Dönitz succeeded *Großadmiral* Raeder as *Kriegsmarine Oberbefehlshaber*
December 30, 1942	Battle of the Barents Sea
December 26, 1943	Naval battle of the North Cape
November 12, 1944	RAF Operation "Catechism" sank the TIRPITZ which lay off Serbotn, by Tromso
May 1, 1945	*Generaladmiral* Hans-Georg von Friedburg succeeded Karl Dönitz as *Kriegsmarine Oberbefehlshaber*
May 4, 1945	***Großadmiral* Dönitz countermanded the order for all *Kriegsmarine* units at sea to scuttle themselves in case of surrender ("Operation *Regenbogen*")**

SUMMARY TABLE OF THE LARGE BATTLESHIPS OF THE KRIEGSMARINE from 1939-1945 (A to G)									
SHIP'S NAME	TONNAGE	LENGTH/BEAM	ARMOR	WEAPONRY	AIRCRAFT	KEEL LAYING	LAUNCH	COMMISSIONING	FINAL DISPOSITION
BATTLESHIPS OF THE SCHARNHORST CLASS (D, E)									
D: GNEISENAU	31,840-38,900	234.9 m/30 m	Deck: 50-110 mm Belt: 45-350 mm Turrets: 360 mm	- 9x 28-cm SK C/34 (3 triple turrets) 12x 15-cm SKC/28 14x 10.5-cm SKC/33 16x 3.7-cm SK C/30 22x 2.0-cm MG C/30 6 TT 53.3-cm (in triple sets)-	3 to 4 Arado Ar 196 A-4	05/06/35 (as battleship)	12/08/36	05/21/38	03/26/45 Scuttled
E: SCHARNHORST	31,840-38,900	234.9 m/30 m	– same –	– same –	– same –	06/15/35	10/03/36	01/07/39	12/26/43 Sunk by the Royal Navy
BATTLESHIPS OF THE BISMARCK CLASS (F, G)									
F: BISMARCK	41,676/50,133	250.5 m/36 m	Deck: 50/120 mm Belt: 320 mm Turrets: 360 mm	8x 38-cm SK C34 (4 twin turrets) 12x 15-cm SK C/28 (6 twin turrets) 16x 10.5-cm SK C/33 16x 3.7-cm SK C/30 12x 2.0-cm MG C/30 (later increased to 20) 6 TT 53.3-cm (in triple sets)	4 Arado Ar 196A-4	07/01/36	02/14/39	08/24/40	05/27/41 Sunk by the Royal Navy
G: TIRPITZ	46,400/52,000	253.6 m/36 m	Deck: 120 mm Belt: 350 mm Turrets: 360 mm	– same – But in 1944 total of 78x 2.0 cm MG C/30	2 to 4 Arado Ar 196A-4	10/24/36	04/01/39	02/25/41	11/12/44 Sunk by the RAF
POCKET BATTLESHIPS (A, B, C)									
A: LÜTZOW (formerly "Deutschland")	11,750/15,900	187.90 m/20.70 m	Deck: 18-40 mm Belt: 50 mm Turrets: 170 mm	6x 28-cm SK C/28 (2 triple turrets) 8x 15-cm SK C/28 6x 8.8-cm (before conversion) afterwards: 6x 10.5-cm 8x 3.7-cm SK C/30 10x 2.0-cm MG C/30 (later increased to 28) 8 TT 53.3-cm (in quadruple sets)	1 Arado Ar 196A-4 (2 possible)	02/05/29	05/19/31	05/01/33	05/04/45 Scuttled
B: ADMIRAL SCHEER	11,900/16,000	187.90 m/21.30	Deck: 16 / 45mm Belt 80 mm Turrets: 170 mm	– same –	– same –	06/25/31	04/01/33	11/12/34	04/09/45 Capsized after RAF bombing
C: ADMIRAL GRAF SPEE	12,000/16,000	186 m/20.60 m	– same –	– same –	– same –	10/01/32	06/30/34	1/06/36	12/17/39 Scuttled
HEAVY CRUISERS									
ADMIRAL HIPPER	14,247/18,208	205.90 m/21.30 m	Deck: 50mm Belt 80mm Turrets: 160mm	8x 20.3-cm SK C/34 (4 twin turrets) 12x 10.5-cm SK C/33 (6 double gun carriages) 12x 3.7-cm SK C/30 (6 double gun carriages) 28x 2.0-cm MG C/30 12 TT 53.3-cm (in triple sets)	1 to Arado Ar 196A-4	07/06/35	02/06/37	04/29/39	05/03/45 Scuttled
BLÜCHER	– same –	– same –	– same –	– same –	– same –	08/15/36	06/08/37	09/20/39	04/09/40 Sunk in Norway
PRINZ EUGEN	14,240/18,400	212.50 m/21.30 m	– same - but Deck: 70mm	– same –	– same –	04/23/36	08/22/38	08/01/40	05/07/45 Conveyed to U.S. Target ship for atomic bomb test

TT = Torpedo tubes; SK - Fast-loading cannon; C = Construction year; RN = Royal Navy; RAF = Royal Air Force

Kriegsmarine
Helmut Neubert
0.554/34-S.
Helmut Neubert
0.554/34 S.
K.T.
Marinehelferin
Marine-Küstenpolizei

More Schiffer Titles

www.schifferbooks.com

German Flamethrower Pioneers of WWI Thomas Wictor. The definitive reference on the topic. Lavishly illustrated, its main sources are the history of the flamethrower regiment, written by its former commander; a manual of assault-troop and flamethrower tactics, by a former flamethrower officer; and the death book published by veterans of the flamethrower regiment. Prewar, wartime, and postwar developments are covered, along with detailed descriptions of weapons, tactics, and epic flame battles.
Size: 8.5"x11" • 300 bw images • 288pp.
ISBN: 978-0-7643-2772-8 • hard • $69.95

Uniforms & Equipment of the Austro-Hungarian Army in WWI S.A. Coil. In addition to the studio portraits shown, the candid photos offer an authentic view of life in the trenches and on the battlefield. Each photo has been carefully chosen and researched to offer the reader detailed information on the k.u.k (royal and imperial) Empire's air, motor and medical corps, as well as infantry, artillery, pioneer and railroad troops. There are chapters covering highly decorated elite units, such as the Bosnian and the Kaiserschuetzen.
Size: 9"x12" • 550 bw/color photos • 352pp.
ISBN: 0-7643-1869-1 • hard • $69.95

Helmets of the First World War: Germany, Britain & their Allies Haselgrove & Radovic. Superb color photos, including multiple full-views and detail shots, depict over 150 helmets of Germany, Britain, France, United States, Austria, Turkey, and others from WWI. Previously unpublished WWI photos show the helmets as they were worn.
Size: 9"x12" • 500 color/bw photos • 240pp.
ISBN: 0-7643-1020-8 • hard • $75.00

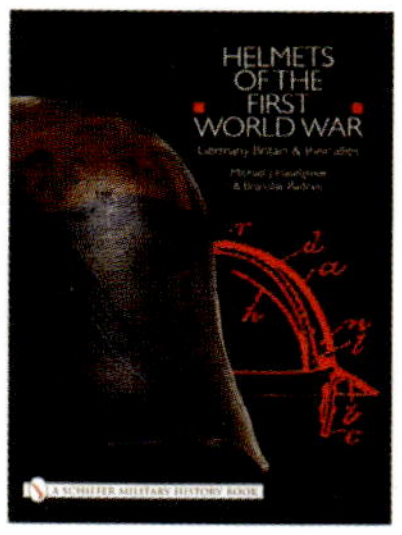

The History of the Steel Helmet in the First World War Haselgrove & Radovic. This illustrated two-volume set is a further detailed look at the helmets of all nations using an identifiable helmet during the First World War, and contains over 1,000 full colour, detailed photos and over 200 period bw photos. Featured are rare and unique helmets, some previously unseen. The text includes a short history of the belligerent countries – setting the helmets and their development in context – as well as details and dimensions of all helmets.

Vol.1: Austro-Hungary, Belgium, Bulgaria, Czechoslovakia, France, Germany
Size: 9"x12" • 550 color/bw photos • 352pp.
ISBN: 0-7643-2528-0 • hard • $79.95

Vol.2: Great Britain, Greece, Holland, Italy, Japan, Poland, Portugal, Romania, Russia, Serbia, Turkey, United States
Size: 9"x12" • 550 color/bw photos • 384pp.
ISBN: 0-7643-2529-9 • hard • $79.95

German Uniforms, Insignia & Equipment 1918-1923: Freikorps • Reichswehr • Vehicles • Weapons Charles Woolley. This volume covers the uniforms and insignia of Germany's military in transition from the trenches of the Western front, to the street fighting in Berlin, Munich and other cities, the bitter contests with the Poles and Communists in the Baltic, the Kapp/Luttwitz Putsch, and finally the campaign in the Ruhr.
Size: 9"x12" • 300 bw/color images • 184pp.
ISBN: 0-7643-1663-X • hard • $59.95

Germany in World War II

German Helmets of the Second World War Branislav Radovic. This two-volume set is a fully illustrated, detailed look at the famous German "stahlhelm" of WWII. Full color photos – including multiple-view, interiors, and up-close detail – show Army, Luftwaffe, Kriegsmarine, Waffen-SS, Paratroop, and many others.

Vol.1: M1916/18 • M1932 • M1935 • M1940 • M1942 • M1942/45
Size: 9"x12" • over 420 color photos • 328pp.
ISBN: 0-7643-1447-5 • hard • $79.95

Vol.2: Paratroop • Covers • Liners • Makers • Insignia
Size: 9"x12" • 480 color/bw photos • 304pp.
ISBN: 0-7643-1448-3 • hard • $79.95

German Camouflaged Helmets of the Second World War Branislav Radovic. This two-volume set is packed with nearly 1000 full-color photos of more than 180 helmets and covers, all shown at full page size and in detail. These helmets are some of the most wonderful and exotic camouflage helmets to be seen in private and public collections.

Vol.1: Painted and Textured Camouflage
Size: 9"x12" • 400 color, bw photos • 240pp.
ISBN: 0-7643-2105-6 • hard • $79.95

Vol.2: Wire, Netting, Covers, Straps, Interiors
Size: 9"x12" • 550 color/bw photos • 328pp.
ISBN: 0-7643-2106-4 • hard • $79.95

SS Helmets: The History, Use and Decoration of the Helmets of the Black Corps Beaver & Hicks. This book presents the combat and parade helmets worn by the SS from its earliest days to the end of wartime production. The examples shown are genuine artifacts of the Third Reich, and most are shown here for the first time. Some of the finest collections and sources globally have been solicited in the construction of this book.
Size: 9"x12" • 300 color/bw photos • 200pp.
ISBN: 0-7643-2476-4 • hard • $69.95

German Headgear in WWII: A Photographic Study of German Hats and Helmets Moran & Maguire. This two volume set illustrates, in full color, over 240 visor hats and helmets of the German: Army, Luftwaffe, Kriegsmarine, SS, NSDAP, Police, Civilian, and miscellaneous formations. Each peaked hat is shown from four angles, including interior, and insignia detail.

Vol.1: Army/Luftwaffe/Kriegsmarine
Size: 9"x12" • over 600 color photos • 312pp.
ISBN: 0-7643-0176-4 • hard • $75.00

Vol.2: SS/NSDAP/Police/Civilian/Misc.
Size: 9"x12" • over 250 color photos • 152pp.
ISBN: 0-7643-0245-0 • hard • $75.00

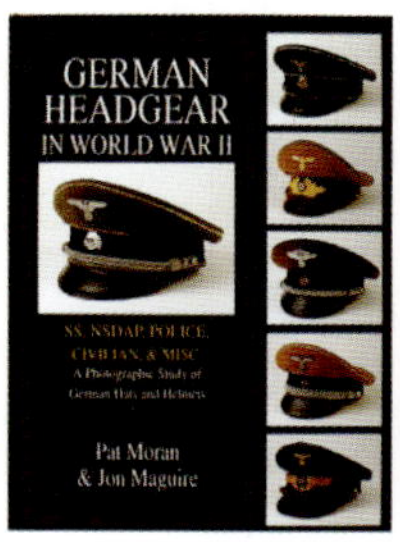

The Collector's Guide to Cloth Third Reich Military Headgear Gary Wilkins. Cap construction basics and materials, descriptions of each model, and comparisons with altered originals, modified post-war caps, and reproductions – all in individual sections for easy reference. For the advanced collector, the book offers historical background about the German cap-making industry, with the first-ever comprehensive listing of German cap makers, maker mark illustrations, and individual histories, including never published info on the history and sad fate of the famous cap maker Robert Lubstein/EREL.
Size: 8.5"x11" • 350+ color/bw photos • 416pp.
ISBN: 0-7643-1428-9 • hard • $79.95

The Collector's Guide to Cloth Headgear of the Allgemeine and Waffen-SS Beaver & Shea. This new book provides an organized, chronological guide to the evolution and development of the myriad types of soft headgear worn by the SS. The overwhelming majority of these photos including many rare original candid period snapshots have never been seen before in any previous publication.
Size: 9"x12" • 600 color/bw images • 304 pp.
ISBN: 978-0-7643-3230-2 • hard • $100.00

German Daggers of WWII: A Photographic Reference Thomas M. Johnson. This four volume set by Thomas M. Johnson, a leading collector and authoritative researcher, has been compiled to serve as a useful and authoritative reference on the daggers of Nazi Germany, and have been designed to aid not only the beginning collector, but also the seasoned collector and specialist. These volumes are the result of many years of arduous research conducted on both sides of the Atlantic, and are a scholarly study that is more than a perfunctory annotation and illustration of the known basic patterns. Also, the series is a study of a culture and the crafts that actually produced the blades, as well as being a manual in the art of collecting them. Within these books one will see coverage of the historical background; the manufacturing techniques; constructional; actual basic patterns; variations and rarities; the art of collecting, and a whole host of other salient facts of absorbing interest.

Vol.1: Army • Luftwaffe • Kriegsmarine
Size: 9"x12" • 240 color/bw photos • 224pp.
ISBN: 0-7643-2203-6 • hard • $79.95

Vol.2: SA • Feldherrnhalle • SS • NSKK • NPEA • RAD • Hitlerjugend
Size: 9"x12" • 470 color/bw photos • 384pp.
ISBN: 0-7643-2204-4 • hard • $79.95

Vol.3: DLV/NSFK • Diplomats • Red Cross • Police and Fire • RLB • TENO • Customs • Reichsbahn • Postal • Hunting and Forestry • Etc.
Size: 9"x12" • 490 color/bw photos • 320pp.
ISBN: 0-7643-2205-2 • hard • $79.95

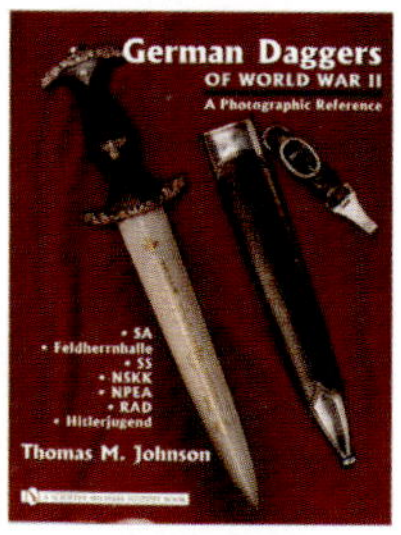

Vol.4: Recently Surfaced Rare and Unusual Dress Daggers • Hermann Göring • Bejeweled Dress Daggers • Reproductions • Solingen Update
Size: 9"x12" • 100 color/bw photos • 112pp.
ISBN: 0-7643-2206-0 • hard • $39.95

German Daggers of WWII: A Photographic Reference – Boxed Set (*see photo below*) Thomas M. Johnson. Also available exclusively from Schiffer Publishing as a four volume limited edition boxed set. Set contains all four volumes as above in a deluxe slipcase. $250.00

German Swords of WWII: A Photographic Reference Thomas M. Johnson. This three volume sword series has been designed to aid not only the beginning collector, but also the seasoned advanced collector and specialist. The series is a study of a culture and the crafts that actually produced the blades, as well as being a manual in the art of collecting them. Within these books one finds the historical background, the manufacturing techniques, constructional information, the actual basic patterns, variations and rarities, and a whole host of details.

Vol.1: Army
Size: 9"x12" • 400 color/bw photos • 304pp.
ISBN: 0-7643-2432-2 • hard • $79.95

Vol.2: Luftwaffe, Kriegsmarine, SA, SS
Size: 9"x12" • 400 color/bw photos • 304pp.
ISBN: 0-7643-2433-0 • hard • $79.95

Vol.3: DLV, Diplomats, Customs, Police and Fire, Justice, Mining, Railway, Misc.
Size: 9"x12" • 400 color/bw photos • 336pp.
ISBN: 0-7643-2434-9 • hard • $79.95

WWII German War Booty: A Study in Photos Thomas M. Johnson. This book contains over 580 beautiful full-color, large-format photos of German daggers, swords, helmets, uniforms, insignia, award documents, weapons, and many other rare and unusual items. Also included is a generous selection of WWII era photos showing many items being liberated!
Size: 9"x12" • 580 color/bw photos • 368pp.
ISBN: 0-7643-1923-X • hard • $79.95

German Uniforms of the 20th Century Vol.1: The Panzer Troops 1917 - to the Present Jorg M. Hormann. All aspects of German panzer troop uniforms in over 200 photos, many in color.
Size: 6"x9" • 126pp.
ISBN: 0-88740-214-3 • hard • $24.95

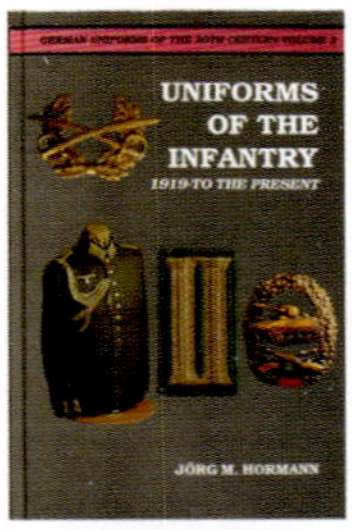

German Uniforms of the 20th Century Vol.2: The Infantry 1919 - to the Present Jorg M. Hormann. Detailed history of all aspects of German infantry uniforms in over 200 photos, many in color.
Size: 6"x9" • 126pp.
ISBN: 0-88740-215-1 • hard • $24.95

Uniforms of the Third Reich: A Study in Photos Hayes & Maguire. This book takes a close look at a variety of authentic WWII era German uniforms including examples from the Army, Luftwaffe, Kriegsmarine, Waffen-SS, Allgemeine-SS, Hitler Youth and Political Leaders. Large full frame front and rear shots, and in painstaking detail to show tailors tags, buttons, insignia detail etc. and allow the reader to see the genuine article.
Size: 9"x12" • over 400 color photos • 200pp.
ISBN: 0-7643-0358-9 • hard • $69.95

SS Uniforms, Insignia and Accoutrements: A Study in Photos A. Hayes. This work explores in detailed color the complex subject of Allgemeine and Waffen-SS uniforms, insignia, and accoutrements. Hundreds of authentic items are extensively photographed in close-up to enable the reader to examine and study.
Size: 8.5"x11" • 800 color/bw photos • 248pp.
ISBN: 978-0-7643-0046-2 • hard • $79.99

Uniforms of the Waffen-SS Michael D. Beaver. This three-volume set is unquestionably the best reference on German SS military uniforms ever produced. This spectacular work is a heavily documented record of all major clothing articles of the Waffen-SS. Hundreds of unpublished bw photos were used in production. Original and extremely rare SS uniforms of various types are carefully photographed and presented here.

Vol.1: Black Service Uniform • LAH Guard Uniform • SS Earth-Grey Service Uniform • Model 1936 Field Service Uniform • 1939-1940 • 1941
Size: 9"x12" • 500 color/bw photos • 352pp.
ISBN: 0-7643-1550-1 • hard • $79.95

Vol.2: 1942 • 1943 • 1944-1945 • Ski Uniforms • Overcoats • White Service Uniforms • Tropical Clothing • Shirts • Sports and Drill Uniforms
Size: 9"x12" • 500 color/bw photos • 368pp.
ISBN: 0-7643-1551-X • hard • $79.95

Vol.3: Armored Personnel • Camouflage • Concentration Camp Personnel • SD • SS Female Auxiliaries
Size: 9"x12" • 500 color bw photos • 272pp.
ISBN: 0-7643-1552-8 • hard • $79.95

Camouflage Uniforms of the Waffen-SS: A Photographic Reference Michael Beaver. Finally a book that unveils the shroud of mystery surrounding Waffen-SS camouflage clothing. Illustrated here, both in full color and in contemporary bw photos, this unparalleled look at Waffen-SS combat troops and their camouflage will benefit both the historian and collector.
Size: 8.5"x11" • 1,000 bw/color photos • 296pp.
ISBN: 978-0-88740-803-8 • hard • $79.99

Camouflage Uniforms of the German Wehrmacht: Manufacturers • Zeltbahnen • Headgear • Fallschirmjäger Smocks • Army Smocks • Padded Uniforms • Leibermuster • Tents • Non-Regulation Clothes • Post War Palinckx/Borsarello. An indispensable guide for historians, collectors and modelers, this book finally resolves the confusion surrounding many of the WWII Wehrmacht (both Army and Luftwaffe) patterns and garments and establishes a complete and concise system of identification and terminology. A comparative section with post-war fabrications is added as a tool for authentication. More than 10 different camouflage patterns are covered, including the super rare carbon overprint and Leibermuster.
Size: 9"x12" • 580 color & bw photos • 288pp.
ISBN: 0-7643-1623-0 • hard • $79.95

Winter Uniforms of the German Army and Luftwaffe in WWII Vincent Slegers. This is the first thorough study to cover all aspects of the winter uniforms issued to and used by the German Army and Luftwaffe during WWII. This book covers all uniform pieces and accessories, their developments, materials, insignia and markings.
Size: 8.5"x11" • 350 color/bw images • 272pp.
ISBN: 978-0-7643-3752-9 • hard • $79.99

Uniforms and Insignia of the Großdeutschland Division Scott Pritchett. For the first time, a comprehensive view of the WWII German Army's most elite formation: Großdeutschland. Exceptional detail of rare uniforms and unique insignia are woven with Großdeutschland's history and development. Its two closest sister units, the Wachbataillon Berlin and the Führer Begleit Battalion are also covered in the same superb level of detail.

Awards, decorations, portraits and personal effects of common soldiers and noted personalities, covering every arm of service within the units, are also presented.

Vol.1
Size: 9"x12" • 2000 color/bw images • 384 pp.
ISBN: 978-0-7643-3342-2 • hard • $125.00

Vol.2
Size: 9"x12" • 1000 color/bw images • 352 pp.
ISBN: 978-0-7643-3343-9 • hard • $125.00

Vol.3
Size: 9"x12" • 1100 color/bw images • 472 pp.
ISBN: 978-0-7643-3543-3 • hard • $145.00

Afrikakorps: Army • Luftwaffe • Kriegsmarine • Tropical Uniforms, Insignia & Equipment of the German Soldier in WWII Robert Kurtz. The ultimate visual guide for collectors of WWII German tropical uniforms! Using actual items from top Afrikakorps collections – tunics, headgear, insignia, documents, field gear – as well as many WWII era photos, this book covers it all in color. From mint issue items, to rare sun-bleached tunics and caps, the wide variety of tropical uniforms used by the Army, Luftwaffe, Kriegsmarine and Waffen-SS are illustrated in superb large format photography, including up-close detail.
Size: 9"x12" • 730 color/bw photos • 300pp.
ISBN: 0-7643-1920-5 • hard • $79.95

Personal Groupings, Award Documents, and Ephemera of Rommel's Afrikakorps: Army • Luftwaffe • Kriegsmarine Robert Kurtz. For German military document collectors this volume has a treasure trove of rare Afrikakorps related award documents, propaganda leaflets, Soldbuchs, Wehrpass and Remembrance/Death cards. Includes both Allied and German/Italian propaganda leaflets, Afrikakorps field newspapers, and two field-made newsletters associated with the Sonderverband 288 unit. Also assembled are several complete veteran groupings and every known document variant of the AFRIKA cuffband and Italian-German Medal.
Size: 9"x12" • 250+ color/bw photos • 144pp.
ISBN: 0-7643-2113-7 • hard • $59.95

German Paratroops: Uniforms, Insignia & Equipment of the Fallschirmjäger in WWII Robert Kurtz. The uniforms and equipment of the elite Fallschirm-jäger is the subject of this detailed, illustrated study. Authentic items – smocks, dress tunics, boots, insignia, helmets, visor caps, gloves, kneepads and more. Unpublished WWII era photos show uniforms and equipment being worn on a variety of war fronts.
Size: 9"x12" • 300 color & bw photos • 192pp.
ISBN: 978-0-7643-1040-9 • hard • $69.99

German Paratroops in North Africa: Tropical Uniforms, Headgear, and Insignia of the Fallschirmjäger in WWII John E. Hodgin. This large-format book is an in-depth photographic study of Luftwaffe tropical uniforms, headgear, and insignia worn by the Fallschirmjäger during the battles for Africa in WWII. Both full-color and war-era photographs illustrate rare uniforms and equipment including tropical jump smocks, Ramcke Brigade jump helmets, and officer's Meyer caps.
Size: 9"x12" • 600 color/bw images • 304 pp.
ISBN: 978-0-7643-2939-5 • hard • $100.00